"*Have You Seen Candace?* is a compelling, fast-moving saga of one ordinary family turned extra-ordinary. It's a story of tragedy beyond proportion, of a chain of events that God used to quietly, slowly, gently, and powerfully bring answers and focus and some sense of understanding to a beautiful child's death. Simply and profoundly written."

Ann Kiemel Anderson, author of *I Love the Word Impossible*

"The invitation to walk hand in hand with someone in the most painful of human grievings—the loss of a child—is both unwelcome and irresistible. Unwelcome because it awakens our own fears for our children and the threat of violence in a violent culture; irresistible because one longs for the reassurance that healing is possible for the deepest of all hurts.

"Wilma Derksen offers that invitation in *Have You Seen Candace?* And she allows us to make our own discoveries as we read. Among the gifts I received: 1) Grieving is spiral; from its beginning in a tight knot of pain, it slowly broadens to allow healing and forgiveness. 2) Forgiveness is never final; it is a process of letting go, opening toward love, reclaiming life, allowing the presence of God to join us in transforming our deepest sufferings."

David Augsburger, author of *Caring Enough to Forgive; Caring Enough N...*

Have You Seen Candace?

WILMA DERKSEN

LIVING BOOKS ®

Tyndale House Publishers, Inc.
Wheaton, Illinois

Living Books is a registered trademark of Tyndale House Publishers, Inc.

Unless otherwise stated, all Scripture quotations are from the *Holy Bible,* New International Version, copyright © 1973, 1978, 1984 International Bible Society. Used by permission of Zondervan Publishing House.

"Friends" by Michael W. Smith and Deborah D. Smith copyright © 1982 by Meadowgreen Music Co., 54 Music Sq. E., Suite 305, Nashville, TN 37203. International copyright secured. All rights reserved. Used by permission.

Library of Congress Catalog Card Number 91-66953

ISBN 0-8423-0377-4

Printed in the United States of America

98	97	96	95	94	93	92
8	7	6	5	4	3	2

To Candace

Contents

CHAPTER 1

Candace Is Missing

Trivia! That's what concerned me—trivia. Tidying the house, paying the bills, shopping for groceries, washing the clothes—all of them were insignificant details. Trivia.

But I didn't realize that then, as I tidied the basement family room. I remember feeling almost overwhelmed with the responsibility of taking care of a family. There was so much to worry about. There was so much to keep in order. I was annoyed when I found a dried-up apple core behind the television set, scraps of paper scattered on the rug, a toy motorcycle wedged between the cushions of the sofa. I visualized and scolded each child. The dried-up apple core I knew was thirteen-year-old, apple-eating Candace's doing. The scraps of paper were nine-year-old, origami-folding Odia's handiwork. The motorcycle belonged to Syras, my two-year-old. It was one of the few toys that distinguished him as a male in a house that up till now had been ruled by dolls.

I dropped the apple core and scraps of paper into the already full wastebasket and put the motorcycle on the step with all the other things I was going to carry up. I could faintly hear Odia and Syras quarreling upstairs. I listened, wondering if this was a small, commercial-length squabble that would subside the minute the cartoon started again or something more serious that I would have to go upstairs and mediate, wasting precious time.

The noise died sharply . . . a commercial quarrel. I breathed a sigh of relief and turned back to my work.

Candace would be back from school soon, and I still had the other half of the room to clean. I'd had two deadlines that past week. I had completed both of them late the night before, and there were remnants of the two projects all over the room. I had left piles of slides on my makeshift light table. They really needed to be organized and sorted, but I scooped them all into one pile and then into a box. I moved a stack of old *Reader's Digest* magazines onto the bookshelf, dismantled the light table, packed away the two projectors, and ripped down the tattered white sheet that I had used as a screen.

It was Friday, November 30, 1984. It was one of those ordinary days that should have slipped obliviously into November's row of days like all the other days of that month, like all the other days of all the other months of that year. Sometimes we may wish that we remembered our days more clearly, more vividly, but it might be a blessing that we don't. I will never forget what happened that day, and there are times when I wish that I could.

The weather was comfortable; the temperature was slightly above normal. It had hovered around a balmy twenty degrees Fahrenheit most of November, and that was considered warm for this time of year in Winnipeg. No one was complaining. We knew the cold would come.

There had been less snow than usual. It had tried to snow that morning but had failed to leave any trace on the ground. However, the forecast was for plunging temperatures on the weekend. Winter was coming, and since it was late, it would probably come with a fury and hold us in its relentless grip for the next two months. We enjoyed every moment of reprieve.

I had spent the day running last-minute errands, and everything had taken just a little longer than I had anticipated. It was already late in the afternoon, and I was still laboring slowly through the basement family room. The only redeeming thought was that it was Friday and I was almost finished cleaning the house. We had a weekend to look forward to.

Heidi was coming for the weekend. Heidi was Candace's friend from Camp Arnes. It would mean a weekend with two giggly teens either lounging around the house or pacing the city. I suspected that I would be driving them shopping, swimming, and skating, but I didn't mind. While I was waiting for them, I might even make a dent in my Christmas shopping.

The telephone rang.

"Mom?" It was Candace.

I glanced at my watch. It was almost four. "I thought you'd be on your way home by now," I said.

"I know," she answered breathlessly. There was a

pause and then a giggle. "David just gave me a face wash, Mom."

"David?" I was hearing that boy's name more and more. "Careful now."

"Oh, Mom," she groaned.

"Shouldn't you be starting home?"

"Aw, Mom," she said, "it's Friday. Can you pick me up?"

I often did pick her up, and I had planned to today, but I had lost track of the time. I paused, juggling the schedule in my mind. If I went to pick her up now, it would mean packing up the kids. . . .

"Mom, someone is waiting for the phone."

"Candace, this is bad timing. If you had called sooner, maybe we could have gone shopping with the kids before picking up Daddy. But right now I'm in the middle of cleaning the family room for you and Heidi, and the kids are cranky. If I pack them into their snowsuits, it means waiting in the car. Can you take the bus?"

"Sure. It's okay."

By the sound of her voice, I knew she understood the situation but couldn't quite conceal her disappointment. I reconsidered. "Look, if Dad can get off early, I'll pick you up. I'll call him. Call back in five minutes. And don't flirt too much." She giggled and hung up.

Why was life so complicated? I was tired. Managing five lives wasn't always easy.

I phoned Cliff. Sometimes on Fridays he could get off by four-thirty. "No, I'm busy," he said curtly, and I sensed he was pushing a deadline. "Pick me up at five."

I looked around the room. There was still more to do. I could hear the kids quarreling again. If I packed up the kids now and picked up Candace, it would mean sitting in the car with three hungry children for at least half an hour. I didn't need that—no one did, I concluded. It was a warm day, probably one of the last. Candace could walk or take the bus while I finished cleaning the room, and then as soon as she came home, the weekend would begin. We'd bundle up the kids, pick up Cliff, cash his check, eat at the kids' favorite restaurant—McDonald's—and then Candace and I would drop the family off and go shopping. I had already promised her I would allow her to choose all her favorite party foods for her and her guest.

I felt good about the plan. Candace would understand.

With new energy I folded the sheet and started to file some of the scripts from my projects. I was startled when the telephone rang again. Right! I had asked Candace to call back.

"Mom?"

"Candace, do you have money for the bus?"

"Yup."

"I can't pick you up now, but tonight we can go shopping alone. Is that okay?"

"Sure."

"Hurry home."

"Yup. See you." The telephone clicked.

Good, she hadn't sounded too disappointed. In twenty minutes most of the tidying would be done, and then there might even be enough time for her to help me arrange the room the way she wanted it before we went out. Knowing Candace, she would have her own ideas about how to arrange things. The family room was already a perfect teen haven: a telephone, an old color TV, a soft bed, and a card table for goodies. The best feature was that the room was far enough away from our bedroom so that they could play their music as loud as they wanted without our hearing. My biggest job this weekend would be to keep Odia and Syras away from them.

I vacuumed and folded the laundry. My thoughts churned, justifying my decisions, planning, worrying about trivia.

Suddenly I stopped. Something was wrong. I dropped everything and went upstairs. The kids were so absorbed in their TV show that they didn't even notice me. I went into the kitchen and glanced at the kitchen clock. Candace would be home any minute.

I looked out of the window. I was shocked. When I had picked up Syras from the baby-sitter's at two-thirty, it had been warm; it was snowing then, but the large, beautiful flakes had melted as soon as they hit the ground. Now the ground was white, and the flakes were growing smaller by the minute. The temperature was plunging as predicted, and Candace hadn't dressed for this weather! If I remembered correctly, she had slipped on just a thin polyester blouse that morning. If she didn't come home soon, she'd freeze. It was unusually dark, too, for this time of the day.

I started to pace the floor from the front living room window to the kitchen window at the back of the house. Which way would she be coming—up the street or down the back alley? I looked at the clock again. Where was she? She wouldn't stop anywhere, at least not for long. Soon it would be time to leave to pick up Cliff; I couldn't wait much longer. Perhaps if I went the route Candace would be taking home, I still might catch her. I walked into the living room. The kids were still mesmerized by the TV screen. I switched it off.

"We have to pick up Candace and Daddy," I explained.

Both of them got dressed slowly.

"Odia," I said as we backed out into the back alley,

"you keep your eyes on your side of the road, and I'll watch mine."

She nodded. "I've got good eyes, Mom. Right?"

"Right."

"Remember the last time we went to pick her up? I saw her first."

I nodded.

We crawled along the back lane and then drove along Talbot Avenue as slowly as the rush hour traffic would allow. I glanced in the windows of the 7-Eleven store, the neighborhood hangout, as we passed, but she wasn't there. The further we drove, the faster my heart started to pound. Where was she?

When we reached Candace's school, Odia turned to me. "Mom, where is she?" The question seemed to resound throughout the whole car.

"I don't know," I answered as calmly as I could. "Why don't you check the school doors?" She jumped out of the car to check, but the school doors were locked.

I now needed to decide whether to turn back and look again or to carry on and pick up Cliff and then come back. I think ordinarily I would have looked for her longer, because the McDonald's we usually went to was right by Cliff's office; going to pick him up without Candace would really put a kink into our evening's plans. But I had this unreasonable sense of foreboding, so I swung the car onto the Henderson Highway. I needed Cliff. Saving time or miles didn't matter.

I met Cliff just as he was coming out of his office. "I can't find Candace, Cliff, and I'm worried."

He took one look at me and grabbed his briefcase. As we left the building and walked to the car, I quickly filled in the details. I told him about her calls, about the scheduling dilemma I had been in, and about my fears.

"Cliff, nothing would keep Candace from coming home from school today. Heidi is coming. She wouldn't do anything to jeopardize this weekend."

He nodded. I didn't need to describe Candace's frame of mind. We all had been aware of it for weeks.

"Cliff, I'm scared. I think this is serious."

We reached the car doors, and for a moment we looked across the car roof at each other. There is something to be said for fifteen years of marriage. Not every thought has to be voiced to be understood. We didn't have time to talk because once we were in the car, we would appear calm for the children's sake. We needed to say it with that one look. I could see that all my fears had been transferred to Cliff's eyes. We understood each other. We were of the same mind. It should have been a comfort, but it wasn't.

Once in the car, I suggested that we backtrack along Talbot. This time Cliff watched the right side of the road and I took the left. Odia watched both sides. There was no one on the road. It had grown very dark.

I had left the house door unlocked just in case Candace had taken an alternate route and got home before we did. I left Cliff to help Syras and ran into the house. "Candace," I called as I opened the door. The house was quiet. I opened the downstairs door. "Candace!" There wasn't a sound. Where was she? I ran upstairs. Everything was exactly as we had left it.

Cliff was helping the kids out of their coats by the time I came downstairs. "Cliff, where *is* she?"

"Tell me again how she sounded on the phone. Was she upset that you didn't pick her up?"

I shook my head.

"Does she have money with her? Could she have met a friend on the way home?"

I ran back upstairs to check her drawer. All the money she had saved for this weekend was still there.

Cliff pulled on his coat again. "I'll drive back to the school. We might have just missed her."

"I'll call her friends."

I switched on the TV so that the kids would be occupied, then I took a deep breath and consoled myself with the thought that Candace was probably with her friends.

Six months earlier I had given every member of the family a piece of paper and told them to write down the telephone numbers of all their friends. Candace had taped hers near the telephone. But now, as I glanced at the names, I realized how drastically her life had changed in the last few months. The change from sixth grade to seventh, elementary school to high school, and public school to private school had given her a whole new set of friends. The names on this list were those of her old friends who lived in the neighborhood. Her new friends' numbers probably would be in her phone book upstairs. Who was I to call first—her new friends or her old friends?

The worst part was that I couldn't make myself believe that she was with any of them. But I had to phone someone. I had to start somewhere. I had to do something.

Deanna was the first name on the old list. Deanna had been Candace's closest friend all through elementary school, and she was the kind of person who knew how to network. She was a natural leader among the kids in the community; if anyone would know where Candace was, she would.

I called her number. There was no answer.

I called the next name on the list: Gitchy. A young

voice answered. I remembered Candace telling me that Gitchy now preferred to be called Krissy.

"Krissy? This is Candace's mother. Have you seen Candace?"

"No, Mrs. Derksen."

"Do you know where Deanna is?"

"She's right here."

"Could I speak to her?"

But Deanna hadn't seen Candace, either. "I can call around for you, though," she offered. I could sense the concern in her voice. Deanna was always quick to catch on.

"Thank you, Deanna." I hung up.

I was disappointed, but not surprised. Even if Candace had met Deanna on the way home from school, Candace wouldn't have been in the frame of mind to go chumming with her. But I did feel a little better knowing that Deanna had been alerted. She knew the community, and she'd let us know if she heard anything.

I ran upstairs to get a list of Candace's new friends at her new school. I didn't know them as well. Using Candace's phone beside her bed, I started dialing.

The choice to send Candace to a private school hadn't been an easy one. It cost money we didn't have.

I had attended a private school, so I had a fairly good idea what a Mennonite private school was like. I knew we weren't sending our child into an isolated paradise of Christian virtue guaranteed to turn her into a responsible adult. There are never any guarantees. There are never any safe places.

We had two reasons for sending her to the Mennonite Brethren Collegiate Institute (MBCI). The first was that we wanted her to make Mennonite friends. We thought it might enhance her life and make it easier for her if her friends shared her values. I knew I had found it easier to relate to friends whose parents were similar to mine. In those days, the difference was perhaps more noticeable. I wasn't allowed to smoke, dance, wear makeup, or go to movies, and it made it easier when none of my friends could do those things either. Friends were important to Candace. Even as a toddler she had been a people person. Knowing that friends would probably be the biggest influence in her life, we wanted her to gain a wide cross section of them.

The second reason was really a hope. We hoped that while she was having fun, making friends, learning, and studying, she would learn a little more about the Bible. To us, good values, good morals, a good system of beliefs, and an understanding of God were as important as a good education. She would get that at MBCI. It was a well-known, well-established school in our community with an enrollment of over four hundred students.

At first, Candace didn't want to attend a private school when all the rest of her friends from George V were planning on going to Elmwood High. So we promised her that if she gave the school a try for one year, we'd discuss our decision again at the end of that year. If she was in any way unhappy, she could then join her friends at Elmwood High.

The first week was the real test. That Friday when I picked her up, she smiled as she said, "You were right, Mom. They're my kind of people."

Probably the greatest determining factor in making a private school a pleasant or unpleasant experience is whether or not a student is accepted into its closely knit society. So even though I would have been irritated if Candace was with one of her newfound friends this time, I also would have considered it a good sign of her ability to fit into her new school. I was still a little concerned about it. This was her third month at the school, and I felt that her relationship with Heidi was still stronger than any she had developed at the school.

I called one of her new friends.

"No, Mrs. Derksen. I left right after school."

After that call I abandoned all reason and just called any name that looked remotely familiar, stabbing in the dark for any kind of clue as to where she could be. Candace had to have gone with somebody. She wouldn't do anything alone. Who could she have met? Who would be so important that they could have persuaded her to do something other than come home today of all days?

By talking to her MBCI friends, I began to gain a picture of what had happened. Candace had lingered after school; she had been seen hovering around the telephone, probably waiting to call me back. One friend said that they had met at their lockers and that Candace had stuffed her gym outfit into her burgundy duffel bag to take home to be washed "because," she quoted Candace, "it's the polite thing to do."

It sounded just like Candace. Most other people would wash their clothes because they wanted to have clean clothes. But not Candace. She washed her clothes for her friends.

Then she had been outside having face washes in the snow. She had last been seen walking down Talbot on her way home—alone.

It seemed just a matter of minutes before Cliff, looking cold and worried, came back from his search. "Is she home?"

I shook my head.

"Any word?"

I shook my head again. I told him about the calls and the information I had gathered, then we looked at each other in silence. Neither of us was able to put into words our deepest fears.

"Let's call the police," he said finally.

I was about to agree, but then I thought of one unexplored element in the whole picture. "Not yet," I said. "There is one person I want to speak to."

"Who?"

"David."

"Why? Do you think she's with him?"

No, it was quite clear that she had walked off alone. But I had never met David, and just by seeing him, I would know more confidently what state of mind she was in when she left the school parking lot.

The other week, when the whole school had been encouraged to attend the evening Terry Winter crusade at the Winnipeg Convention Center, Candace had come home from the crusade walking on air. David had introduced her to his mother. "Mom, he's crazy," Candace had said over and over again, paying him her highest compliment.

After that I asked Cliff to casually check him out with Lily Loewen, the outdoor education director at Camp Arnes. I knew that they went to the same church as the Wiebes. We learned that he was in eleventh grade and a good kid. Of course we wondered what an eleventh-grade boy was doing taking notice of a seventh-grade girl. But then again, we knew that Candace was able to relate to a wide range of people.

Just by the way Candace lingered over his name and described every detail of every encounter that she had with him, I gathered that she had a crush on him. An innocent attraction. Younger girls often idolize the older fellows. Possibly David didn't even know he was slightly bewitched by a younger girl's charm or in some innocent way trapped into noticing her.

Cliff couldn't quite understand what I would learn by meeting him now. We probably knew all that we needed to know to go to the police. But he handed me the keys. "I'll feed the kids."

I drove slowly to the school, searching each side of the street. I remembered Candace telling me about the time David sat with her during a basketball game after school and about how he caught her arm when she was going to volley the ball over the net during a volley-ball game, making her so nervous that she missed the next two serves. But when I asked if she was in love with this David, she laughed. "Mom, don't be silly. He's in eleventh grade."

Now the school was buzzing with evening activi-ties. Harry Wall, the principal, looked a little tired as he supervised the students. I asked him if he knew where David was. He pointed to a boy fumbling with his lock at the lockers.

My heart stopped. I had never seen David before, but he was exactly the kind of boy I had always imag-ined Candace would fall in love with someday. Ever since first grade there had been a parade of little boys in her life. All of them had similar features: fair hair, twin-kling eyes, and quick smiles. David was a carbon copy of them all, the oldest one in the long string, and it caught me by surprise. His age was just another reminder of how quickly she was growing up. No won-der she called me silly when I asked if she loved him. She adored him.

I approached him. "You must be David."

He nodded, and I wasted no time.

"I'm Candace's mother. Candace hasn't come home from school today. She mentioned that you were with her after school. Do you know where she is?"

His face grew concerned. "I thought she was going home."

"Was it after the face wash? She told me on the phone that you gave her a face wash with snow."

He flushed a bit guiltily. "Actually, I gave her two. One before she called you and another one when she went out."

Two face washes! Wow! Candace would have been walking home inches off the ground.

Quick to recognize the gravity written all over my face, he said quietly, "Mrs. Derksen, the last time I saw her she was walking down Talbot in the direction of your home. I had driver's training after that so I didn't hang around." He watched me closely. "This is serious, isn't it?"

I nodded.

"I'm so sorry." And with a sensitivity way beyond his young years, he gently touched my shoulder in an effort to comfort me. Barely able to control my emotions, I turned and walked out to the car. It was seven o'clock. I had my answer. The night seemed blacker than I had ever seen it as I slid behind the wheel of the car.

David had been my last hope in the gathering mystery. I had just met the other most important person in Candace's life. I knew she wouldn't have been interested in being with anyone else. Nothing could have distracted her from coming home and waiting excitedly to tell Heidi all about it. After an intimate face wash from David, she would have walked home smiling, in a state of absolute ecstasy, totally lost in her daydreams and oblivious to anything or anyone else around her. Totally vulnerable.

I slammed my fist on the steering wheel. "No, God! No! Not my Candace!"

I could feel my heart sink down somewhere to the

bottom of my being and throb there, murmuring unintelligible prayers. There are no words for such moments, just pain. There was a terrible sense of futility, knowing she was in danger—possibly struggling for her very life—and I didn't even know where she was. I was helpless, so totally helpless.

What do you do? Where do you start?

I remembered once when Odia hadn't come home from school. We had called her network of friends and found out that she had last been seen walking out of the school yard carrying a box of chocolates she was supposed to sell.

I had been worried, but not like this time. We knew Odia. Odia and Candace were different. Just as Candace was motivated by people, Odia was motivated by achievement. Her little eyes would gleam with determination when she was presented with a challenge, and then nothing could deter her from her goal. She was going to sell those chocolate bars.

Cliff and Candace had combed the neighborhood looking for our little girl while I manned the telephone, but she eluded us. Every few minutes a friend would call in: she had been sighted at the corner of such and such street. Another few minutes and another friend had seen her at another place.

At nine o'clock, she had come through the door. Her button nose was red, her shoulders sagged, and her mouth trembled as she said, "Mom, I sold only two." She had absolutely no idea that she had missed supper and that we had been frantically looking for her.

At that time, I had been paralyzed between the emotions of utter joy that she was home and pure fury that she had been so inconsiderate. Later, when I had calmed down, I sat down with the girls, and we talked about the responsibility of letting us know where they were at all times. I repeated over and over again that if they developed the habit of letting us know where they were, then if they didn't show up, we would know something was really wrong and would start searching.

I remember Candace asking, "Okay, Mom, let's say someone did take us. How would you find us?"

I had answered, "I don't know. But we'd try everything humanly possible."

Now that question was a reality. It probably had been a reality for some time now. It had become a reality while I was downstairs concerned about dried-up apple cores, scraps of paper, and motorcycles—matters that in hindsight were so trivial. Nothing mattered anymore—bills, grocery lists, food, guests—nothing. In one dark, lonely moment, our lives had been totally refocused, and we hadn't even known it was happening.

Frantically I turned on the ignition. We had to call the police. They would know what to do.

CHAPTER 2
A Question of Faith

Somewhere I once read that it is often when people are in a crisis that they throw their faith away—at the very time when they need it the most. I had read that and wondered idly how I would react in a crisis. I didn't know. I don't think any of us know what we are going to do in advance. The last time I had been in what I perceived to be a life-and-death crisis, I hadn't thrown my faith away, but I certainly had rethought and revised it afterward. The crisis revealed that my faith wasn't based on reality and that it needed to be revamped. But since that time, my life had been routine: a domestic scramble to make ends meet.

As I faced this new crisis, I wondered vaguely if

my revamped faith would hold. Was it based on reality this time? Would it give me strength? Would it give me direction? Or would I, after all of this, have to rethink it again, revise it, or throw it away? I knew I was about to find out.

When I came home from seeing David, Cliff immediately called the police. It was about seven-thirty.

"Are you sure she isn't with friends?" the desk officer asked.

"Yes, we're very sure. We've checked with all her friends," answered Cliff, projecting a control and calmness he wasn't feeling. "We are absolutely certain she isn't with friends. We've checked everyone and everything. We're up against a wall. Something is wrong."

"Was she upset?"

"No, she wasn't upset. She was looking forward to having her best friend come to our place tomorrow morning. They were going to spend the weekend together."

The questions were precise and systematic, and all of them were fashioned to confirm the underlying supposition that every disappearing thirteen-year-old is a runaway. Cliff answered them all patiently and explained, "Her best friend lives in Arnes, fifty miles away from here, and she won't be in until tomorrow. They haven't seen each other for weeks. I know she wouldn't have run away today."

After a long pause, the officer on the phone finally said, "If she isn't home in half an hour, we'll put this out to the Transcona fleet of police cars. Can you give me a description?"

Cliff described her. "She's petite, about five feet one inch, slim—a hundred to a hundred and five pounds, maybe. She has light brown hair and blue eyes.

What was she was wearing?" He looked over at me, and I mouthed the words to him. "A black wool jacket with burgundy raglan sleeves, tight blue jeans, and runners that are never tied. She was carrying a burgundy duffel bag—and she had black gloves."

The description seemed so inadequate. He was describing half a dozen teenagers roaming all over the city at that very moment. How would anyone recognize her from that description?

I knew what I had to do next. The police would need pictures, and there were boxes of pictures downstairs waiting to be filed into albums. But, rummaging through them, I couldn't find one that was adequate. The most recent school picture showed a child grinning into the camera. Candace was almost an adult now. Then I stopped at one picture and stared at it for a long time.

The picture had been taken on a warm summer's day when we had been living in Calgary. Candace was about four years old, and she was wearing an outfit I had just finished sewing. It was a cute, brightly colored outfit with a midriff top, butterfly sleeves, and a short skirt with attached panties. Miraculously, it had turned out. It looked wonderful on her, and she knew it. She strutted, twirled, and floated through the house like a miniature model.

To celebrate the success of my creation, we planned a shopping trip for just the two of us. We hopped into our little blue Datsun and headed for the mall. Candace rolled down the window and rested her arm on the window ledge just the way I did. We grinned at each other. The slight breeze lifted her long curls lightly, and her big blue eyes sparkled with happiness.

She had seemed so much older than her four years. But then she had never been much of a baby. By the time she was five months old, she was walking along the furniture. At six months she took her first step, and at seven months she was walking confidently. It was the cutest thing to see this tiny baby walking. To get any attention, all we had to do was set her down in a mall on a Saturday afternoon and all the shoppers would stop to see this smiling, bright-eyed, tiny baby waddling about with diapers that were bigger than she was. We could have charged for the entertainment, and—of course—she loved the attention.

I was amazed at how many people still smiled at my little girl. There was nothing remarkable about her. She was just an ordinary, pretty four-year-old with a new outfit. It must have been her infectious smile that attracted them.

As we were wandering down the mall we heard western music. We came upon a grandstand where four singers, complete with ten-gallon hats and guitars, were crooning to the shoppers. They were fairly good, and since there was standing room close to the side of the stage, we stopped to listen.

One of the singers noticed Candace, and, as they were singing "If you happen to see the most beautiful girl in the world," he smiled down at her and sang the rest of the song to her. She was utterly captivated and stood motionless even after the last notes had faded away and the band had said their good-byes.

I looked down at her. Her eyes were shining. "They were singing about me," she whispered in awe.

I nodded. To us, she was the most beautiful girl in the world, and again I marveled at her capacity to glow with happiness.

I put the picture down. I knew why I was being haunted by this particular picture and these memories. I was afraid that this time, too, she had been so happy. . . .

Had she been radiating? Had she been glowing

with so much happiness that she stood out in the crowd? Had her happiness made her vulnerable, less alert? Had she attracted unwanted attention?

I put the picture of Candace in her cute outfit back in the box and picked out some recent pictures of her. Her school picture was the clearest and best, but it was a year old, so I picked out a few recent candid pictures, including some with Heidi in them. I found myself wishing we had taken more pictures.

I went upstairs and spread them out on the dining room table. By that time, Cliff had let the police know that half an hour had passed and Candace hadn't come home. He asked if they would please put a missing person alert out to the Transcona fleet of cruisers. The desk officer said she would and asked us to call back in two hours.

Mechanically, Cliff and I gave the two younger children their bedtime snack and tucked them into bed, promising them that tomorrow, when Candace was back, we would do all the fun things we had promised to do today. I think they believed us, because they fell asleep almost immediately.

Time passed slowly. Cliff went for another quick search. This time he decided that he would have a better feel of the community if he walked and tried to retrace her steps exactly. I paced inside.

He was back in an hour, his step wearier than before. We tried to watch TV, but it was a blur; we couldn't concentrate. The minutes seemed to drag and race all at the same time.

At nine-thirty Cliff telephoned the police again, and again I could hear him trying to persuade them that this was not just another runaway case.

I couldn't listen anymore. I remembered that I had taken out a few other boxes while looking for pictures and had left everything strewn all over the basement floor. If Candace did come home, the place needed to be neat. So I went down and started to pack things away.

Cliff came down to the basement to tell me that the police had put out a citywide missing person alert for Candace and that they'd be dropping by around eleven to pick up a picture. We went back upstairs together. We were both tremendously relieved. It was ten o'clock.

"There's still time for me to walk to the school once more," Cliff said, pulling his winter jacket out of the closet.

I went to look at the thermometer outside our kitchen window. "It's cold, Cliff; the temperature is still dropping. What if she's outside? She wasn't dressed for this weather."

"She won't be."

"Then what are you looking for?"

He shrugged. "I don't know—tracks, anything that looks suspicious. I'll check the stores. I don't even know what to look for. I've just got to go."

I nodded. I wanted to go with him, but someone needed to be by the phone and with the kids. So I shut the door behind him and shivered as the cold air swirled through the house.

The two uniformed police officers knocked on our door at approximately eleven o'clock that night. Since we thought we had convinced the desk clerk—twice—that Candace hadn't run away, we assumed that the two officers would already be briefed on the details and convinced as well. We didn't have any more reason to doubt that this was serious, and we thought they wouldn't either. We even wondered if they would reprimand us for waiting so long to notify them.

Since time was of the essence, all we expected to do was brief them on our fears and give them Candace's picture and a precise description; then they would radio the main station to mobilize the entire police force for a full-scale search of Winnipeg, perhaps even bringing the dogs out.

We had scattered all the pictures of Candace on the dining room table, and we invited the officers to sit around the table with us. We spoke quickly, urgently shoving pictures in front of them.

But instead of taking a picture and rushing out the door, they sat back, relaxed, and watched us closely. They wanted to know what kind of parents we were. What was our relationship with Candace like? Had we argued with her? Was she upset that I hadn't picked her up?

Our hearts sank. We started over, trying to answer the questions as best we could, but how do you convince someone that you are a capable parent? It seemed everything we said incriminated us. The more we tried to convince them, the worse it got.

And they just listened to our panic as if they had all the time in the world.

After a few more questions, they more or less told us that they thought it was extremely unlikely that Candace had been abducted. They told us that there are approximately a hundred runaway teens on the streets of Winnipeg at any given time; any child over twelve who disappears is probably a runaway. We were also told that there hadn't been any abductions in Winnipeg for seven to ten years, so what made Candace any different than all the other cases with which they were dealing? Why couldn't we just admit to ourselves that we'd had a quarrel with Candace and she had run away?

We groped for our most credible references. We told them that Cliff worked for Camp Arnes, the largest

Christian camp in Manitoba, and that he had been a pastor at North Battleford Mennonite Brethren Church. We thought that if anything would immediately impress on them our solid family values, integrity, and love, it would be our Christian commitment.

The more outspoken officer perked up and said, "I know what the problem is."

We both straightened. "What?"

"You," he answered, glancing at both of us.

"What do you mean?" I groped to understand.

He spelled it out. "You're both religious, and Candace is rebelling."

How incredibly naive we'd been! The minute they caught the slightest whiff of our religious background, especially the words *Mennonite* and *pastor*, they instantly classified us as fanatical, overreligious hypocrites. Maybe they even believed we used religion as a cover for deviant behavior. I wouldn't normally have cared about their skepticism, but our daughter's life depended on their believing us. We had to convince them.

"Okay. Maybe you're right," I conceded. "But you know what teenagers are like—how important friends are to them. Candace is expecting her best friend, whom she hasn't seen for weeks, to spend the weekend with her. They planned this weekend a month ago, and she hasn't talked about anything else since. No kid would run away if their best friend was coming the next morning. You're used to looking for motives; well, the motivating force in Candace's life this weekend was to come home and get ready for her friend."

"Is she religious?" the officer asked.

"Who, Candace?"

"No, her friend."

What could I say? I guess according to the broad sweep of the brush—the same brush he used for us—

yes, he would define Heidi as "religious." She went to church; she believed in God; she was just as religious as Candace was. Neither one was fanatical or a Bible thumper; they were ordinary Christian girls with a simple faith in God.

They were at the stage of life where it was a little hard to define them. One minute they were preening themselves and flirting with the boys at camp; the next minute they were racing through the tires on the playground octopus like two carefree elementary kids. They seemed to go from one extreme to the next. One day they would dress up in absurd clothes and clown around the campground; the next day they'd be dressed fit to knock the boys dead, but within minutes they'd slip into jeans and cowboy boots and go help groom the horses at the corral. I'd hear them listening to rock, and I'd overhear them discussing their relationship with God. But whatever they did, it was with a giggle, a laugh. They were experimenting; they were finding themselves; and what better place to do it than in a Christian camp setting. But no matter how I might try to describe them, I knew this policeman wouldn't understand. So I said nothing.

It seemed as if my moody silence was answer enough for him.

"Are Heidi's parents religious?" he probed.

According to his definition, yes, they would be perceived as religious too, so I nodded.

"You see, that proves my point. Maybe Candace is rebelling against your whole religious community, and so she is rebelling against Heidi, too."

I was horrified.

"No," Cliff and I insisted.

In desperation I picked up a picture of the two girls sitting underneath a tree. "Look at them. You can tell even from this picture that they are kindred spirits. Even though they only spend the summers together, their friendship survives the long winters apart."

I could see we hadn't convinced them, but they changed their tactic. What about school? Was Candace a good student? Was she having trouble at school?

We admitted that, if anything, we were concerned about her academic adjustment to MBCI. We had been considering private tutoring—their eyes widened with interest—but we told them that her marks were improving. We had begun to tutor her, Cliff one evening and I the next, and her marks had improved drastically. Her last marks had been in the *B* range. We were all extremely encouraged.

I don't think any of our arguments convinced them. At least, if they did, the officers didn't let on.

They asked about family. Might she have gone to be with a relative? We told them that we didn't have any family in Manitoba. All my family lived in British Columbia. Except for one brother in British Columbia, all of Cliff's family lived in Saskatchewan. We had relatively little contact with our cousins in the city; Candace certainly wouldn't have known them. And we had already checked with friends.

Eventually, still looking skeptical, the two officers took her picture, promising to put it on citywide computer and to cruise the community. At that point we were grateful for crumbs.

After they left, I found that their questions had depressed me; they'd had an opposite effect on Cliff, however. They had given him new ideas, and now it was his turn to verify her state of mind and to explore some of his leads. He called a whole new set of people, and one of them told him that Candace had talked to the school counselor that day, so he called Dave Teigrob.

I paced aimlessly around the house. I had never dreamed that I would ever hope Candace would be a runaway. But I found myself praying underneath my breath, *Lord, let her just be angry with me. Let it be something I said. I can always retract my words or drown them out with hundreds of better ones.* I even prayed that it might be problems at school. We could always find a new school. We'd sell our house and hire the best experts. Any problem was solvable if only she were alive, if only we could have her back again.

I heard Cliff say to someone on the telephone, "I'm sorry if Dave is sleeping, but this is an emergency."

I was surprised that it was so late. I could see that most of the houses in the neighborhood were dark.

Cliff joined me at the window. "Teigrob said he didn't say much to Candace. He said she was in good spirits and that he's as puzzled as we are."

We were again at a loss for ideas. We just stood there looking out into the dark and processing over and over again what steps we had taken, what we thought might have happened, trying to think of something else to do. Our options were running out. We knew that soon everybody, like Teigrob, would be asleep, and we couldn't think of anything else to do. It was an unusual situation for us to be in. Cliff was creative—he had a natural art ability—and I had spent the last two years studying communications. We were idea people. We always had ideas. Our problem usually was that we had too many ideas to pursue. Now, we had none.

There was a thump on the other side of the wall. Living in a duplex, we could hear our neighbors' every movement. From the traffic in and out of the house, we had deduced that there were a few fellows taking up residence together. Exactly how many, we weren't sure. They were the noisiest neighbors, constantly thumping and bumping around the house in the strangest way. Cliff and I had often tried to guess what those unusual bouncing noises were. The only thing we could think of was that bodies were being hurled around the floor and against the walls. But that couldn't be. Surely no one could be thrown around like that without getting hurt, and we never noticed any ambulances.

Cliff went to check on the kids, and I saw one of our neighbors coming up the sidewalk. I opened the door and asked if I could speak to him.

He stepped inside, and Cliff came down to join us. Our neighbor introduced himself as a wrestler from eastern Canada and explained that he was staying with his wrestling buddies next door while he was training for a match to be held the next weekend. He told us that his match had been well publicized. I was a bit embarrassed that I didn't recognize his name. He said he would be leaving town after the match.

We told him that our teenage daughter hadn't come home from school and asked him if he had noticed anything unusual. I watched carefully for his reaction. Would it be guarded? Did he know something?

He was immediately sympathetic—genuinely so, I thought . . . I hoped.

"If you need help," he said before he left, ". . . if she's in trouble, just call me." Had I imagined it, or had he actually flexed his muscles ever so slightly? I nodded thankfully. He said he would ask around. We said our good-byes, and he disappeared into his side of the house. We heard voices, and the thumping stopped.

Wrestlers. Why hadn't we thought of that? It explained the sound of bodies flying against the wall. How I wished that I could search their house. Suddenly I wanted to go out and search every house in the neighborhood. Even though most were good neighbors, could one ever be certain? I wondered about the neighbors on the west side, but their house was dark. No one was home.

Again we wandered around the house. We tried watching TV, but we couldn't concentrate.

When the front doorbell rang around midnight, we both rushed to the door. Hope! But it was only Dave Teigrob, the school counselor and vice president of MBCI. "I couldn't go back to sleep," he explained simply. After the initial disappointment, we were amazed that he had come all the way from his home on the outskirts of Winnipeg to talk to us.

He had nothing to offer us, he said, other than to stay with us. So we sat down in our living room and went over every detail of the day again. I can't remember much of what we talked about, but his presence was like an anchor in a storm, a rock, something solid to hang on to. He assured us over and over again that his last encounter with Candace had left no reason for alarm. She had seemed pleased with herself and hopeful her problems could be worked out.

There wasn't much we could do but wait together and convince each other that by now she must be inside a building, that whatever situation she had been in was resolved, that the police were looking for her, that there were police cars everywhere in the city and surely they would notice something.

By two o'clock there was nothing left to say, and Dave urged us to try and sleep. We reassured each other again and again that in the morning we could begin calling around again and, after a good rest, we would be fresh with new ideas. By then Candace might have called.

We thanked Dave for coming; we were truly grateful.

I think Cliff was probably more comforted than I was. I think he felt confident that Candace was safe by now and that the police would find her soon. I tried to believe it. I really did. But after Cliff fell asleep, I slipped out of bed to take up my vigil by the living room window.

Candace wasn't safe. She needed me. I could feel her struggling. I put on the porch lights, left the door unlocked just in case she needed to run into the house, and put out all the lights so I could see outside without being seen. I watched every move of the community. I watched every car that drove over the Nairn overpass.

I was truly alone. It seemed everyone else was asleep. There are no words to describe those long, torturous hours.

And that was when I asked, "God, why?"

When I was a little girl, one of my friends had a picture of two children crossing a dangerous bridge in the middle of the night. Hovering over them with huge protective wings was a beautiful angel, and I remember often thinking of that wonderful picture of total protection when I was frightened. To me it had communicated that as long as we remained innocent and good, God would protect us. He would keep the bridge from breaking and little feet from stepping off into the canyon. My favorite verse was "The angel of the Lord encamps around those who fear him, and he delivers them" (Psalm 34:7). I quoted it every time someone asked me what my favorite verse was.

But as I grew up, that image hadn't held up to reality. There didn't seem to be any angels to protect innocent children from suffering, abuse, neglect, and broken bridges. There didn't seem to be any protection from anything, anywhere. I tried to get around that one by rationalizing that those who had faith in God and who tried to lead a pure and good life would be protected by their good works. But I learned differently in a little isolated Indian village in northern Manitoba.

After college, Cliff and I, thinking that we had something to offer the native people, decided to manage the Pauingassi Trading Post and to do volunteer service for the village church on the side. We believed we had all the answers and were going to solve all their problems.

None of that happened, of course. It quickly became apparent that we were ill-suited for roughing it in the wild. Our paternalistic attitude toward the native culture became quite obvious, and we soon realized that we didn't understand any of their problems, much less our own. One Sunday afternoon, needing to get away from it all, we decided to go on a joyride on our snowmobile.

The day was beautiful. The snow was like soft powder and the sun was bright as we headed for Fishing Lake Lodge, which was abandoned during the winter. We hadn't been there before without a guide, but we were told that it was quite easy to find if we followed the north shore of Fishing Lake through the island straits and across some bays. For the experienced traveler, it was about a four-mile journey.

The winter had been an unusual one. It had snowed a lot after the first thin freeze in early winter, and the snow had insulated the ice on the lake, keeping it from freezing any thicker. The ice was thick enough to travel on, but the weight of the snow had caused huge cracks to form that allowed the water to seep through the ice and lie hidden between the ice and snow. We were advised to avoid these cracks and the surrounding slush spots.

In the beginning of the afternoon, our powerful

machine just skimmed over the snow, and we wondered why everyone had been warning us. But as we passed through a strait between the mainland and the island where the stronger currents kept the ice even thinner, I happened to turn around and see the brown trail of slush we were leaving. I pointed it out to Cliff, but he just gunned the motor, and we sailed blissfully into the fishing camp.

The camp was truly a winter paradise. We had the time of our life roaming through the drifts, exploring the forlorn sight, and enjoying our freedom.

As the shadows lengthened, we decided to go home. We swooped down a bank of snow onto the lake again and headed for the wide white spaces. Cliff was careful to cut a new path, but we weren't even near the strait before the snowmobile bogged down.

We had never encountered slush before; to our horror, slush is to a snowmobile what mud is to a car. We couldn't move.

Cliff told me to get off and push. I did, and it worked. As I pushed, he gunned the motor and steered the machine onto a fresh patch of solid snow. I ran to catch up, and we were off again.

But in the strait there were no dry patches. We would get stuck, and I would get off. Cliff would gun the motor, and he wouldn't even wait for me. I'd catch up before he got too far.

The shadows were getting longer, and I was getting colder. I looked at the shore with the dark trees and remembered that the natives had told us to be careful because there was a wolf in the area—a big wolf who could walk in the unusually deep snow without his belly even touching the snow. He was also a hungry wolf. Some dogs had disappeared.

To top it off, I wasn't really properly dressed.

Cliff's snowmobile suit had arrived, but mine hadn't. I had put on layers and layers of clothes as protection against the cold, but they offered no protection from the wet slush. I didn't need a degree in outdoor education to know that, with the sun setting and the already low temperatures plunging, I was in danger.

This is it, I thought. *This is the time for God to help us.* I had followed God faithfully all my life. We were in this place because of our desire to be of service. Now he would give us a miracle.

Cliff asked me to push again, and I prayed quietly under my breath. Expecting great things, I gave one hefty push. Cliff gunned the motor, the snowmobile leaped out of the slush, and I lost my balance and fell flat in the murky water. I was soaked. Before I even got up, the snowmobile was mired in slush deeper than we had yet seen. This time the motor sounded different, and there was a thin wisp of smoke coming from the drive belt.

I gave up praying after that.

I wanted to abandon the machine and start walking. Cliff wanted to try over and over again. And we did until both of us were soaked and bone-tired. Cliff eventually realized how hopeless it was. We tried building a fire, tried screaming for help, and tried thinking of different ways to work the machine; but we finally gave it all up, realizing our only hope was to walk the six miles back to the village.

The snow made it a bright evening. Every once in a while both of us would stop and study the distant shoreline for movement. It became a test of endurance. I could take only little steps in my armor of ice-encrusted clothes, and each step was an effort.

When we finally stumbled into our tiny cabin, Cliff and I plopped down in front of our wood-burning barrel stove to melt. Just as I was beginning to feel warm again, my toes began to thaw. Oh, the pain! I nearly lost my toes that time.

There was one more interesting fact. The next morning when they rescued the snowmobile, they found big wolf prints following ours. This last bit of news verified my fears, and I was furious. God hadn't heard my prayers. We had been in danger, serious danger, and if God couldn't or wouldn't help us, then what good was he to us?

We moved out of Pauingassi a short time later.

That's when my understanding of theology had to be revamped. I had to go back and rethink. "The angel of the Lord encamps around those who fear him, and he delivers them"—from physical danger, I had thought. But when I reread the stories about the saints of the Old and New Testaments, it became apparent to me that God works on a different level. He is more concerned that we remain spiritually protected. Job is a good example. God allowed righteous Job to lose every material thing he had, but Job emerged victorious because his faith in God remained intact.

Slowly I began to understand that if the spirit is victorious, there are no prison walls or bars that can contain it. Even death cannot destroy it. To choose God's way is to choose a different set of values; it is to recognize that even though the body may suffer, the spirit will remain content.

A police car was racing over the Nairn overpass with its red lights flashing. I jumped up from the sofa. Candace! Had they found Candace? Was she hurt? I rushed over to the phone to wait, pacing circles in the kitchen.

It didn't ring. I pulled up a kitchen chair and just sat and looked at the telephone, terrified it would ring with bad news, terrified it wouldn't ring at all. I was trembling. I'm not sure how long I waited. Time was meaningless.

Eventually I realized there would be no call and that the emergency had been for someone else. I went back to the sofa to take up my lonely vigil.

It was one thing to choose a set of values for myself that allows for suffering and pain, but to choose it for my children? I wanted to be the angel that protected my children. I wanted to take their pain. That's what my going back to school these last two years had been all about. I had gotten up at six and had gone to bed at two so that we could give them a better life, so that we could spare them some hardships.

But the question I now had to face was, Could I entrust my daughter's life to a God who doesn't promise us a bed of roses, but who promises that through suffering we will be made whole? Had my beliefs and values been strong enough to be transmitted to her? Would I allow her to suffer pain?

It's not an easy decision for any parent.

But I remembered the story about how Abraham was willing to sacrifice his promised son at God's request, and I knew suddenly what that was all about. Our children are not ours to keep. We are to give them back to God for his purposes, purposes that we don't always understand.

I was fully aware that as a mother I could struggle against what was happening, fight it every inch of the way. But that would be selfish. My needs weren't important now. The sooner I could look past my own desires, my own mothering instincts, the sooner I would be able to look for God's purpose and God's comfort in all of this.

That's when I remembered that observation about people throwing their faith away at the very time when they need it the most. Now wasn't the time to question or throw my faith away. I needed God. More than at any other time in my life, I needed the direction, comfort, wisdom, and strength my faith in God could give me. Later I might have to rethink it all again. But right now I just needed to hang on and to pray as best as I knew how.

So I did. I prayed that God would be with Candace. I told God that it didn't matter what happened to Cliff or to me; the important person was Candace. I told God that, more than anything in the world, I wanted my daughter safe at home; but if that wasn't to be, then my request was that he would protect her from pain. She couldn't bear pain.

As I thought of the implications of what I was praying and the possibility that she might die, I was frightened. It was totally possible that she might already be dead. I wondered how we could bear it. Our lives were so intertwined; the police were already involved; the public would know. How could we cope with the aftermath?

Then I prayed that God would be with us; that, if this was what lay before us, he would guide us every step of the way.

There was silence. The struggle wasn't over, but my struggle was. For the first time, I felt God was crying too. It seemed the whole universe was crying with me. I sat for a long time; though I could only hold Candace in spirit, I wanted to stay awake with her. I got colder and colder. I put up the thermostat and grabbed a few blankets, but nothing could stop me from shivering. Finally I thought of Cliff, warm in bed. Maybe he could warm me. I could still be with Candace if I went to bed and snuggled up close to Cliff. I didn't plan on falling asleep. I wasn't tired, just cold.

Before I went upstairs, I glanced at the kitchen clock. It was five-thirty. Almost morning.

I lay in the darkness beside Cliff's warmth, but it didn't help. Just as I was about to get up and go back to the window, I noticed that the wind had stopped. I hadn't even realized there had been a wind. Had the wind been in the house? Had there been a noise? Now in its absence, the silence, the stillness, was deafening and horrific. The struggle had stopped.

I sat up in bed. It could mean only one thing. "Candace!" my soul shrieked. "Are you in heaven?"

Somehow the heavens were still open, and her presence seemed to fill the room. She was close, but yet so far—just out of reach. I wanted to enter fully into the next dimension, to ask her if she was okay, to ask her who had taken her away; but a soft, black velvet curtain fell between us and shut me out. She was gone. I couldn't penetrate the wall again no matter how hard I tried. But she was safe, I told myself over and over again. It was over. Whatever had happened was over. I closed my tired eyes, and the room went black.

CHAPTER 3

The Search Begins

The alarm went off at six o'clock.

It seemed as if I had been in limbo for hours, but it must have been only ten or fifteen minutes at the most.

We lay in our bed remembering the nightmare to which we were waking up.

"She's not home?" Cliff asked.

I didn't answer. I couldn't.

"She could be at a friend's place," he said quietly.

I broke into sobs. Should I tell him? What was there to say? Had it been real? Had I been hallucinating?

When I gained control again, I told him about my all-night vigil at the window, my struggle to accept the situation, my exhaustion, and how, during the final moments of the night, I had felt the end of the struggle. I told him that the wind had stopped and that I had felt Candace's presence, but she had slipped away where I could not follow. I told him that meant only one thing to me. She probably had died. She wasn't coming home again.

He sat without moving. "Then it's all over?"

"I can't say for certain. It's all feelings."

But the energy had drained from his face, and tears started to ooze from the corners of his eyes. Candace had always been her father's daughter. Maybe that's why I had always found it so easy to love her and get along with her. She was so much like Cliff, so athletic, fun-loving, and outgoing.

There was nothing else we could do but cry together.

"What do we do now?" I asked. "Do we continue to look for Candace?"

"How certain are you? Do you have any doubts?"

It was hard to explain. Yes, I was certain, and yet I wasn't. I didn't doubt that God could perform miracles. I could believe that this kind of thing could happen, especially during those critical moments when the soul hovers between heaven and earth. But the one thing I wasn't certain about was myself. I had been extremely overwrought the night before. I had been tired, exhausted, terrified, and frantic. I had been nearly out of my mind—maybe I *had* been out of my mind. Maybe I had imagined it. I could have created the whole experience so I would have answers, something solid with which I could cope. I didn't know.

"Can you tell me without a doubt that it didn't happen?" Cliff probed.

I shook my head. Even though I was certain that I would never be able to prove the reality of the experience to myself, I couldn't deny it either. I shook my head and then turned the question around. "Do you believe me?"

"Yes," he said simply. "You obviously experienced something."

I was truly amazed. He believed me! It was the most beautiful gift he could have given me. "But what do we do now?"

We were both quiet for a long time. Cliff finally answered, "We carry on. We look for Candace. We aren't 100 percent sure that Candace is dead, so we can't ignore the possibility that she might still be alive and need us. But we can keep the knowledge that probably she is safe in heaven as an inner comfort. Maybe we'll need it. Maybe God knows we will need it."

Then we reached out for each other. Perhaps Candace's struggles were over, but ours were only beginning. I could see the terror of my own heart reflected in Cliff's eyes, but he was the one who put it into words. "I wonder what must lie ahead of us that will make the knowledge of her death a comfort?" It was a question that would haunt us for weeks to come.

I'm not sure how it was possible to get dressed and carry on as if everything were normal, but we knew that the children would be up soon and that they would need an explanation. They would need breakfast. And the police would be checking in soon. The day was going to be demanding. We had to be ready.

I still wonder how people can operate with so many conflicting emotions. We must have an automatic pilot built in that takes over when we can't think straight. I think it was only adrenalin that kept me going. I wasn't eating and I hadn't slept, yet I wasn't tired. I needed to keep moving.

We showered and made the bed, and all the while

the questions churned inside of us. If the police didn't believe us, who would? Was there anyone who would take us seriously?

Since we had heard nothing from the police, we were now convinced that the missing person alert the night before had only been a pacifier, not an offensive move. We were no longer satisfied with that. We needed direct action. We had already wasted one precious night. But if we did find someone who believed us, would they have the resources to help us? It hadn't taken us long to come to the end of our own resources. We didn't have the experience to find a missing child; we didn't even have the concentration to think up a plan, and we were already numb with despair and grief.

The first call that morning was to Dave Loewen, the director of Camp Arnes and Cliff's employer. Cliff briefly told him what had been happening, and, after a few questions much like what the police had been asking, Dave announced, "You need a search party. You need a lawyer. I'll make some calls." With the same questions, the same answers, he had come to an entirely different conclusion than the police had. He believed us!

We didn't know the full extent of his plans, but it didn't matter. Something was being done. "Anything you can do would be appreciated." That was the understatement of the year. I could tell immediately that Cliff's mood had changed.

I called my parents. Cliff checked with the police. Dave Teigrob checked in, expecting Candace to be home or at least to have called. People we had called late the night before were now calling to see if Candace had come home. Things were beginning to move quickly. Cliff and I knew we both had poor memories for details, so we put a new notepad by the telephone and began to list all the visits and calls with their times.

We knew that if anything turned up, the police would need a detailed account of all activities.

We fed the kids breakfast. Odia was old enough to be alarmed, and I didn't try to spare her. "This is serious, Odia," I said. "We're going to do everything possible to find her. You can help us by looking after Syras."

She nodded.

The same police officers who had visited us the night before dropped in after breakfast, and we sat around the dining room table. Some of Candace's pictures were still strewn over the table exactly where we had left them. We went over every detail again. They hadn't changed their minds. It seemed that they were more convinced than ever that Candace was a runaway. One officer went into a lengthy speech about his problems with his own daughter and how shocked he was when he discovered she had run away, insinuating that we, too, would be shocked to find out that our daughter had run away.

But I noticed that our attitude was different. Even though we were still desperate, the inner panic wasn't there; when they didn't believe us, we didn't react as strongly. I realized that we had shifted our loyalties. We were going through the motions with them, but our hope now lay with Dave Loewen, someone who we felt believed us.

One of the officers asked to see Candace's room, and I took him upstairs. Candace and Odia shared the same room, and it was a mess. But I shelved my pride. Nothing mattered. I hoped that because of our complete openness with them, the officers would soon realize we had nothing to hide. Then they might believe us, and maybe, just maybe, they'd spend their time looking for Candace rather than questioning us. But my openness backfired.

We found some old notepads Candace had used as diaries. I handed them to the officer triumphantly. He would meet Candace through her writing.

But just glancing over his shoulder at the first page made me realize again that my expectations were based on my own experiences. I was the writer. It was my medium of communication and part of my identity. Candace was a people person, not a literary person at all, and her diaries were a poor reflection of her. She had used her diaries not as a record, but to vent. During her twelfth year, she had really struggled a lot with her identity, with her faith, and with us, her parents. I hadn't been surprised. My twelfth year had been my worst too, and I knew it wasn't easy growing up. But there wasn't anything that I read there that I didn't know about. Often Candace would read me what she had written or at least tell me about it.

The officer read a little of it and laid it down. "See, she did have problems."

I smiled. I had never said she didn't have problems. I had never said we didn't have problems. But I had maintained that her problems weren't any bigger than anyone else's and not big enough to make her run away when her best friend was coming for the weekend. I had a stack of notepads of my own, written at the same time in my life, that would have alarmed him, my parents, and everyone else as well. My problems probably had been worse than Candace's were.

But I could tell by the officer's face as he read, that, out of context, Candace's writing was incriminating evidence. If only Candace were here to explain. I realized how quickly things can be misinterpreted when a person isn't around to defend himself.

"This girl's in trouble," the officer concluded, and

I knew there was nothing I could say. Only Candace could lay his fears to rest.

While he was going through one notepad, I picked up another one and began reading it over. Candace had used her diaries to indulge in the usual teenage nobody-likes-me-everybody-hates-me pity party, and there was a lot of the daisy-petal-pulling routine of "he loves me, he loves me not." There were complaints about friends, complaints about life—but the officer was missing some important sections.

There was a prayer written in an obviously tired evening scrawl:

> *Dear Lord, Thank you for getting me through the day. Thank you for my friends, for Mom and Dad, Odia, Syras, for food, and your support. Help my grandmas and grandpas, and relatives and all the new babies. Give me the strength for the days and nights to come. Help me in my basketball games and my practices. . . . And now I close with a clean heart, I pray.*

There was another poem, printed in a hurry. I could barely make it out:

> *I want to fly,*
> *I want to soar,*
> *I want a horse,*
> *I want the highest score.*
> *I want to live,*
> *I want to die,*
> *I want to hug,*
> *I want to cry.*
> *But to do all of the wants,*
> *I have to help.*

I have to live a right life
. . . and that's what I want most.

It wasn't great poetry, but it was Candace. I continued to page through the diary.

"You shouldn't be reading her diary," the officer said accusingly and took it from me.

"I want to see if there is anything in here, a clue that will help us find her."

"A mother should never read her daughter's diary," he stated flatly, refusing to give it back.

"Normally, I wouldn't. But she has shown this to me before, and nothing like that matters now. We have to find her."

"How will you explain it to her when she comes back?" he pressed.

I answered him evenly. "When she comes back, I'll tell her that I ransacked her room looking for clues. She'll understand. She'll know that we did it because we cared."

"When she comes back, will you promise me that you will go for counseling?"

I bit my lip. It was too much. I wanted to scream at him, *How can you hurt me like this? Don't you know that she's dead? She's never coming back! It doesn't matter if we turn the whole world upside down; its all over! Here you are thinking I'm the abuser while the real culprit, the killer, is out there somewhere!*

I caught myself. If I went off the deep end, it would only convince him that I was an unfit mother. There was too much at stake. I calmed myself with the thought that someday he would probably know the truth. I wasn't being fair. He didn't know Candace. He had never met her. He had never witnessed us as a family during normal times. I knew things he didn't know. I had an unfair advantage.

"I promise you," I answered quietly, "if you find her and bring her back to me, I'll go and see six psychiatrists if that's what you want me to do." And I meant it.

He smiled wryly. "One will do."

The officers asked for a list of Candace's friends and then they left. Cliff wanted to go out and walk the route once more. We checked the thermometer outside the kitchen window. It was hovering around minus four degrees Fahrenheit and dropping.

The back doorbell rang. Who would use the back door? I ran through a mental list of everyone it could possibly be, and before I opened the door, I knew who it was. We had forgotten to call Heidi, Candace's friend! I had thought of calling her first thing that morning, but I had decided to wait until a more reasonable hour; then, with the police coming and all, I had forgotten. I opened the door. She was standing there impatiently, looking so happy, so full of expectations. It should have been such a wonderful moment. She looked past me, obviously wondering why Candace hadn't come to the door. I could see her father, Dave Harms, waiting in the car. I waved for him to come in. He seemed puzzled but signaled back that he would first park the car.

"Heidi, come in. I'm so sorry I didn't call. Candace isn't home."

"Isn't home?" she echoed in disbelief and confusion. "What do you mean, she isn't home?"

I groped for words. I should have thought of a way to break this to her. "We don't know what has happened to her. She didn't come home from school yesterday."

Dave stepped inside. I began again. "Candace

didn't come home from school yesterday. We don't know where she is."

Both of them looked at me in total disbelief. "She knew I was coming," Heidi said in a cold voice.

Then I realized that they thought she had chosen not to come home. "Heidi, I don't think she had a choice. She was looking forward to your coming so much; nothing would have kept her from coming home. That's why we think something terrible must have happened to keep her from coming home from school. But we're having a hard time convincing the police that she didn't run away. You know she wouldn't run away."

"Candace wouldn't run away," Heidi said in a dull voice. "I just know she wouldn't run away. We were going to have so much fun . . . ," and she broke down into frantic, disbelieving sobs.

I told them in detail what had happened, and after we had cried together, we thought it best that Heidi go back with her father to stay with their relatives in the city. If the police needed to talk to her, they could contact her there.

They left. Just the way Heidi walked to the car— shoulders drooping, head bent—tore my heart out. I wasn't the only one who had been robbed.

The telephone rang. It was Mary Wiebe.

"You don't know me," she said, "but I'm David's mother. Did Candace come home?"

"No."

"David is worried. He introduced her to us at the Terry Winter crusade."

"Yes, I know."

There was a long pause. I didn't know what to say.

"Is your family with you?"

"No, Cliff's family lives in Saskatchewan and mine

lives in British Columbia. We really don't have anyone in the city." My voice quavered. I needed my family.

"You shouldn't be alone now. You need your family."

"It's really okay," I tried to reassure her, wondering what she meant. Why should she be concerned? Did she believe us? Could she tell by my voice how desperate I was?

"Can I come over?"

"Oh yes, that would be nice." A stranger would be better than no one.

She came, and I soon found that one doesn't stay a stranger long with Mary. She helped take care of Syras as Cliff and I continued to make calls and answer the phone. She was truly a godsend. But the most wonderful thing she brought was her faith in us. I'm not sure what she thought at first; she must have had her doubts. We were strangers to her, too. But she never expressed them. She kept saying that Candace was in God's hands and that we didn't need to worry, and I would nod. It wasn't important to define exactly what we meant by *God's hands*.

One of the police officers called us again at lunchtime and said that in the process of contacting Candace's friends, he had become more convinced than ever that Candace had run away. Cliff had taken the call, and I watched his face carefully. His eyes dulled as the officer repeated, "We are convinced more than ever that she ran away and that you, her parents, are the problem."

I didn't know where he was getting that. Who was he talking to? What were her friends saying? What kind of slant were the police putting on the questions? What kind of pressure were they putting on those young kids?

But there was something else that was beginning to trouble me. I was becoming increasingly alarmed by his choice of words, the tone of his voice, and his attitude. This situation had become a contest between us and them. We were no longer discussing whether Candace had run away or not; we were arguing. His parting words that morning had been, "Look, who do you want to have egg on the face, you or me?"

I had answered, "Me."

He had grinned back as if he had won some kind of point. But I had closed the door knowing that if this became a contest, we were both losers. This wasn't a matter of winning or losing, right or wrong. This was a matter of finding Candace. Shouldn't both of us be looking at all angles at all times? We weren't closing our minds to the possibility that she had run away. We couldn't understand why these officers weren't pursuing both directions as well.

As Cliff hung up the phone, I wondered if we had erred in our approach the night before. Had we pushed too hard? Had we turned it into an argument? Had we polarized the situation? I could tell that I was panicking. One tends to find only what one is looking for. If the police were looking for a runaway, then they would only find a runaway. If Candace wasn't a runaway, then no one was looking for her. A trail of evidence disappears very quickly under such circumstances.

Cliff was thinking the same thing. Feeling helpless, he decided to walk the streets again. He grabbed for his coat, but just then the telephone rang. This time it was Dave Loewen calling to tell us that he had organized a search party. A group of people were meeting at Candace's school at one o'clock in the band room.

Dave Loewen had called the president of the Camp Arnes board, Dave DeFehr, a member of the prominent DeFehr family that owned Palliser Furniture. DeFehr had offered his help. Dave had then called two lawyers for legal advice and to establish the parameters of a private search. He had also called the police for their support, asking if they would brief the search party on what to do. They had agreed.

Dave had also called the rest of the Camp Arnes board, the MBCI teachers, and everyone else he could think of. He asked Cliff to join them and to bring as many pictures of Candace as possible. Cliff was only too glad to go. Fortunately, we had a lot of pictures. Candace's sixth-grade picture had been retaken, but by the time her package had come, picture trading was over and she had never distributed her pictures.

Between twenty-five and thirty people showed up at one o'clock that day. First they were briefed by a police representative. They were told that they could look along any back alley and into any trash can that they chose because such were considered public property, but they were to be extremely careful when they approached private property. They needed to ask permission to search any yard, and if they wanted to search an abandoned shed or garage, it was important that the owner accompany them. Under no circumstances were they to wander around private property or look into windows. If they did see anything suspicious, they were to write it down and report it to the police.

The group was divided into teams of twos and threes, and each team was given different streets to search. They were given an area map and a picture of Candace. Everyone was told to report back to the school at a given time.

Waiting by the telephone that kept ringing but not with the message I wanted to hear was one of the most difficult things I have ever done. However, it was made immeasurably easier by my knowing that there was a group of people out there, braving the cold, looking for our daughter. The most amazing part of it was that they believed us. None of them questioned our conviction that Candace hadn't run away.

It was dreadfully cold, and some members of the search party hadn't dressed properly. They had to keep their vehicles running as they went from house to house. Those who dropped by our house, half-frozen, looked like angels to us. None of them had ever done anything like this before, and to their surprise, many of the residents they questioned responded with hostility.

Later, back at the school, each one of the groups reported their experiences. They hadn't found anything concrete, though they had come across two abandoned houses that they wanted the police to check.

Dave and Ester DeFehr had encountered one suspicious family. While they were talking to a man at his door, his son, approximately twenty to twenty-five years old, came in, and when he heard Candace's name, he dropped the money he was carrying. Ester asked the son some questions directly, but the father intervened, seemingly to protect his son. Dave and Ester reported this to the police.

Before the group dispersed they asked Harold Jantz, editor of *The Mennonite Brethren Herald*, to see if he could use his media contacts to get Candace's picture in *The Winnipeg Sun*. Since the next day was Sunday, each person was to go back to his or her church and request prayer for Candace.

During the day, our house had become a center of activity. The community communications network was working well. People from every segment of our community started calling to see if they could help. The most obvious need was groceries. We hadn't shopped the night before, and there was nothing in the house. Two of our friends asked me to write down a list of what I needed. That was probably the second most difficult assignment of the day. I just couldn't concentrate on trivia like whether we needed tea, coffee, and milk. Those things suddenly seemed so unimportant.

The police kept coming and going. As I was making coffee for everyone, a call came in for one of the officers. Though I don't make a habit of eavesdropping, the telephone was in the kitchen, and it was hard to miss the conversation.

"You can't take me off the case," I heard the officer argue. "I've just started, and I've got a good handle on it."

I rattled the cups to distract myself, but it didn't work.

Eventually he said, "Yes, sir. I understand, sir." He was off the case!

I was so relieved; new officers might mean we had another chance. I was puzzled as to why he had been pulled, though. What had changed? Did this mean that those at headquarters were starting to believe us? Did headquarters even know what we were saying or wanting? No, it wasn't that. Suddenly it dawned on me; it was the search party. Our friends were making a difference. Whether the police actually believed us or not wasn't important anymore; sheer numbers and people force were enough to get us heard. Our friends were weighing the case in our favor.

The Wiebes stayed with us the entire day, making sure we ate and making sure the guests who came and went were all taken care of. They listened to us as we repeated our story over and over again. It seemed important to them that we weren't alone. But when

Reverend John Epp and his wife, Katie, came later that evening, the Wiebeses finally felt free to leave.

As with each new person who arrived, we again went through our story and our reasons for believing that Candace had been abducted. I was amazed that the Epps, too, believed us. We were part of a large church; they really didn't know us well enough to put that kind of confidence in us, but they did.

There was also something very comforting about having the Bible read to us and hearing someone else pray. I don't think it mattered very much what was read or even what was said. I was cold and trembling with emotional shock, and those old familiar words were like a soft warm blanket.

Just before they left, Pastor Epp turned to me and said, "I know you couldn't sleep last night. I also know that you are very tired and that you are going to need your sleep to keep up your strength for the days ahead. You can sleep now. You can be at peace. There are others who will be praying for Candace tonight. Now there are others to help carry your load."

How did he know how afraid I was of the night? All day I had dreaded the time when everyone would go home and leave me alone. Cliff would sleep, and I would pace the house again. I had seriously wondered if I would ever sleep normally again.

His words were powerful. I had never realized how wonderful it was to have a loving community to whom I could entrust the special responsibility of prayer. They were probably much better at it than I was.

As we prepared to go to bed, Cliff, who is always so levelheaded, said, "If we can't sleep, it means that we don't need it. Let's continue to talk it out." So we went over every little detail of the day's activities and told each other our insights, our fears, and our interpretations. We released our anxiety by agreeing that though we didn't understand what was happening or what was going to happen, God did. God would lead us through.

I was doing most of the talking and Cliff was doing most of the listening by the time we crawled into bed. I was still talking when he eventually fell asleep. I glanced at my watch; it was two o'clock. I could feel my fatigue slowly outweighing my anxiety. The 90 percent of me that believed Candace was in heaven had cried all day and had run out of tears. The 10 percent of me that wondered if Candace was still struggling somewhere, waiting for us, was now supported and soothed knowing that now there were many other people who understood us, believed us, and were willing to help us carry the load. It was my first glimpse of our supportive community.

Candace's picture was slated to appear in the next day's edition of *The Winnipeg Sun*. I found myself wondering if the public would believe us. Would the cold, windy city of Winnipeg believe us?

CHAPTER 4

The Need for Community

How does one prepare for a crisis? Usually we think of stockpiling money, food, and basic supplies; but that wasn't what we needed in this crisis. As we faced the police and our loss, we needed something else. We needed support, wisdom, human resources, and confidence. But how do you stockpile such things?

I woke the second day, Sunday, at five-thirty, feeling shaken, unnerved, and emotionally distraught. I could hardly perform those simple, habitual tasks of showering, curling my hair, and preparing breakfast.

When the two newly assigned plainclothes detectives came to the door around eight, we were still doing our morning chores. They slipped out of their over-shoes but kept their coats on as they accepted our invitation to sit down on our sofa. Their pant legs kept riding up to reveal tiny handguns strapped to their ankles. They watched us as carefully as we watched them. Since they were new to the case, we had to describe in detail everything from the beginning. I fought for composure as we rehashed Candace's disappearance.

I had thought the previous, uniformed officers were set in their thinking and unbending, but these detectives were no better. They were worse.

"She's coming back tomorrow," they assured us over and over again. "Trust our experience. Kids her age stay with friends for the weekend and then come back Monday for school. It's happened over and over again. Besides," they informed us, "she's been sighted by two people. What do you think of that?"

Tired of the games and of being accommodating, I responded, "They're lying. They didn't see her."

My response must have seemed strange. They paused and eyed us carefully. "There is something in this case you aren't telling us. There is something missing here."

Cliff assured them that we were being honest, that we had nothing to hide.

I was finding it increasingly difficult to remain calm. I felt that we had been raped; that every inch of our house, our lives, and our friends' lives had been pried open, analyzed, and exposed for their viewing. But I didn't say that; instead, I tried to use their question. "Yes, it doesn't make sense, does it? There *is* something missing. There *is* something wrong. It just doesn't add up, and that's the dreadful part of it. We don't have that answer either. The piece that you think is missing is the piece that is scaring the living daylights out of us."

I could tell by the way they shifted their eyes that they were discarding our comments. They continued their line of questioning. Did we have problems in our home?

Yes, we had problems.

Did we have insurance on our daughter?

They didn't need to do a credit check to know that we didn't have much money. Our furniture looked as if it had been rescued from the dump, and frankly, most of it had been. No, we didn't have insurance on our daughter.

They told us a vague story about a conservative family in southern Manitoba who happened to be Mennonite or Hutterite, they couldn't seem to remember which, who also had reported their daughter missing. The detectives described them as a very staunch churchgoing family. But the man had taken advantage of his own daughter's running away and had produced a ransom note asking for the exact amount that he owed on his tractor. The daughter was later found in another city.

They watched our reaction as they told the story. I didn't know how the story applied to us, but I had a sinister feeling that it was some kind of test.

We shrugged our shoulders. We pointed out that there was no way we could gain from our daughter's disappearance. We hadn't produced a note, and we weren't about to.

One of the officers turned to me and said, "We've been questioning all her friends. Some of them believe she could have run away. Did you know that you could be described as overbearing?"

I paused before answering him. They were building a case against me. I wasn't without faults, and they were probably finding out every little mistake I had ever made. I wouldn't have minded admitting to every mistake that they could produce—I'd even have accepted a few of their own—if it would have helped. But I wasn't a factor in this case. How was I ever going to divert their attention away from me to where the real evidence lay? Why weren't they doing as much research about Heidi and her relationship with Candace? Why weren't they asking about Candace's love for her friends? I caught myself. I reminded myself that they were just doing their job.

"Yes," I answered. "I know I can be overbearing. But Candace has always prided herself that she can handle me." She could, and she did. I remembered our last quarrel. She had said almost those exact words.

Eventually the officers closed their little black notebooks, telling us that they were going to stake out our church just in case Candace showed up there. We thought it ironic that they would even consider watching the church. They had made it abundantly clear that their first assumption was that Candace was rebelling against us because of our religious beliefs.

Their questioning had unsettled us, and as we closed the door behind them, I turned to Cliff. "It's a pity they're going to spend all morning out in their car, in the cold weather, watching a church for nothing."

Cliff smiled. "They should wait inside. They might learn something."

We smiled at each other. It made us feel better.

As we ate breakfast, I brooded over the conversation. I wondered if they were slotting us into some Mennonite stereotype. As with the other policemen, it seemed as if they associated fanatical religiousness with Mennonites. It wasn't unreasonable. As a people we have a history of being slightly fanatical. That reputation was warranted. Though I was proud of my heritage, I felt uncomfortable being defined only as a Mennonite. It was too broad a sweep.

I remembered the first time I'd heard the word *Mennonite*. I was in first grade. My three cousins and I were swinging on the swings when an older boy came by and sarcastically remarked, "Isn't it just like the Mennonites to hog the swings."

Mennonite. I had never even heard the term. At home I asked my sister, "What is a Mennonite?"

She paused, took a deep breath, and recited in her big sister tone, "They're a people who wear black bonnets, won't own cars, and only ride in horse-drawn buggies. They don't have electricity in their homes, the women aren't allowed to wear any makeup, and they all live together in a large community. They are known for their quilts."

"Are we Mennonites?" I asked cautiously.

"Yes."

"But we don't live like that."

"We're a different kind. There are thousands of different kinds. We're more modern, but we're still Mennonites."

I listened to her incredulously. I couldn't believe that she was dead serious. She wasn't making any sense, and she didn't even realize it.

Dad always made sense, so I went directly to him. He was bent over his workbench fixing a small motor. He listened to my question, and he did give me a straight answer. He explained that, yes, there were many different types of Mennonites, but the one thing they all had in common was that they believed in *nonresistance*.

"What's that?" I asked.

"We don't believe in going to war." He went on to explain that "to true Mennonites it means more than just not going to war. It means believing that peace is part of believing in God. We take it seriously when the Bible says that you should love your enemies, that when someone hits you on one cheek you should turn the other."

But I had hit back. I had hit the neighbor boy. Actually, we fought a lot. Did that I mean I wasn't a Mennonite? My Mennonite cousins fought, too. "Does everyone who is a Mennonite believe that?" I asked.

"No. Very few really understand and live it."

I wondered how we could be known for something we didn't understand.

"It's part of our history," Dad said simply, already guessing my next question. Then he went on to describe the rationale behind pacifism, and the discussion never really stopped. It was something we often discussed after supper, in the evenings, or when something happened in the community that tested our beliefs.

I learned about our history as a people: how our beliefs had sent our people on a pilgrimage from one country to another—eventually moving them from Russia to Canada; how the years of isolation had created a culture of sorts; how some Mennonite cultures were extremely severe and austere while others, like ours, could hardly be distinguished from mainstream Canadian culture.

My own roots are Russian Mennonite, which means my grandparents emigrated from Russia in the early 1900s. Cliff's roots are Canadian Mennonite, which means his grandparents were born in Canada. Both of us consider ourselves Canadians and have lost most of our Mennonite cultural distinctives. We understand a little German but can't speak it fluently, and I can count the times I've made borscht. Cliff wears a beard, but I think that comes more from his creativity than from his historical roots. But both of us are baptized members of the Mennonite Brethren denomination, making our Mennonite identity not only a heritage, but also a choice.

To be honest, much of the basis of that choice was that the church does feel like one big, extended family to us. The other reason is that we still adhere to and appreciate the strong emphasis that faith does not include just a personal relationship with Christ, but also the peace that God gives reflected in our day-to-day life. Responding in love to whatever happens is one of the basic premises of my Christian faith.

I didn't have long to brood. Dave and Fran Harms and their daughter, Heidi, came over soon after the police had left. "We didn't feel like going to church, and we didn't think you would either," they explained. Dave's first wife had died, so they were a family well acquainted with grief. We cried together.

The minute church was out our phone began to ring. News seemed to be flying around the community, and I wasn't sure anymore where people were getting their information. Candace's picture had appeared in *The Winnipeg Sun* that morning, and some of the callers mentioned it. Others mentioned hearing it announced in church as a prayer request. It was a toss-up as to which line of communication was stronger, that of the well-developed church-community network or that of the media.

About mid-afternoon Dave Loewen called and offered us a plan of action. He said he knew a constable in the juvenile division who had four days off and wanted to help with the case. He also suggested that we try Crime Stoppers, an excellent media public service announcement that alerted the public about different crimes.

Dave said that some people he knew were suggesting that a citizens search committee be formed to spearhead the community's response and to organize the search. He also wondered if the committee could act as a liaison in our dealings with the police. It was already apparent that the police communicated more openly with Dave than with us.

Dave thought that this committee could organize a more comprehensive ground search. The students of MBCI could be utilized to search the outlying areas, the railway tracks, the back alleys, the riverbanks, and the empty fields. Of course, he reminded us, this would all have to be cleared with the police, but what did we think?

We were ready for anything. Dave was going to pull it together for a meeting the next morning. Did Cliff want to be part of it?

"Yes," Cliff answered quickly.

Just before he hung up, Dave asked if we would check with the principal of George V School to see if Candace had been at that school's dance on Friday. We said we would. It was grasping at straws, but it could lead to something.

Taking Syras and Odia, Cliff went to get my parents from the airport at 3:44 that afternoon. When I had called them early on Saturday, they had immediately promised to come as soon as they could make the arrangements.

While he was gone, the two city papers called for more details about Candace's disappearance. The questions behind the questions were obvious: Who were we? Who was Candace? What was she like? I answered them as best as I could.

It kept coming back in a thousand ways. We were being forced to identify ourselves, to define ourselves.

As far back as I could remember, my parents had never been questioned like this by others—had never really questioned themselves. They knew who they were. When they had encountered problems, they had seemed so sure of what their response should be.

Before he retired, my father had owned a Shell service station on South Sumas Road in Greendale. Our house was surrounded by climbable apple and chestnut trees. Behind the house was a delicious grape-vine that draped itself over a little cellar that was always full of boxes of apples. It was a wonderful mix of rural and urban life. We could run over to the garage for candy from a tiny confectionery and then go to our little barn and watch a newborn calf learn to suck milk from a pail.

I remember how extremely proud and self-suffi-cient my father was. He worked six days a week—some-times up to twelve hours a day—to feed, clothe, and educate his five children. But more than anything else, I remember my father's integrity.

As my three sisters, one brother, and I grew up, we all were trained to serve gas at the pumps. This was during those marvelous days when the price of gas was thirty-three cents a gallon. It was a time when there was a trust that allowed the customer to call out "charge it" and drive off without bothering to sign.

Our particular bookkeeping system was to fill out a bill and file it in a huge gray account book that Dad tabulated at the end of each month. It didn't take me long to assess where the entire community stood with regard to each one's financial obligations.

I soon noticed that one particular person, consid-ered a responsible community member and a church member in good standing, was far behind in his pay-ments. I watched the account rise far beyond most of them—and then stop. My father suddenly insisted that we ask the customers to sign their bills. I finally asked my father about it.

He just shook his head sadly. "He isn't paying."

"But it's wrong," I insisted. "Why don't you do something about it? Can't you take him to court to have them settle this?"

My father was horrified. "No, Mennonites don't take people to court. It says in the Bible that in the church we are to settle it among ourselves peacefully."

"Then why don't you take him in front of the church? That's in the Bible too."

"Then what would come of it? I would get my money, but how would he feel? How would the church feel?"

"But you're out of a lot of money!"

He just shrugged his shoulders.

Every Sunday I would watch the delinquent man sitting near the front of the church, and I would wonder how in the world God could tolerate such injustice in his own house.

But I learned a lot about Dad.

I think children are able to perceive their parents' values better than the parents are themselves. I knew that money was very important to my father. As a twelve-year-old boy he had seen starvation in Russia, and he had encountered it again in Canada during the Dirty Thirties. It had left him determined never to be without money again. So both of my parents skimped and saved. My mom would wash and reuse plastic bags, can all our vegetables and fruit, sew our clothes, bake our bread, and do without.

I also knew that Dad wasn't a coward. He was actually quite small (I only realized this much later) and slightly shy, but I had seen him stand strong and coura-geous whenever anything threatened his value system. I knew that he would always live up to his convictions. He was a man of principle.

One evening, I heard him say to Mom, "That man has more problems than I have." The issue of justice becomes obsolete when a bad debt turns into a gift. Dad was no longer wronged; he had given the money away.

Years later, the man eventually paid.

My mother exemplified the same convictions and integrity. As a child, I had seen her walk back into a store and return the ten cents that she had been overpaid. Except for April Fools' Day when she often played practical jokes on all of us, my mother, to my knowledge, has never even smudged the truth.

When the door opened and all of them swirled in with the cold wind, and we had hugged and kissed, tears rolling down our cheeks, I noticed that my usually calm, reserved parents were as shaken as I was. They looked drained and absolutely weary. Yet underneath I could feel their strength.

Over tea, Cliff and I went through all the events of the last two days and described the current status of the investigation.

The telephone continued to ring and interrupt us.

When we were through, Mom started to set my kitchen straight, Dad gave his attention to the children, and I drifted upstairs to finish cleaning the bathroom. It was a project I had started a few times but could never seem to finish; I would just drift out and do something else.

In the evening, once the kids were in bed, we sat down again and began to really process the situation. I noticed that my parents kept asking questions about Candace almost as if she were a stranger. What was she like? What was she interested in? I finally stopped the conversation.

"Mom, why all these questions? You know Candace. She stayed with you for almost two months. Of all our children, you know her the best."

"Yes, we knew Candace as a child," Mom agreed. "But she must have grown up a lot in the last years. Children change, especially between the ages of ten and thirteen, so I don't feel I know Candace as a young lady."

I understood, and I tried to describe her, but my words were the words of a mother. How could I describe Candace?

I had been trying to answer this question for the last two days, and I hadn't done very well. Showing Candace's diaries to the police hadn't been convincing or adequate. I needed to find something that Candace had done recently, preferably something that she did every day, something she loved.

I wandered upstairs to look. How could I capture Candace for them? Since she shared her room with Odia, showing them her room wouldn't really do much. The decorations hanging from every corner of the room showed her creativity, but they didn't capture her attitudes or her philosophy. Suddenly, I knew. Her music. Her love for music. Her choice of music.

About a year and a half earlier, when Cliff had been in charge of music for Camp Arnes's roller-skating night for the young people, he had haunted the Christian music stores, bringing home all sorts of demonstration tapes. Of course Candace had loved Cliff's new responsibility. She had helped him pick out songs that kids her age liked.

I still remember that sunny day when she came

into the kitchen where I was quickly stirring some cookie dough.

"Mom, I found *my* song, and I want you to hear it."

"Play it while I put these on the pan before they harden."

"No, I want you to listen. I'll wait."

She curled up on the chair to watch and nibble.

"Is it rock?" I asked.

"No, you'll like it. It's by Michael W. Smith." The name didn't mean anything to me. "It's a song that's just mine. I like the words and the music."

"What's it about?" I asked.

"Friends."

I had to smile.

After the cookies were finished, I followed her into the living room and sat down. She put the tape on, and the song floated through the room. I tried hard to listen to the words. Though most of them escaped me, the theme was unmistakable. It was about the value of friends.

When the last note faded, she sat smiling smugly. "It's me, isn't it?"

I nodded. It was a lovely song, and I was thrilled with her taste.

Candace incorporated that song into a theme song for her life. A year and a half later she was still playing the song as often as when she discovered it. We heard it every night before she went to bed. I knew that if Mom heard it, she would know Candace.

The tape was still beside the bed in my old battered tape recorder that Candace had claimed. I took it downstairs and introduced the song to my family. When the familiar beat began, it was as if Candace had walked into the room, swaying slightly to the music, the hint of a dreamy smile on her lips, and a faraway, peaceful look in her eyes—totally absorbed in her music. The words floated into the room. I thought the pain would rip Cliff and me apart.

I had never really listened to the words. Now it was as if she were singing them to us.

Packing up the dreams God planted
In the fertile soil of you
Can't believe the hopes He's granted
Means a chapter in your life is through
But we'll keep you close as always
It won't even seem you've gone
'Cause our hearts in big and small ways
Will keep the love that keeps us strong

It was a good-bye song! She had chosen a good-bye song! Had she known? Had she in some way chosen this song for us because she knew she was going?

Then the chorus:

And friends are friends forever
If the Lord's the Lord of them
And a friend will not say "never"
'Cause the welcome will not end
Though it's hard to let you go
In the Father's hands we know
That a lifetime's not too long to live as friends

We sat stunned, the tears streaming down our faces.

Mom broke the silence. "She listened to those words every night?"

"Yes," I answered quietly.

Mom nodded, and I knew I had found the right vehicle to portray Candace to them. They knew the importance of music. They knew the importance of those words. They knew that one's choice of music often reflects the inner workings of the soul. They had just become reacquainted with Candace.

I also realized that the song was Candace's parting gift to us. It was her last message. I also knew that I'd never be able to listen to it again without being torn apart. It would both comfort and destroy us.

Candace had used the song to center herself at night, to find some peace before sleeping, and now the song had worked its magic on us.

At eleven o'clock that night, the two detectives came back. They told us that they had nothing new, they would call us again tomorrow, and a new team would meet with us. They asked us to let the staff at MBCI know that they would be at the school in the morning. They were still positive that Candace would show up there, and I knew that they really believed that. I wished I could. It would be so much easier to sleep with that thought than with the thoughts I had.

During the day we had remembered that Candace probably had been carrying her clarinet in her duffel bag. We told the detectives about it, and they felt it was important. They agreed with us that it might show up somewhere, hocked for money. To follow that through, we needed to check her locker to see if she really had taken it with her.

They also asked if we would check with the principal of her former elementary school to see if she had been at a party there on Friday night. We said we would. We didn't bother to tell them that Dave had already asked us to check. We sensed that there were two parallel investigations happening simultaneously, and we decided we would cooperate with both, not discourage either one or mingle the two, and perhaps we could cover twice as much ground.

With that, they left. Like the day before, they had been our first visitors in the morning and our last visitors at night. We were beginning to shape our days within the parentheses of police visits. It seemed so contradictory to everything we were. I was sorry to see my parents drawn into this, and yet I was glad for everything they were. Amidst all the contrary winds, my parents were the most integral reminder that we came from a tradition of honesty and truth and that if we held onto these values, perhaps we would survive.

As we prepared for bed, I noticed that only half of the tub had been scrubbed. My mom, the best housekeeper in the world, was here, and I had left half the tub unscrubbed all day. I knew it didn't matter. It was only trivia.

CHAPTER 5

The Role of a Mother

There must be millions of books on how to be a good mother—how to breast-feed, how to look after a sick toddler, how to deal with a teen—but I have never run across a how-to book on how to be a mother when your daughter is missing. I have read a few things about missing children and about some of the dos and don'ts in such situations, but I have never read anything about the role of the mother involved.

I gathered from Cliff's telephone conversation with Dave Loewen, Sunday afternoon, that the newly formed citizens search committee, which was meeting on Monday, had asked for Cliff's presence and not mine. But after a Sunday of mourning and waiting, I wanted to do something. I needed to feel I was doing something. I wanted to be where the action was.

I was also concerned. If these people were going to be the leaders in looking for our daughter, I wanted to make sure that they were the right people. Misfortune attracts all kinds of attention—some of it helpful, some of it not so helpful. I trusted Dave Loewen, but I wanted to see the whole group, and I wanted to assess them in action.

So at breakfast that morning, I told Cliff that I wanted to go with him. He hedged. In a long, roundabout way, he carefully let me know that this was going to be a working committee, that they would not be mincing words, and that they couldn't afford the time to be sensitive to my feelings. Would I be able to handle it?

I could tell that he didn't think I could. I couldn't blame him. I had been crying on and off, uncontrollably, since the first night. All day Sunday I had been an emotional wreck.

"I promise I won't cry or make a scene. I won't act like a mother. I'll be part of the working team. I'll be totally professional."

"That's not what I want," he said. "You *can* be a mother. You don't have to put yourself through this."

I didn't give up, and eventually, knowing how determined I could be, Cliff gave in.

Before we left for the meeting, I took my parents aside and gave them explicit instructions about what to do if, by chance, Candace called. I gave them all the pertinent telephone numbers: the police, the school, the emergency number. I was torn. I wanted to be by the telephone. I wanted to be there if Candace called. I didn't think anyone could replace Cliff or me, but I needed to go. More than anyone else, Mom and Dad could handle the home front.

They assured me that they could.

I had only been housebound for two days, but when I stepped outside into the freezing cold that morning, I felt as if I had been in the house for a year. Everything had changed in the last two days. Last week it had meant nothing to get in the car and drive all over the city, but now I was grateful that Cliff was driving. I had changed. I felt vulnerable and incapable.

Driving down Talbot was painful. Everything was so full of memories. The last time I had driven down this street, I had just been to see David. I had screamed at God.

I was extremely weary. Thursday I had worked through the night on my projects. Friday I hadn't slept at all because of worrying and praying for Candace. Saturday I had slept three and a half hours at the most. And Sunday I had slept four hours. I could tell that my edges were ragged. I knew I was going to have a tough time controlling my emotions. Even at the best of times, I'll cry buckets if a tiny dog dies in a movie; and here I was, tired and hurting. The meeting hadn't even started yet, but just thinking about it made a knot of emotion start to grow in my throat. But I had promised Cliff.

During my teens, when I had dared to go to a tear-jerking film on a date, I had learned a few tricks so as not to cry and smudge my mascara. When the movie started to tear at my emotions, I would distract myself by noticing details. I'd count the boards in the ceiling, the folds in the drapes, the colors in the room, or the rows in the theater.

Now, as I felt the pressure mounting, I wondered if it would still work. I looked around at the houses as we drove. One homeowner had bundled his evergreens up in sacks, another had only tied them up. One house had a new roof, another needed painting. And so it went. It was working. It took more effort than before, but it still worked.

I kept it up as we walked into the school: *that girl is wearing five different colors; the janitor must have waxed the floors over the weekend. . . .*

I was so absorbed in my details I didn't notice that everyone in the school halls stopped talking as I passed by. Suddenly I was aware of it, and I felt awkward and conspicuous.

Inside the office, two police officers passed us, their heads bent. There were tears in the female officer's eyes—or did I just imagine it? The tension continued. It was almost as if people were frightened of me.

I sensed that everyone was much more at ease with Cliff. *Does a mother play a different role than a father does in these kinds of cases?* I wondered. Everyone seemed genuinely frightened of me, and I wasn't quite sure why. But whatever it was that was frightening them, it would stand as a barrier to us all working together. It would block communication. I tried to smile.

We were ushered into a meeting room. There were introductions: Dave Loewen and Dave Teigrob representing MBCI and our church, River East Mennonite Brethren; Harold Jantz, editor of *The Mennonite Brethren Herald*; Henry Wedel, a schoolteacher; Dave DeFehr of Palliser Furniture; his wife, Ester.

Winnipeg is a city of around 650,000 people, set right in the middle of Canada. It's probably best known for its extreme temperatures: hot, dry summers and frigid winters. For those of us who are part of the Mennonite community, it is also known for having the highest Mennonite population in the world. There were nineteen thousand Mennonites in forty-seven churches in 1984. Usually this wouldn't be particularly important. But with our daughter missing, we were looking for the largest support base we could find. Looking over the composition of the committee, I knew that at least one Mennonite conference was behind us. We had representatives from the largest camp in Manitoba, the largest private school, one of the more powerful churches in Winnipeg, the Mennonite paper, and the largest western-Canadian furniture business. This group was nothing to sniff at.

But what was far more important was something else I knew about them. I knew that all of them were known for their integrity.

Ester was first on the committee's agenda. I didn't know her that well. We had met only once, but we had clicked. I liked her easy casualness and the way she could cut through all the blarney and the social games and get right to the point. Even at our first meeting, I had sensed her caring. She seemed to have a heart that enveloped the whole world. Now she was concerned about Candace, a girl she hadn't even met. And as the only other mother at the table, she understood things that no one else could but me.

Barely taking the time to notice me, she gave a report on her discussions with the police and voiced her frustrations. She had discovered an organization called Child Find that she was sure would be able to offer valuable information on what to do in this case.

I was amazed at how much she had been doing while I had been sitting at home, crying and fielding telephone calls and visitors. I felt a pang of guilt. She was more serious about looking for Candace than I was. I was jealous. I wanted to do what she was doing.

I caught myself. I couldn't do what she was doing. I couldn't concentrate, and I was constantly being interrupted by the telephone. I realized that I had my own unique role, and I was suddenly very grateful that she was there to do all the things I wanted to do, but couldn't.

I scanned the group. This was community. This was what that beautiful Bible passage about bearing each other's burdens was all about. This was what Scripture meant about each believer having a different gift and each having a different role to play. Everyone playing his or her part makes for a powerful team.

As I looked at the people around the table, I was satisfied with what I saw: Dave Loewen with his organizational ability, Dave Tcigrob with his school counseling experience and interchurch connections, Harold Jantz with his media know-how, and Ester DeFehr with a mother's perspective. The committee was complete. I was satisfied that they didn't need me.

I felt the constriction in my throat begin to choke me. My emotions were slipping, so I tried to notice details. . . . Dave had a worn brown folder . . . Ester was wearing a green dress—moss green, an autumn color.

Then they started talking about the media. They delicately asked me if I would go on television, and I recoiled in horror. Talking to the press the night before had been bad enough. We had just picked up the paper and read the results of my conversation with the reporter. It had been good; the tone had been excellent. But the writer had called David Wiebe Candace's boyfriend. What would David think? Candace would have been horrified to find her secret crush talked about in the paper. It was a minor slip—not even a mistake, depending on one's definition of boyfriend. But what if I made a bigger mistake on television? We wouldn't have any friends left. Besides, they didn't know that all that was holding me together was a small veil of details as fragile as a soft mesh of cobweb.

They had Candace's picture, and they had Cliff. Cliff loved speaking in public. He had always been the public person in our family. I said something of the sort, and they all nodded their heads. But, they insisted, the mother's plea is the most powerful.

Harold Jantz reminded us that in this case the media wasn't hostile. They would be sympathetic and want to help us.

They asked me to think about it some more. They said the stations were asking for an interview. They reminded me that the police and the school were doing their part, but it was the public that was everywhere. If we could gain their attention, we had a much better chance of finding Candace soon.

I promised to think about it.

I could feel my tiredness growing. The choking was growing. I was losing my concentration, and I knew I would lose control soon. I excused myself and asked Cliff if he could find another way home after the meeting. A committee member quickly said that he'd take Cliff home. Did I need a ride? Did I need someone? No, I answered quickly. I was fine. I had been away from the phone too long.

Somehow I managed to get to the car. My fingers were trembling as I started the motor, and for a minute I wondered if it would start in the cold. It did. As I inched out into the road, the dam in me burst. The street literally swam with wave upon wave of emotion and tears.

I cried all the way home as I carefully considered the request to go on television. Somehow it had been all right to talk to a reporter on the telephone, but going on television was another thing! The image on television, even if it is only three minutes long, is so powerful. If we did it, our privacy would be completely shattered. It had been hard enough just going to a meeting with friends, with truly concerned people. How could I ever face the public?

Besides, I had been taught that a reporter needs to be there for the follow-up to his or her story. A good reporter sees the story to the end. Here I was at the beginning of a story whose end I didn't know. Did I really want the media around when we found out what had happened to Candace? If I went on television now, they would be with us till the end. If the police were right, we would be the most embarrassed couple in Winnipeg. If we were right, we would be the most traumatized. Neither ending would be good, and the cameras would only make it more difficult.

By the time I turned into our driveway, I had made my decision. I was not going to go on television. Cliff would have to do it.

My parents met me in the kitchen. "Any calls?" I asked.

My mother knew what I was really asking. "No," she answered quietly. "But there were some other calls you can take care of later. You have guests in the living room."

I took off my coat. "The committee thinks I should go on television. You don't think I should, do you?" I was positive that my private, conservative parents would agree with me.

But they both shook their heads. "We think you should," said Mom with conviction.

I couldn't believe what I was hearing. Not only were they advising me to go public, but Mom wouldn't have said "we" if she and Dad hadn't already discussed it.

I went into the living room. I don't know who I expected, but I wasn't expecting my former instructors from Red River Community College. I couldn't fathom that Alice and Sheila, my journalism and public relations instructors, had abandoned Monday morning classes to drive across the city and visit me. I was both stunned and moved.

I went through the story, explaining everything to them as best as I could. I found that the stress of the morning on top of four days' accumulated weariness was interfering with my concentration, and I had a hard time focusing on my own story.

But I realized that they had come at the perfect time. I could ask them, the experts, whether I should go on television. They would say that under the circumstances—being unprepared, under duress, and tired—I shouldn't go on television. Both of them had always stressed being prepared for the occasion.

"This is different," they said firmly but sympathetically. "The public is out there. You need to solicit their help."

I didn't want to hear what they were saying.

By this time, Cliff had come home from the meeting. "Wilma, you have to go on television. You have to do this for Candace." Cliff rarely uses my first name. It's usually something like "sweets" or "wifey." By using my name, he was signaling in a room full of guests that he wasn't speaking a husband. As Candace's father, he was letting me know it was his opinion that I had no alternative but to go public.

"Will you be with me?"

"Yes, I'll be here," he promised.

Both Alice and Sheila said that they would also stay.

For a moment I recalled how I had stood in front of the living room window that first dreadful night, pleading with God. I had said that I was willing to do whatever was required of me, but I had also asked for two things. I had asked that Candace wouldn't have to suffer physical pain and that God would guide us. I wondered if it was only coincidence that now, when I had to make one of the biggest media decisions of my life, I had my communication instructors come and visit.

I finally nodded my head.

Cliff immediately went to the door and waved to the two vans waiting in the street. I hadn't realized they were outside the door waiting.

I ran upstairs to freshen my makeup and to catch my breath. I tried to pull my thoughts together, but I couldn't. I could hardly comb my hair.

When I came down, a television crew was setting up lights in our tiny living room, which was beginning to look like a dilapidated studio. Cliff, always interested in photography, was giving them some suggestions as to lighting.

For one brief moment, I was intrigued. It was interesting watching them set up. I had always been the one to write the stories, to draw the story out of others. Now *I* was the story, and I wondered what it would be like. What would they ask me?

Cliff and I sat down on our chesterfield sofa. The reporter asked the first question . . . and I couldn't answer.

One second after he had spoken, I couldn't for the life of me remember what he had asked. My mind was a total blank. All I could think was, *I don't want to do this. Why don't they all get out of my living room and leave me alone? Don't they know that there is no hope? Candace is dead!*

Cliff picked up the question and answered it. I looked over to my instructors. Their eyes mirrored my pain. They were suffering with me. One of them mouthed the words, "For Candace."

She was right. If there was a slim chance that she was alive, I had to do it for Candace.

I answered the next question. I was strangely calm.

After the interview, I heaved a sigh of relief. Our fate was sealed. Whatever would happen, would happen. We could now relax.

But we weren't finished. My teachers excused themselves as another camera crew took over our living room. Our house had turned into a studio. The phone was ringing, the doorbell was ringing, and we were giving interviews, talking freely, not even capable of weighing each word carefully. We were going for broke. Things became a blur.

The police stopped by the house to pick up a shoe. I gave them a boot that Candace had worn recently. They didn't need to say what they were going to use it for, and I didn't ask. There was a certain hopelessness in the gesture. There had been fresh snow since Candace had disappeared, and the temperature had plunged. No dog would be able to pick up a scent with those odds. But I was grateful that they were trying.

That afternoon the police did an aerial search of the area. I suppose we could have claimed some kind of victory. Public pressure seemed to be forcing the police to act on our case.

The radio stations had picked up our story. We were getting calls and more food. The kitchen began to fill up with dainties.

At this point it surfaced that there was a girl living in the community who looked very much like Candace. There were at least five people who had thought Candace's picture was of this other girl—a girl who was into drugs and lived a shady life. Could Candace have been picked up by someone thinking she was the other girl? Was this person afraid to release Candace for fear she would talk? Every theory was worth checking.

That night we watched the news. I was scared that they would show me sitting there in stunned silence.

Would they highlight the tears that had glistened in the corners of our eyes? Would they capture our stammering and make us look like two silly, overwrought parents who couldn't own up to the fact that they were inadequate parents and so were making an abduction case out of their daughter's running away? It could be done so easily with one comment, one opposing view by the police.

But they didn't. I was amazed at how calm and controlled we appeared. The most important part of the whole news blurb was that they showed Candace's picture. It was the best possible way of getting her picture into the community.

Even though I still didn't know where we were going, I was already glad that we had done it. As a mother, I had done something constructive.

That night, once the children were in bed and I had prepared a night snack for my parents, Cliff, and myself, we settled down in the living room to rehash the details of the day. I finally asked the question that had been bothering me all evening. My parents had surprised me completely when they had encouraged me to go public. All my life I had seen them as the most private people I had ever encountered. On Sundays they were the last to arrive at church and the first to leave. They never told us children their "secrets." We never knew about any of their personal problems. They would openly discuss their dreams, their ideas, and their aspirations, but problems and tensions were always discussed behind their bedroom door. And I had always admired their control. It wasn't that they ever tried to deny that they had problems; it was a courtesy on their part. Yet they had almost pushed me in front of the television cameras to tell the whole world that we had a problem.

So I asked them why. Why had they thought it would be good to go public?

"It must be hard to go in front of the cameras. I would never have thought to do it. But we had Clifford Olson in British Columbia. . . . " Dad's voice trailed off, but he didn't have to say anything more.

Clifford Olson, a well-known serial killer, had stalked Fraser Valley, killing eleven children. I remembered my sister who lived in Clearbrook writing about how terrified she was for her children and how they had organized car pools. At the time, I had thought, *I'm so glad Winnipeg is safe.*

I also remembered that only one of the victims had been the subject of an extensive police search, even though others had been reported missing. The others had been dismissed as runaways. Now I understood.

I also understood why my parents had been so sad when they arrived. I realized that right from the beginning they were comparing the two cases; having heard the end of one dreadful story and knowing the possibilities, they were preparing themselves for the worst.

We watched the late night news. It aired a documentary about the most wanted man in Canada. I don't remember all the details, but it described his violence, his criminal record, and his uncanny ability to disguise himself. We all sat watching in horror. Murder stories now had a special significance to all of us.

By the time everyone went to bed, it was extremely late. Once I was sure that everyone was asleep, I slipped out of bed and started to wander around downstairs in the dark. It was becoming a ritual. I still had too much to process, and I could do it best when everyone else was asleep.

It seemed as if by the end of each day I had accumulated all the hurts, all the fears, and all the questions all over again. Each night I had to go through each one and decide once again that it wasn't I who was important here, it was Candace.

Even though I felt good about the media exposure because it would help in our search for Candace, it also made me feel we were making our entire family extremely vulnerable. Someone had taken one of our children; was there another person waiting to take Odia or Syras?

I sat at the kitchen table and looked out at the black night. The face of the most wanted man in Canada was haunting me. It seemed so familiar. I wondered if it was the wrestler from the East who was staying next door and whom I had called in the first night of Candace's disappearance. It all made sense: his living in the area, his flexing muscles. . . .

In many of the stories I had read, it was the neighbor. What if Candace was next door? What if she had been that close the whole time? I wanted to grab my coat and run over and bang on the door and demand to search the house immediately—or at least call the police and have them do it. But every time I tried to convince myself, I had to admit to some doubts. I needed to be certain.

Our neighbors usually got up early, about the same time we did. While making breakfast, I could watch; and when this guy walked down the sidewalk, I could double-check. Then I would call the police.

CHAPTER 6

Suspicions and Psychics

I don't think I slept at all that night. I heard every start of the furnace, every snore, every deep breath on our side as well as the other side of our duplex. Somewhere in the night I heard some dull thuds, and I wondered if it was Candace, bound and gagged, trying to get loose from a closet just on the other side of the wall. It would be driving her crazy to think that we were so close and yet so far.

Our neighbors started to stir unusually early Tuesday morning, and I was down in the kitchen in a flash. I made some coffee and sat on our kitchen table so I could watch every movement in our backyard. There was a street light in the alley right behind our house, and it was placed perfectly for my little stakeout.

He couldn't have eaten much of a breakfast, because the back door opened at almost the same time as the kitchen light went on. I moved closer to the window, hiding in the shadows. For one desperate moment I wondered what would happen if he saw me. What if he suspected we knew who he was? Would our whole household be in danger?

A man stumbled down the sidewalk, shielding himself from the bitter cold. Just as he moved into the alley, he turned to look both ways and to look back at the house. The street light shone brightly on his face. It was the wrestler, but he didn't look at all like the man on the news the night before. There was not even a close resemblance.

I drew back from the window and went into the living room with my cup of coffee. *Is this what happens?* I wondered. *After a crime, does a person become obsessively suspicious?* I wondered what would happen if I suspected one of my friends. Would I stake out their house, sitting in the dark night after night? Would I ever be able to sleep in peace again? It was more than concern for my daughter that had kept me up the night before; it was my own basic need for answers.

Sitting there alone, before my family began to stir, I knew that I needed a resolution. If not a solution, then at least some guidelines or a philosophy to help me through this. I needed some kind of model, some kind of map of a path through this mystery. And that's when I remembered Jake Plett.

When Cliff was a pastor in North Battleford, we'd had friends who sold books from their home. One day they told us that the author of *Valley of Shadows* was coming to town, and I quickly offered our home as a place for him to stay. I was interested in writing and wanted to rub shoulders with anyone who knew how to write, hoping some of their magic would rub off on me. My friends were relieved not to have to host him, and they gave me his book to read before he came.

I wasn't so sure that I wanted to meet Jake Plett after I read his book. It was about the disappearance of his wife from their home in Edmonton. Plett's wife had been a real estate agent who had never come home after showing a potential customer a house. After a whole winter of searching, her body was found on the outskirts of town. There was no doubt that it was murder. The book was about Jake's journey through the valley of shadows.

Plett arrived at our home Saturday afternoon and didn't have any plans till a presentation he had to make that evening. Cliff had to put the finishing touches on Sunday's program, so I was elected to entertain him. I asked him if he might like to have a cup of coffee in the kitchen while I finished baking my pies, and he didn't seem to mind at all. He was the most amiable, carefree, and happy person I had met in a long time.

After the usual talk-about-the-weather, get-to-know-each-other conversation, my curiosity got the better of me and I started to ask questions about his experience. He seemed quite willing to answer my initial questions, so I went for the story behind the story—the unpublished version. He never flinched. In fact, he seemed to enjoy talking about it.

How had he felt? Why had he done what he had? How had he coped with his children? How had the church helped? How had he dealt with his anger, his grief? Why had he written the book? Why had he remarried? What did he feel was the purpose in it all? Somehow I continued to peel the apples and slice them, even though I was completely enthralled with his story and his responses.

When I asked about his children, he said that he had felt sorry for them at first. "How could I discipline two little boys who had just lost their mother?" he explained. "So I let them do what they wanted, when they wanted. I gave them candy, didn't make them go to bed, and just let them run wild. It shouldn't have surprised me, then, that they began to really be wild."

"What did you do?"

"One of my friends was kind enough to tell me that children need routine. With their mother's death, they had lost the security of her presence; I was compounding that loss by discarding her routine. I needed to put our lives back together and carry on as if she were still there as mother. I needed to make them eat their vegetables and get to bed on time, and I needed to discipline them if they did wrong. So that's what I did, and it helped."

According to his book, his wife's killer had never been found. I wondered what it would be like to live with that kind of question, so I asked. Was he actively looking for this person? Was it his preoccupation?

I watched him closely. I watched for hidden stress, for hidden anger, but Plett seemed so open, so free. He was sitting on the kitchen table, one leg swinging, the other on a chair. He said, "I'll always be alert. Sometimes I see a strange person, and of course I wonder if it could be him. But I have better things to do. I wasn't called to be a policeman, and I have no skill in that direction. The police keep telling me that they'll find him, but I have my doubts. Still, it's really their responsibility, not mine."

Tears glistened in his eyes. "I decided that, by taking my wife's life, this person had already taken too much. I wasn't going to let him disrupt the rest of my life as well. If I had started trying to solve this case, I'd still be at it. And what would I accomplish if I found him? It wouldn't bring my wife back. He would only have been successful in robbing me of my own purpose in life."

Since his wife's murder, Plett had remarried. I wondered if he felt he was betraying his wife's memory. Did he feel guilty for continuing?

His answer was the same. "I needed to carry on. My present wife will never be able to replace my first wife. She wouldn't even try. My sons needed a mother, I needed a wife. My first wife and I had decided together that should one of us die, the other would be free to remarry. Remarriage only means that I loved my first wife."

I couldn't understand all of that, but I believed him. He was walking proof that life can go on.

Then we went on to other topics. He told me about the media and how he had coped with them. He told me about the police and their limitations and about the psychics who seemed to come out of the woodwork.

I could hear the family begin to stir upstairs. I shook off my memories, amazed at how vivid the experience was after all these years. I wondered how similar our stories would end up being. We had already encountered the police and the media. If Plett's story was to be any kind of model, we would have psychics calling soon.

After our television appearance on Monday, we sensed a totally different attitude from the police. Inspector Heintz of the juvenile division told the media that the police were more concerned about Candace's safety with each passing day. "Statistics show that kids who run away usually return within two days," he told the media. "While there's no evidence suggesting foul play, we're certainly concerned about the situation."

The search committee printed posters with the captivating question "Have you seen Candace?" at the top and a big picture and a brief description of her underneath. They were printed on bright orange paper that could be spotted miles away.

Their next project was to organize another search of the area, this time by the students. The police were very cooperative in helping to brief the fifty MBCI seniors who wanted to go out and search on Tuesday. Five students from Kildonan East Regional Secondary School also joined in the search. The school had decided to recheck the entire area that Candace walked home from school. This time the search included the nearby riverbank and the railway tracks. The police supervised the entire search.

While searching, the students distributed the fly- ers and asked the residents near the school if they had seen or heard anything unusual during the last five days. The students did a marvelous job. In an hour-long blitz covering a twelve-square-block area, they distrib- uted approximately one thousand flyers to residents of the area and business people. Many of the businesses posted the picture in their front windows.

Afterwards, the students said that many of the people they approached already knew that Candace was missing because of the media coverage. There were also many who hadn't heard, and the students felt good that they had alerted the community.

The publicity was beginning to have the effect we hoped it would. People were responding by calling in any kind of information that they had. Many of the reports were "sightings." At first, we were a little baf- fled by the strange places that Candace had supposedly been seen, until we realized that most of these sightings were really just the response of a caring community wanting to become involved and grasping at straws.

On one hand, all of these calls were exactly what we wanted; on the other hand, there were so many of them that it was hard to deal with them all. We began to understand the police when they complained about their work load. Each sighting and each report had to be investigated thoroughly, and this created more work for them and sometimes distracted them from working on the more serious leads.

One of these sightings became public. An Elmwood couple, who lived near us, reported that they had seen a young girl being dragged from a Watt Street bus stop by two teenagers at about four o'clock Friday afternoon. The two teens had been wearing parkas with their hoods up, so the Elmwood couple hadn't been able to see their faces. At first the couple had presumed that the kids were just fooling around and having a good time. But after hearing the media reports about Candace, they wondered if indeed it had been Candace struggling with her abductors, so they reported it to the police. However, someone at the police station had told them not to worry, because "Candace is just another runaway." The couple couldn't believe this response and pursued the incident by calling *The Winnipeg Sun*. The story appeared in the paper as a complaint about the apathy of the police.

When we heard about it, we were immediately concerned that the police hadn't taken this lead seriously, and we asked them about it. They assured us that they had gotten back to the couple and reassured them that they were taking Candace's disappearance seriously. However, after getting further details on the sighting, the police had good reason to dismiss the story. Apparently the couple had seen the struggle on the way to a four o'clock appointment, making the incident somewhat before four o'clock. Candace had called me from the school right at four o'clock, and then again five minutes later. They couldn't have seen Candace.

The police never did publicly clear up the apathy complaint. I guess it just didn't seem important to them. However, it made it clear to us just how much effort and time it took to investigate each new bit of information.

We were getting calls at home as well; people with horror stories of other abductions, people with theories as to why and how she had disappeared, and people with vague sightings that were almost impossible to verify called to share what they knew. We simply passed on all the information to the police.

There were also a lot of calls meant to give support. A mother from Steinbach whose daughter had disappeared from home called to say that her daughter had walked into the school two weeks later as if nothing had happened. Someone called to tell us a story about a fifteen-year-old who had hidden in a farmer's barn and had suddenly returned. We were grateful for the stories; we understood that people were trying to help, and we thanked them, but they were little comfort.

Tuesday evening a radio station called to ask if we would speak to Peter Warren on his radio show the next day at 8:40 A.M. I think every city must have a Peter Warren, a crusty radio journalist to whom everyone listens—whether they liked him or not—because he makes things happen. He had an open-line talk show on CJOB, and it seemed that there was nothing too sacred or too private to be talked about. He was brilliant and formidable.

Television had been bad enough. I was not going to go on his show. What if I drew a blank? He, more than anyone else, would make mincemeat out of me.

I'm not sure who did the convincing this time, but when 8:40 rolled around the next morning, I was sitting beside the phone, trembling. Cliff was on an extension.

Warren seemed friendly enough. He asked about Candace. He wanted to know her description. He wanted to know why we didn't think this was an ordinary runaway case, and we told him. I thought it was going well.

Then he said slowly, almost hypnotically, "Mrs. Derksen, I have an audience of ———," and he gave a number in the tens of thousands, "who listen to me every day. What if Candace is listening right now? What would you like to say?"

A picture flashed through my mind of Candace, bound and gagged, listening to the radio. But a stronger picture followed, a picture of her body lying inert in the bushes. I burst into a sob. I wanted to scream, "She isn't listening! She's dead," but I caught myself again. What if she were alive? I had to act as if she were alive. Somehow, I managed to say, "Oh, Candace, come home. We're waiting for you."

How inane! If she were alive, I would be screaming, "I love you! I love you! I'm so sorry." We signed off, and I vowed I'd never be caught off guard again.

We listened to the radio to see if anyone would call in. There was one call directly afterwards. A man with a deep, dull voice, who identified himself as an ex-convict, said, "If anyone has harmed one hair on this girl, he will have to answer to me and forty-five thousand others, so he had better be careful."

The search committee met again Wednesday afternoon. They were meeting every day, having taken on the huge task of keeping track of the investigation as well as coming up with new ideas for finding Candace.

Ester reported that she had contacted the Child Find organization as well as the Tania Murrel Missing Children's Society in Edmonton. She had also been in contact with the National Center for Missing and Exploited Children in Washington, D.C., and we were given the forms to register with them.

The committee decided that they should formally organize and call themselves The Candace Derksen Citizens Search Committee. They would begin to raise funds to cover expenses; receipts would be given for all donations, which would be handled by Camp Arnes. There was also talk about the possibility of offering a reward for information, but they hadn't really thought through the concept. They decided to consult with the police; unless the police supported the idea fully, they wouldn't even attempt it. They also talked about raising money for a private detective, about stepping up the poster distribution, and about organizing a press conference.

But the most important item of the day was to contact prayer chains and update the information before the weekend.

Prayer chains! I had forgotten about them. These chains are probably the best means of church networking that has ever been conceived. It is simply a listing of the names of those who are interested in supporting each other in prayer. To link up, one only has to phone the person next on the list, pass on the prayer request, pray together, and then hang up. That person will then phone the next person on the list, who phones the next, and so on. A cynic might say that it's just an organized gossip chain, but for us, every bit of information and every earnest prayer was so important.

Pastor Epp asked Cliff to attend the church prayer meeting Wednesday evening to tell the congregation firsthand what was happening.

My heart skipped a beat when the first psychic called.

The call came in from Kenora. The man asked if we would be willing to send him a strand of Candace's hair. He had devised a scanner that could give a coordinate within three thousand miles of Candace's location. He said he had already been instrumental in helping to find a downed aircraft.

"Three thousand miles! That isn't exactly what one would call terribly accurate," I said to Cliff.

Cliff was more tolerant. "At least we'd know if she's still in the province."

I nodded. While everyone was searching the riverbanks, the railway tracks, and the city, I often wondered if she had been taken out of the country.

But we politely declined his offer.

It wasn't much later that the police called and said that they had gone to some "card people" and that these people had said that "Candace is with someone she knows." A young fellow showed up at the Camp Arnes office and said that he was a "born again believer" and that he had prophetic powers. He wondered if someone would drive him around because he had seen Candace in a dark place, probably outside the city limits.

It seemed as if we were suddenly bombarded by requests to give something of Candace's to these psychics so they could get more accurate readings. Then I remembered Plett; I remembered my conversation with him.

Plett had confessed that at first he had been tempted to cooperate with the psychics. It had been so hard to live with the unknown. Now I understood what he meant. It was tempting. When it appears as if there is no one on earth who can help you, the supernatural element becomes a very strong alternative. I don't think there has been any other time in my life when I have been so aware of our dependence on something bigger and larger than we are. We needed God.

But how were we to recognize God?

There was another supernatural presence making itself known, and in the confusion of the moment, in our time of greatest need, I wasn't so sure we could trust ourselves to be discerning. Would our fears, panic, and desire to find Candace cloud our judgment? To cooperate with the other power, the destructive power, would destroy everything we were attempting to do.

But how does one distinguish between them in such instances? Both do miracles, both have their prophets, both have their priests.

We discussed it with the police. They told us that while they cooperated with the psychics and took them seriously, they didn't rely on them fully. They maintained a cynical objectivity. As one officer put it, "We have all of these psychics making all these predictions: by a railway, by a bridge, in a dark place. Face it; with all the guesses, one of them is going to hit it lucky, and in hindsight it's going to look like he knew it all along. But when you think of all the railway tracks, all the bridges, and all the dark places in the city of Winnipeg, that kind of forecast looks a little obscure on this side of things."

Finally, we decided that the best tactic was simply not to become involved with or cooperate with these prophets, psychics, and futurists. We listened to them and talked to them politely, but we declined their offers of help. There was too much at stake to put our loyalty to God at risk. And if, in the process, we were overlooking one of God's personal messengers, surely God would understand and use another way.

As far as the police were concerned, we felt that

they were responsible for their own choices as we were responsible for ours. When the police forwarded requests from the psychics to us, we told them that we preferred not to cooperate with the psychics. The police could, but we wouldn't. They respected our wishes.

So we listened, we wrote it all down, and we waited.

On Tuesday and Wednesday there were nine sightings and seventy-five calls with which we had to deal. I was glad my mother and father were there. There just didn't seem to be enough time to deal with them all. Wednesday night, when I slipped out of bed for my nightly ritual by the window, I remembered Plett again. He had been right about so many of the things we were encountering, including the psychics. He had also talked about the waiting.

Plett had told me that he had known in his heart right from the beginning that his wife was dead. I could relate to that. He also said that there was a comfort in knowing that she was dead and not suffering. I could relate to that, too. He said that he had grieved through the whole searching process, knowing that she was dead, and no one knew the hell that that conflict had created for him. He also said that he had guessed that they would find her body that next spring, if ever.

I had naively asked, "Why spring?"

He had explained that Edmonton is extremely cold in winter (much like Winnipeg), and that people don't stray very far from shelter until spring. In the spring, people move outdoors and into the woods, the fields, and the outskirts of the city. That's when he had believed they would find her. It usually happens that way, he told me. And for him, it had. His wife's body had been found in the spring, in a deserted part of the countryside.

I wondered if his story was our model. Would our waiting end in the spring? Would we find her body, unprotected. . . ?

Plett had said, "But it was only her body that they found. She had been in heaven all that time."

CHAPTER 7

Rumors, Routines, and an Ugly Black Angel

Our lives couldn't have been more devastated if someone had set a bomb in our house and it had exploded into billions of pieces. That's how we felt.

But by the middle of that first week, the seventh day of our search, our need for sense and order, to find reasons and explanations so as to gain control again, was beginning to emerge.

We started to look for handles. And amazingly, we found them. Faint patterns of repeated actions, repeated problems, and repeated thoughts began to organize themselves into small groupings. Once we noticed the groupings, we could organize around them.

Our sleeping habits were a small but major concern. They had changed. Even though we were tired, we weren't falling asleep until two or three o'clock in the morning, and we were waking up at five. At first we worried that not being able to sleep was disorienting us. But that wasn't necessarily so. High all day on adrenaline, the energy that enabled us to deal with the demand of the search, meant that we needed four or five hours at the end of the day to process events and wind down. Less sleep wasn't a sign of falling apart; it was a necessary coping mechanism. We had to accept the fact that, for now, our lives had reversed. Life was now the nightmare and sleep the escape. So instead of worrying about the tiny snatches of sleep we were managing to capture, we began to relish them. And slowly, because we were relaxing with our new routine and our new sorrow, the hours of sleep began to lengthen naturally.

We saw patterns in our pain as well. Cliff loves the mornings. He and Candace had always been our early birds. They would wake up fighting over the washroom and playing jokes on each other, making a regular nuisance of themselves. Odia and I had cringed at their mistimed sense of hilarity and had ignored them as best we could. Now it only made sense that Cliff felt his pain the greatest when his senses were most alive and alert. He did his crying in the morning.

My nature is to move slowly in the morning. I don't wake up until my second cup of coffee or ten o'clock, whichever comes first. Now I welcomed the numbness in the morning and dreaded the pain that intensified as the day progressed. I cried late at night.

Percy, the neighborhood alley cat, was one of the first to notice and take advantage of the altered routines and new movements in our home. Every time someone came to our door—and our door seemed to be a revolving door—she would jump up onto the steps, sneak through all the legs, and make one wild dash through the living room and up the stairs. She got so good at it some of our guests didn't even notice her. Those who did had the strangest expressions as they felt that tiny thundercloud swirl between their legs and into the house.

"What was that?" someone would ask in horror.

Usually there were more pressing things to consider than Percy, so we would just shrug our shoulders. Percy was a little hard to explain.

One evening, as we were visiting with friends, she came slinking down the stairs and stopped conspicuously in the hallway to survey the guests sitting in the living room, expertly assessing when they would be ready to say their good-byes and she would be able to make her escape. One of the guests gasped when he spotted her and said, "That has got to be the ugliest cat I have ever seen."

I had said those exact words not long ago. With her arched back, long legs, stubby body, batlike face, and matted, scraggly fur, she was the ugliest-looking cat I had ever seen, too. Silhouetted against a moon, she would have been a perfect Halloween cat. Our guest was right, and I nodded in agreement, but I looked away hoping he wouldn't see the pain in my eyes.

I had first seen Percy that past spring. It had been warm that day, and there had been puddles in the driveway. For some reason I had decided to take all three kids shopping with me.

The kids stuck close to me in the store, where they wanted everything they saw, but it was another story when I drove into our driveway and wanted them to help me carry the grocery bags inside. They chose all the light bags and fled into the house before I could say anything.

While I was struggling to lift three of the heaviest

bags and close the trunk at the same time, I looked up
in time to see a horrible-looking black cat streak into
our house between Syras's short legs. Instead of being
alarmed, Odia quickly closed the door behind them.

I scrambled up the walk. There was a wild cat in
our house with my children! I had visions of a wild black
animal clawing up my drapes, hissing at the kids, and
hiding behind the furniture never to come out again.

I burst into the kitchen. "Where's the—!" It
wasn't what I expected. The bags, of course, had been
dropped in the middle of the kitchen floor, and the kids,
all three of them, were squatting on the living room rug
crooning over this cat.

I had this uncanny feeling that the cat knew my
children by name and that it was familiar with my living
room. I put down my three bags. "Candace, has this cat
been in here before?"

Candace stood up and faced me defensively. She
looked terribly uncomfortable, but she nodded slowly.

The scene looked too cozy! "This thing has been
in our house . . . a lot?"

"Well, . . . not that often. Aw, Mom, she's not that
bad. She's a stray. She doesn't have a home, and everyone in the neighborhood loves her. Her name is Percy."

"Percy is a male's name."

"We all thought she was a male, but she had kittens."

I wanted that cat out! It looked as if it carried
every flea in the neighborhood, not to mention every
disease. I grabbed a broom and moved behind her to
scare her through the open door, but Percy flashed
behind the couch. When I poked at her, she streaked up
the stairs. There was no way I could catch her.

Candace gave me a disgusted look, went upstairs,

and called the cat gently. It came to her, and she carried it to the door.

"I don't want that cat in our house ever again," I said, matching Candace's look with one of my own.

Through the window, I watched as Percy scampered undaunted down our sidewalk to another friendly house. I couldn't help but stare. She was so odd-looking. She must have been in an accident at one time, because she was slightly deformed and humped along like a strange-looking weasel, and her long black tail had a kink at the tip.

"She has got to be the ugliest cat I have ever seen," I said and turned from the window in time to see the pain in Candace's eyes.

"Mom, don't say that. Percy is a wonderful cat. She's had it tough. Her kittens died. But she plays with us kids."

"You don't think she's ugly?"

"Once you get to know Percy, she doesn't look ugly anymore."

I turned back to the window. Now Percy was sitting on a white fence post.

"Mom, can we play with Percy? She really is good with kids. Syras loves her."

One could never be sure what kinds of diseases a stray cat might bring into the house, and I shuddered at the thought of that black hair against our pale yellow rug.

"She's been around for a year, and she's great, Mom," Candace pleaded. The other two kids stood on either side of her. "Please."

It's amazing what you will do for your children. Those three sets of eyes were so appealing. I turned back to the groceries. "As long as I don't know about it."

Candace smiled. It was all she wanted.

I didn't see Percy much after that. I never found her in our house, and I never detected any black hairs on our rug. I assumed she had moved on to another neighborhood.

The day Candace disappeared, the temperature dropped, and Percy was frantic to find a warm place. Since our door was opening and closing so often, she chose our house as her winter home, and we had little choice in the matter because, without Candace, it was impossible to catch her. So we chose to ignore her.

It didn't take us long to realize that Candace had been right. There was something special about Percy. She didn't like us adults any more than we liked her, but she loved children. Syras would follow her around the house, and she knew how to stay one short, chubby arm's length away from him, keeping him amused for hours. She made the children laugh; she made us smile. She was an ugly black angel—but an angel nonetheless. A few days after she had adopted us, I asked Cliff if he would pick up kitty litter and some cat food on his way home from a search committee meeting. She had become part of the fabric of our lives.

Thursday we realized that the national Canadian Press service had picked up our story. Some of my cousins in Alberta called to say they had read about it in *The Edmonton Journal* and were wondering how we were doing.

Other calls were coming in from friends in other provinces. Were we okay? It was a hard question to answer on long distance rates. Those who called were good friends, friends who deserved more than glib answers. No, we were not okay. Our daughter was missing. But we were handling it, I assured them. We had a good community behind us. We were perplexed, but not abandoned. At least the publicity saved us the trouble of writing our friends or calling them with the news.

But there is a negative side to publicity, and we soon encountered it. We soon began to hear the different responses people had to our plight. The fabricated stories, rumors, misconceptions, and misinterpretations started to filter back to us. Some thought that we had abused Candace and so she had run away; that Cliff wasn't Candace's father; that I'd had an affair some time ago; that Candace was a native Indian foster child of ours; that Cliff and I were separated; and so on. At first, we were horrified. We couldn't believe that stories were circulating that weren't remotely close to the truth. Who would start them? From where did they come? As the stories accumulated, I noticed that most of them were an effort to blame the family somehow. People needed to do that to feel safe.

But it was frustrating. At least when the police had first accused us we could fight back, we could try and explain ourselves; but how do you confront a rumor?

Mom must have seen my pain. We were having coffee in the kitchen when she said, "You know, Dad and I had stories circulated about us, too, in Greendale a long time ago."

Stories about my parents? I couldn't believe it. "What kinds of stories?"

She shook her head. "They aren't important anymore. But they were then, and I wanted to go and clear my name. I wanted to make sure everyone understood. But, of course, I couldn't."

I still couldn't imagine anyone saying anything about my parents. They were so transparent, so withdrawn, so kind. They would never have hurt anyone.

"Dad said that we shouldn't do anything, that we

should remember the truth and hold our heads up high and eventually the truth would come out."

"Did it?"

"It took a long time. But, yes, it did. Wilma, just be true to yourself."

I recalled how Mom and Dad used to sit in the shade of our white, one-cow barn in the cool of a summer's evening. They would sit and talk softly to each other for hours. To me it had always been the perfect picture of serenity. They had carried their problems with such dignity.

Suddenly, all the stories didn't seem as bad. The people talking didn't know us—would never know us—and probably were making the best judgments they could with the information they had. What mattered was what our friends thought, and they seemed to have faith in us. One of my childhood friends, whom I hadn't seen for at least twenty years, told us, "I know that if you say Candace didn't run away, she didn't." Miraculously, the people most important to us understood us and believed in us.

There was no pattern to the food that kept walking through our door. My mother is rarely at a loss to know what to do with food in the kitchen, but all the gifts of food were getting too much for even her to organize. I don't think anyone who came to visit came empty-handed. In one day, the MBCI volleyball team dropped by with cookies; a woman, who could only speak German and whom I had never seen before, brought the most delicious freshly baked buns and a whole pot of borscht; and two couples, the neighborhood leaders and organizers, came in with a whole box of assorted foods that they had collected from the neighbors.

At first there was always enough company to eat

the food that arrived. But with the increased publicity, more and more food kept arriving. Cliff and I weren't eating, so it began to accumulate.

Finally my mother called me into the kitchen, pointed at a few boxes, and said, "This is everything that has come in today. I'm not going to be here forever, and when I put things away, I keep wondering if you'll ever find them again after I'm gone."

My first response was, "Mom, I really don't care." Food was the last thing on my mind. But I could see my mother's concern. I knew that all of it had been lovingly packaged and we needed to cherish it. So we started to go through it all, organizing it, pushing it into the cupboards, taking it downstairs to put in our huge freezer. But then the telephone rang, and it was for me. Half an hour later, when I thought I could get back to it again, the doorbell rang.

My mother shrugged her shoulders, and I thought I detected a glimmer of mischief in her eyes. "When you're hungry, you'll find it."

Our view of our friends and of people in general had changed. Now we had an entirely new screen to sift things through. The one thing we were quickly trying to figure out was who was courageous enough for the big questions. I'm sure our friends were trying to figure out the same thing. In fact, I know now that many of our friends thought early on that Candace had died the first night, but they didn't mention it to us for fear we would be hurt. We, in turn, out of consideration for their feelings, didn't mention it either. Yet we needed to process some of those issues, so we looked for those who could handle it.

There was one fear I needed to verbalize to someone, but no one seemed to let me say the words. Cliff and I had referred to it the first evening; we had mentioned it occasionally and had read it in each other's eyes a million times, but it was too painful for us to really discuss it. It was almost as if her death was easier to deal with than our fears of what might have happened to her just before she died. It was almost as if we were afraid to talk about it for fear that by saying it we would be making it a reality.

Had Candace been raped? Had Candace been tortured and abused? How had she dealt with those last minutes? How had she died?

Ester came over to report on what was happening with the investigation and to ask some questions. She was becoming a major investigator. She had a skill in dealing with young people and was somehow managing to tap their network. She was also totally dedicated and was working on the case full-time.

We started to talk about some of the possible scenarios of Candace's abduction. She seemed to feel, as I did, that since none of Candace's friends seemed to be involved, the motive for taking her must have been sex, drugs, money, or revenge.

Like many other children, Candace had experimented with smoking, but I just couldn't imagine her taking drugs. I had never seen any evidence of the sort. On the contrary, I had a hard time getting her to take even an aspirin.

She didn't have any money. We didn't have any money. It couldn't have been for money.

And I didn't think Candace was the kind of person ever to have enemies. Some people might not have liked her, might even have been irritated by her, but no one actively hated her enough to deliberately take revenge. She just wasn't important enough. She was too naive. Basically, she was too kind.

We were left with sex. Candace was thirteen and vivacious, and she had that friendly sparkle that attracted smiles, that attracted attention. Had it attracted some unknown, unwanted attention?

Ester let me talk about my fears. I told her that I was finding it more and more difficult to cope with my fears that Candace might have suffered, that she might have been raped, that she could still be being abused.

We were standing by the door. Ester still had her coat on, and she fidgeted for a moment with her wrist-size key ring full of keys before clearing her throat. "Was Candace experienced?"

What a question. I didn't think so. In fact, I was pretty sure she wasn't. But parents know so little about what really goes on—in the boat house, on the beach, at the corrals. I flipped through my memories quickly.

Candace knew about sex. I had told her about sex.

One evening when we were having our routine evening chat, she had asked, "Mom, what is sex?"

I had read child-rearing books that said if the child is old enough to ask the question then she is old enough for the answer. At the time that made perfect sense, and I had promised myself that I would answer all questions honestly. But so young? I had expected this much later. Maybe any age is too young in a mother's eyes.

While I was stammering, she asked more questions, and they were all so direct. "What does *making love* mean? Is it the same as sex?"

I answered, and she continued to ask. How? When? Where?

I knew I had been too explicit when she asked, "But, Mom, why would anyone want to do *that?*"

I wanted to be truthful, and I didn't want her to be left with a bad impression, so I answered, "It feels good."

"Feels good?" Her eyes grew big. "What does it feel like?"

I knew I was in trouble. "It feels like . . ." I groped for words. What image could possibly portray it to a child? I tried to think of an image within her experience and yet accurate. We had just been to a fair the day before, so I said, "It feels like the rush of a roller coaster going down the steepest hill."

Her eyes nearly popped out.

I bit my lip as I realized I was talking to a child. My sex instruction, horror of horrors, had turned into a promotion, so I backtracked. "But, Candace, it can be a cheap thrill. Sex is only wonderful when it's with someone you really love." And I spent the next hour drilling her on the importance of finding the right father for her children. I told her that trust is the basic ingredient in love and that sex is only really fulfilling within the parameters of a secure marriage.

My only consolation after that talk was the knowledge that a child forgets. She was so young. Kids forget everything the minute after you tell them. How many children remember to brush their teeth or to pick up their jackets? She would forget.

But one night years later, when I had turned off a movie that had become more raunchy than I thought was suitable for her young eyes, she looked at me with a glint in her eyes and said, "Like a roller coaster, huh, Mom?" She laughed and then quickly escaped from the room before I could give her the half-hour lecture she knew would follow.

Yes, she knew about sex; but had she experimented?

I remembered a conversation the past summer. Odia was with her two little boy friends out in the front yard when suddenly Candace, standing at the front window, gasped, "Mom, I really think you should send Odia's friends home."

It was still quite early in the evening, so I asked why.

"I just saw one of the boys kiss Odia."

"You're kidding." I went to stand beside her so I could see what she was seeing. The boys must have seen the movement at the window, because they had disappeared down the sidewalk.

Candace pouted. "I can't believe this. Odia is younger than I am, and I haven't been kissed."

I searched her eyes to see if she was telling the truth. Candace always seemed so sure of herself with boys. She always had a lot of good friends who were boys, and it was obvious they liked her. There must have been ample opportunity. Not that I was disappointed that she hadn't been kissed; rather, I was delighted. She still had plenty of time.

"Ester," I finally answered, "I don't think Candace was experienced. I think she was much more innocent than other people knew. I can't be certain, of course."

Ester nodded. "It really doesn't matter." She didn't skirt the issue as she continued. "Even for someone who is sexually active, rape is violent. Wilma—" somehow we both had sunk to the floor by the front door—"I work for Pregnancy Distress, and I've talked to girls who have been raped. They all have said that while it's happening, the body goes into some kind of shock. It's like they leave their bodies to hide."

I had heard that before, but I had forgotten. "You mean she wouldn't have felt . . . ?"

Ester shook her head.

"She would have been so scared. She really wouldn't have understood."

Ester remained quiet.

"I wanted her first experience to be wonderful."

Ester understood.

"I wanted her to be with someone who would love her."

"The emotions go numb, Wilma," Ester said in a low voice. "It would have been dreadful, but it doesn't mean that she can't have a good marriage still, if . . . Girls do get over rape—with counseling, with help."

Then she told me stories about the girls she was counseling, about their pain, and about how they had learned to survive. We took the time to discuss all the different effects and consequences, and again and again Ester assured me that Candace would have been protected in some way from the harsh reality. There would have been some physical, emotional, or spiritual buffer between her and her abuser.

We stood up. We had to stamp the circulation back into our feet again. Ester still had her coat on, and I apologized for being such a dreadful hostess, making her sit on the floor beside the drafty door. What had I been thinking?

"It's okay," she said graciously. "I'm not that old that I can't sit on the floor. In fact, I like to sit on the floor." Then she paused. "It wouldn't have been right to sit on a comfortable couch and talk about what we were talking about. It was just the kind of conversation that needed to be done on the floor."

I loved her for that. And I loved her even more when, as I closed the door behind her, I noticed she was limping slightly as she walked to her car.

Even the search committee was finding its routine and was meeting every day. They were in constant contact with the provincial Child Find offices, coordinating the pictures of Candace to be aired on Child Find's publicity programs across Canada.

Two prominent Mennonites had each donated a large sum of money; because of this, it became apparent that the committee needed a person to take charge of the search fund. Len DeFehr, Ester and Dave's cousin, was asked to come on as administrative secretary for the committee.

The two biggest items dominating the discussion at the meetings were whether to establish a reward fund and whether to cultivate more media attention. Finding the money for the reward didn't seem to be a concern; it was how to actually do it. The police were quite encouraging. They gave certain tips, such as to use the phrases "for the safe return of" and "giving whereabouts" and not to use the phrase "leading to whereabouts."

Though the public was responding to the media exposure, it was disappointing that all the calls were still leading to dead ends. The director of Child Find Alberta suggested to the committee that a mother's direct appeal would be helpful. She said that people would respond to the pain of a mother and her plea for help.

Another idea was to distribute posters all over the city instead of just in the area where Candace had disappeared. The committee realized that by now she could be anywhere. Since the pictures on the first poster had been taken in sixth grade and Candace had changed so much in one year, the search committee asked the company that had taken this year's school pictures to rush Candace's order and to double it.

The police delivered her picture at noon on Thursday for us to see.

For one moment my heart stopped as I opened the sealed envelope. There she was—so recent, so alive, her eyes shining. The photographer had captured her essence. She was even wearing her tarnished locket that I knew she loved so much.

We kept one picture and gave the rest back to the police and the committee to distribute all over Winnipeg. This time almost all the students, four hundred of them, distributed more than three thousand posters to Winnipeg businesses. The search was beginning to be called one of the biggest search efforts for a missing teenager that Winnipeg had ever seen.

For me, it wasn't big enough. Others thought it was too big. There was a backlash to all the attention: Why was Candace getting all the attention? What about all the other runaways?

At the time Candace disappeared, there were 76 juveniles reported missing: 29 boys and 47 girls. The police had opened a total of 4,455 missing-children cases the previous year, 1983. Juvenile division Staff Inspector Bill Heintz confessed to a reporter that "to a certain extent, we're hearing from the parents of other missing children asking for similar attention." But he said that most of these juveniles had gone to stay with friends or family.

The same reporter asked me if I was concerned about the publicity. How would Candace feel about the attention? I supposed that behind the question lay another question: Would I be embarrassed if Candace suddenly turned up and we found out that she had been with friends the whole time?

I answered, "No. Candace would love the attention." Little did he know how we would have welcomed that kind of embarrassment.

We didn't want to steal the attention from the other missing teenagers, and I didn't think we were. Every parent had the right to do what we were doing. I kept wondering what was really going on. Were the other cases being overlooked, or were they really not as serious as ours?

The calls were still coming in. By the eleventh day of the search, the police reported that they had received eighty calls. Some of the calls were still coming to our home. Some of them were prank calls. I answered one call. At first, the line seemed dead. Then, after a long pause, a voice whispered faintly, "Mom, Mom!"—plaintively, as if in pain. It was obviously poor acting, and I immediately knew it wasn't Candace and quickly put the receiver down.

We considered putting a tracer on the phone.

The psychic calls were seemingly without rhyme or reason. At first they served as comic relief. We had funny names for them: the culvert man, the pendulum lady, the white house ghost, the dreamer, the old voice. We didn't want to be disrespectful, but to us it was all a bit bizarre.

Then we appeared on a local television show called "It's a New Day," hosted by Willard and Betty Thiessen, a religious show with a strong charismatic leaning. At the same time, the search committee submitted Candace's picture to the national equivalent, "100 Huntley Street," hosted by David Mainse. At this point we started to get calls from psychics who used our own Christian terminology to describe what they were doing. The calls increased and became more persistent. We were forced to consider them more carefully than we had at first. Because of their frequency, we felt we needed to develop some routine way of dealing with them.

I can't stress enough how vulnerable we were; how, suddenly, things we had never taken seriously—claims of fortune-telling, prophecies, superstitions, powers that reached into the beyond—were now enticing, tempting. We began to wonder if maybe there were people who had direct access to God's plan for the future. It certainly was a tempting thought. Perhaps we were saying no too quickly. Had we closed the door too tightly?

About this time, a friend, Gary Brumbelow, called. Gary and his wife, Val, had lived in the other side of our duplex before they moved to Edmonton to be missionaries to the native Indians. We had grown to appreciate and respect them as a couple.

Gary asked, "What can I do to help?"

"Thanks, Gary. We have friends here who can search, but we appreciate—"

He was insistent. "Surely there is something we can do to help, even if we are in Edmonton. Look, I'm going down to the States soon. Is there anything down there? Any resources we can tap into? Any research?"

I was impressed by his determination, and I had to think for a moment. The word *research* had triggered an idea. Gary was a theologian; he could find out if there really were spiritual, God-loving psychics and prophets and how we could recognize them.

He liked the challenge. "Sure thing," he said as he hung up.

I was delighted with the idea. In a crisis there just isn't the time, the concentration, or the energy to do any research. Once again, I had reason to appreciate what a rich resource it was to have so many friends.

It didn't take Gary long to call back. He had called a few theologians in the States. His findings were simple and concise. Gary said that there is evidence for the existence of modern-day prophets. These prophets exhibit the fruits of the Spirit in their lives, and their predictions can never be wrong, because God is truth. If a prediction fails, it is a sure sign that the prediction and the prophet are not of God. Gary also emphasized the Bible's warning about cooperating with Satan's prophets. While all this was not new to me, Gary's clarification was reassuring.

Cliff had been at a search committee meeting when Gary's first call had come through, but he liked what I had done. Both of us agreed that the problem was how would we recognize these godly prophets if they did show up. Most of these psychics were coming out of the blue, and it would take another committee to research each one's reliability.

Yet I wanted to leave that door open. Was there anyone we knew already? I rephrased the question. If someone were to say that he or she had seen a vision and knew that Candace had been kidnapped and was being held in a hotel in Japan, who would that person have to be for us to trust him or her enough to make a flight reservation on that scanty bit of information?

Just then Dad walked into the kitchen.

Dad!

I had known him all my life, and I couldn't remember once when he had ever misdirected us children intentionally. He was fastidious about telling the truth. And I knew from the stories he told of his past that there were a few times when Dad had stepped out on a limb because he knew God was talking to him. One time his motorcycle broke down in a tiny town and he had to stay in a motel. In the middle of the night, he felt God urging him to get up and roll his motorcycle to the edge of the little town. A man had come by in a truck and offered to haul him and his motorcycle exactly where he wanted to go.

He certainly hadn't publicized the story, and he always seemed a little baffled by it himself. But it told me that if God wanted to communicate with Dad, Dad would be listening.

A small incident had happened once when Mom

and Dad were camping in our area. We had met them for a barbecue at their campsite. Just before we were about to leave, we discovered our keys were missing. Syras, a toddler at the time, was fascinated with keys. We knew that if he had taken them, then there was no way of knowing where they might be. He had been all over the campground. We were in a hurry to get home, and I was ready to panic. While we combed the tiny campsite, my dad wandered off in a totally different direction—and found the keys. I asked him what had possessed him to look where he had, when none of us had seen Syras go in that direction. He gave me a slightly bewildered look and was a little apologetic. "I prayed," he explained simply.

Dad took his faith in God into the smallest corners of his life. Whether God answered his prayers the way Dad wanted him to or not wasn't important. What was important was for him to listen and act on what he heard.

I made up my mind. Dad would be my choice. If God was trying to communicate to us and we were too overwrought to hear him, maybe he would speak through Mom or Dad.

I told Cliff what I was thinking. He smiled a little. He finds my reasoning a little quirky at times. But he said it wouldn't hurt, especially if it gave me some peace of mind.

In a heartfelt prayer, I told God that I could no longer tolerate all this uncertainty. I wanted it to be clear in my mind to whom we were to listen. I explained that I knew I could trust my parents if he chose to communicate through them.

I then went to my unsuspecting father and mother and told them about my uncertainties and asked if they would be open to God's leading and pray that God would speak to them.

Dad looked up at me and said, "Wilma, don't you think we have been praying?"

I knew then that he had already interceded for us; he was our self-appointed prophet. I also knew from the heavy silence in the room that there had not been an answer. Why would God take the time to answer Dad's prayer about a small set of keys but then be silent when Dad prayed concerning Candace?

That is a question that defies real understanding.

Still, it was good to have our own minds made up. Now, when we had calls from psychics, we could, without hesitation, decline their services with confidence. When all was said and done, I think I was glad we didn't know—yet. I was finding it difficult enough to deal with the truths of each day. Did I really want to know how Candace had died? Was I ready to accept the truth? Was I strong enough? Maybe it wasn't God who needed more time; maybe we needed more time.

Candace (on right)
and a summer
girlfriend, 1979.

Candace (on right)
and Heidi, 1983.

Candace's seventh-grade school picture, taken during the fall of 1984. Candace never saw this picture.

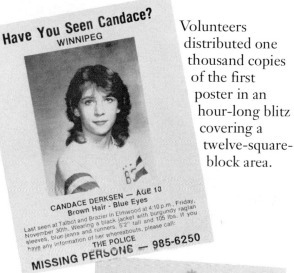

Have You Seen Candace?
WINNIPEG

CANDACE DERKSEN — AGE 13
Brown Hair - Blue Eyes

Last seen at Talbot and Brazier in Elmwood at 4:10 p.m. Friday,
November 30th. Wearing a black jacket with burgundy raglan
sleeves, blue-jeans and runners. 5'2" tall and 105 lbs. If you
have any information of her whereabouts, please call:

THE POLICE
MISSING PERSONS — 985-6250

Volunteers distributed one thousand copies of the first poster in an hour-long blitz covering a twelve-square-block area.

Four hundred MBCI students distributed over three thousand reward posters in one day.

REWARD
MISSING PERSON
$2000 $2000

CANDACE DERKSEN - WINNIPEG, MANITOBA
13 Years (DOB. July 6, 1971)

At approximately 4:15 p.m., Friday, November 30, 1984, Candace Derksen was
last seen in the Elmwood area walking east on Talbot Avenue from Brazier Street
on her way home.

DESCRIPTION:
Female, caucasian, 160 cm (5' 3"), 47 kgs (105 pounds), brown shoulder-length
hair, blue eyes. Last seen wearing black wool jacket with burgundy sleeves, blue
jeans with yellow piping on sides, white baseball type runners, size 8 black
leather gloves, carrying burgundy gym bag containing school books and a
clarinet.

The Candace Derksen Citizens Search Committee offers a reward of $2,000.00 for
information as to the whereabouts of Candace Derksen. All information to be forwarded to the Winnipeg Police Department, Youth Division, Missing Persons
Unit. (204) 985-6250 or your local police agency. Reward expires midnight
February 1, 1985.

The Chief of Police of the Winnipeg Police Department will be the sole arbiter as
to whom, if anyone, this reward will be paid and in what proportion, if there is
more than one claimant.

H.B. Stephen, Chief of Police

Cliff, me, and Odia at Candace's
funeral, January 17, 1985.

Winnipeg Free Press

Glen Eden Memorial
Gardens. A freak
storm accompanied
the funeral procession.

Winnipeg Sun

David Weibe
at Glen Eden
Memorial
Gardens, 1985.

Memorial plaque displayed at Camp Arnes.

(Left to right) Cliff, me, Vern Koop,
Dave Loewen, and Dave DeFehr
looking over plans for the Candace
Derksen Memorial Pool, March 1986.

Camp Arnes.

The Candace Derksen
Memorial Pool.

CHAPTER 8

Endless Waiting

Mom and Dad left on Saturday, nine days after Candace's disappearance. It was a signal that the state of emergency was over. As they were leaving, Mom casually mentioned something about going home and quickly preparing for Christmas and leaving us to do our own preparations.

Christmas? It was a totally new thought. Only after that did we notice that Christmas carols were playing on the radio and many of the homes had Christmas lights on. The world hadn't stopped; Christmas hadn't been postponed. The radio announcer went through the usual commercials, mentioning over and over that there were fourteen more shopping days until Christmas. We had been counting too, but forwards—and from a totally different significant day.

The next day, Sunday, there were barely any calls, and we wondered if everyone had naturally and understandably turned their attention to Christmas. But the doorbell rang that evening, and Dave Loewen walked into the house followed by friends. They had organized a surprise prayer meeting, and they came laden with goodies and smiles. Eventually they all found seats; someone made coffee and tea, Dave led in a short Bible meditation, and then everyone prayed.

Those simple words, "We are praying," had come to mean so much. Now, with a whole room full of praying people, I no longer had to wonder if people might forget when they went home.

That week we had a visit from a couple with whom we had only a casual, over-the-fence kind of relationship. We were delighted that they came, and we could feel our friendship deepening. I think most people would have found it quite difficult to picture this couple sitting in church, singing hymns. In fact, I think the husband wouldn't have been caught dead admitting to his buddies that he had any inclination whatsoever towards sentimentality. But as we were having coffee and wondering what had happened to Candace, he said with tears in his eyes, "I'm praying she'll be found." He must have anticipated our surprise. "Sure, I believe," he said simply, and that was enough for us. I couldn't help but remember Christ and how he treasured the faith he found in the most unlikely places.

We were learning about prayer. We were discovering that we weren't the only ones who believed in prayer. This whole experience was systematically breaking down our religious stereotypes, and I appreciated every prayer that people offered. Anglican friends, charismatic friends, friends from different Mennonite conferences, and complete strangers had all joined us in praying; and I had this image of a huge bowl of prayers accumulating somewhere in the heavens that someday would tip, at the right time and at the right place, when God's work needed to be done. Sometimes Cliff and I were convinced we could feel the sheer force of those prayers like they were a tangible thing, and we held out our own little personal cups to catch the drips and to drink for strength and nourishment.

I'm sure there will be some who think that we should have been more discriminating. But, when one is desperate, none of those boundaries seem to matter; we unashamedly took without questioning what was offered to us.

On Monday morning, refreshed and encouraged, I started to straighten the house. It had been good to relinquish the kitchen to Mom, but it felt just as good to take ownership of it again.

As I wandered from room to room, I found Candace's belongings mixed in with ours as if she were still coming home from school. I wanted things to remain like that always—ready and waiting for her. But they were also a constant reminder of the pain we all were feeling. I decided on a compromise. I gathered all her things from every corner of the house and organized them in her room as if she were coming back. I lovingly washed all her clothes, even the clean ones, so they would be fresh. I straightened her closet and drawers and took the time to display her favorite things on her dresser. I set her collection of koala bears close together, warm and hugging, so they wouldn't miss her too much. I untangled her necklaces and organized her earrings. I separated her books from Odia's.

I was glad there were no calls that day, because I

needed that time to be alone, to continue gently to cry my way through the good-bye.

I had done most of my Christmas shopping in November, and as I contemplated wrapping those presents, I wasn't quite sure what to do. Should we wrap Candace's gifts and expect her home for Christmas? If she didn't come, would those gifts be more painful than the gesture of hope was worth? It was the little decisions, like this one, that I found so difficult. I decided my guideline was to act on the 10 percent hope that we would have a wonderful Christmas.

I made a list of some of the things we still needed, and I was even beginning to muster some Christmas spirit, when reality crashed in on us again that evening.

The detectives came to our door after ten o'clock that night. They apologized for coming so late, but they said they had something to show us. One of them was carrying a bundle of what appeared to be dirty clothes. We all dropped onto our knees on the living room rug, and they opened up the bundle.

"These were found in the Logan area," said one of the detectives, "between McPhillips and Kewatinn. We want you to look at them to see if anything in here belongs to Candace."

I recoiled from the bundle.

"They're just clothes," the detectives said.

It was an assortment of socks, tops, and panties. With horror, I picked up a pair of flimsy white bikini panties that could have belonged to anyone. There were blood stains on it. I think I would have freaked out at that point if I hadn't remembered Ester's words, "It's like they leave their bodies to hide."

The bundle told us a curious and sad story, but it wasn't Candace's story. We didn't recognize anything. When the door closed behind the officers, we shivered from the cold blast of air—and the horror of the experience.

Cliff was pale. "I wonder what we will eventually find," he said slowly.

I gave up on the Christmas spirit. We would go through the motions, but not much more.

I don't think we were the only ones who had something other than Christmas on our minds. People hadn't forgotten us.

Tuesday morning there was a new excitement in the search. A fifteen-year-old girl came forward to say that she knew Candace and had recently run into her in the Zellers parking lot. She said that she had asked Candace why she had run away and that Candace had responded with a laugh, saying that she was staying with friends and was doing fine. She had asked the girl to pass on the story that she had been kidnapped and then had warned her, "If you tell them the truth, I'll kick your head in." Then Candace had left with her friends.

Everyone was optimistic.

"Kick your head in." The words rang through my mind over and over again. That wasn't Candace. Those words weren't familiar. I didn't believe the girl had seen Candace. Still, all the old doubts came back. Was it possible that we had lived together for thirteen years and I didn't even know my own daughter? Would it have been possible for her to lead such a double life? But I always arrived at the same conclusion: I knew my daughter, and what that girl had said was not what Candace would have said.

Eventually the verdict came back: the fifteen-year-old girl was lying. For some strange reason she made up the whole story.

The police were finally taking some strong action.

A helicopter made another search of the riverbanks on Tuesday. Though public attention wasn't quite as intense as the first week—the calls dropped from an average of thirty a day to approximately twenty a day—there were still constant contacts with the media, the police, friends, and family.

One teenager called to say he had seen Candace in a dream or vision, he wasn't sure which. She had been walking along a road crying and had a cut lip. There had been trees in the background and a little shack. Someone else called to say that she had woken up in the middle of the night and God had asked her to pray.

Suddenly we had a wave of calls from friends asking if she had been found. We discovered there was a rumor that she had been found at the floodway.

Near the end of the second week, CBC television asked our pastor if they could come and do a story during the Sunday morning service on how a church helps its members during a stressful time. Pastor Epp called us to see if we would mind.

We didn't mind; we would carry on as usual.

Our Sunday morning services at River East Mennonite Brethren Church were hardly newsworthy. The church of four hundred members gathered in a plain, nondescript church building and worshiped in a nondramatic—some even might say staid—way. We were fortunate to have professional church leaders from the college, MBCI, and the conference offices; so if there was anything unique about our church, it was the lineup of high-profile preachers who treated us to stimulating and challenging academic sermons every Sunday. Some said it was too academic, but we liked it all: the sermons, the casual style of Pastor John Epp, the good music, and the crowded foyer.

I wasn't sure what the press were looking for;

were they looking for God? And I wondered about the wisdom of it all when the cameras zoomed in on our row as we tried to worship. They had found us. Our concentration was gone.

I'm not sure what they found that Sunday. But we didn't find much peace of mind during the service.

But later on in the evening when we watched the news clip, we were moved by how they were able to portray and put into words the support of our church and the importance of our faith.

By the beginning of the third week, none of it seemed enough anymore. Everything that had been done—the ground searches and the posters—had all been done with public effort and within the public domain. We had exhausted all the possibilities within public jurisdiction, but not necessarily all the possibilities. If Candace was being held on private property, she could be right next door and no one had been able to check.

Dave Loewen expressed his frustrations to the media. "It's no longer realistic to think she would have voluntarily disappeared. There had to be others involved, and I find it hard to understand why no information has come forward."

In desperation, Dave said that he wanted a search done of every home on the route she would have taken home. He asked the police if they could go and search dwellings, but he was told that it was impossible to get a search warrant unless there was a reasonable cause to think that an offense had been committed in the vicinity.

The media constantly asked us if we felt the police were doing their part. We were able to answer honestly, yes, we felt that they were doing their part. We did believe that the police were working conscientiously within the framework of their own experience and knowledge, and we accepted that. Privately, we were happy that we didn't need to depend totally on the police, that we had good friends who supplemented the police force and did what needed to be done.

The search committee began to pressure the police to do a more thorough search of the community. So far they had confined their search to public property even though they had the authority to go beyond that—to search private property—an authority the search committee didn't have.

That week David Wiebe and his friend Andy DeFehr dropped by to give me a rose. We talked and we hugged.

David had every reason to be upset with our family. Just because he had given a seventh-grade girl a face wash, his life had been suddenly turned upside down. He had discovered that Candace had a crush on him and that he was one of the main suspects in her disappearance. He had been questioned over and over by the police—and not always that gently. It would have been so easy for him to be angry at us, but he never complained. The entire Wiebe family had become very close to us, sending flowers and calling in. Candace's friends had become so special to us.

We could see how the attention and the publicity were beginning to have an effect on all of Candace's friends. After the initial shock and terror, we noticed that Candace had become almost a heroine, a celebrity of sorts.

One of her friends, Kiersten Loewen, wrote a poem that was published in *The Free Press:*

"I knew her,"
I claim.
But did I really?

Candace, always smiling, laughing,
Giving of herself,
To strangers and friends alike.
Candace, the one who didn't seem to need anything.
No one thought that anything would happen to her.
"Not to Candace,"
They say.
"She's so sweet, kind and giving.
Not to her."
Well they were wrong.
Something did happen to her.
And now I fear she might be dead.
No more to see the sun again,
Tho rain again,
Feel pain again,
No more to cheer me up again,
Praise God again.
Candace
Where are you?

We caught wind that some of the students of MBCI were planning to throw a huge homecoming party when Candace was found. It was a lovely thought, a lovely gesture, and so typical of youthful optimism. We didn't want to dampen their enthusiasm, yet we were struck by the unreality of it. We cautiously reminded those who talked to us about it that the ending to this story in all probability was not going to be a happy one. We very carefully tried to explain that if Candace had run away, then we were dealing with an extremely troubled person; if she had been abducted, most likely she would be hurting emotionally and physically, and we could be looking at a hospital stay; we also might not find her alive.

They continued to send us poems and cards and to visit us.

The search committee kept pushing. They started to investigate the street life of Winnipeg. Was there a sex ring in the city? No, the police weren't aware of any organized prostitution. Then they started looking into the idea of a private investigator. One organization again suggested a reward. "It could be bait for people on the fringe, but it should be done in conjunction with the police," they told us.

The committee moved on this suggestion and found it wasn't easy setting up a reward. Just establishing the amount of the reward had many ramifications. The reward couldn't be overwhelmingly large so as to tempt a law-abiding citizen to lie, yet it had to be significant enough to appeal to someone on the fringe of society and make it worth their while to speak up. We finally settled on a reward of two thousand dollars.

A contract was set up with the police and the wording was approved. The reward money was sponsored by The Candace Derksen Citizens Search Committee and was to be raised through private businessmen, but it was to be administered by the Winnipeg police. A poster similar to the ones first distributed was designed. The initial print run was for five thousand copies, and MBCI students were again solicited to distribute most of the posters. The reward was announced on December 19, nineteen days into our search. The police also announced at that time that they had placed our case on a North America–wide alert.

The committee didn't stop there. They lobbied politicians Jake Epp—then Canada's minister of health—and Bill Blaikie, a federal member of Parliament. Blaikie responded by sending a letter to the minister of justice, John Crosbie. He wrote, "[Candace's disappearance] has, however, provided members of our community with a tragic opportunity to become acquainted with the facts concerning the numbers of missing children, and the not unreasonable fear that many such children have been abducted for purposes of child pornography and child prostitution."

Cliff's parents came from Saskatoon the week before Christmas. We were having coffee in the living room one evening when, at about ten o'clock, the doorbell rang. It was a stranger, and Cliff invited the man to join us. Just the way he dressed, the language he used, and the way he looked us over made it obvious that he lived in a world quite different from ours. He explained his mission quickly.

"You don't know anything," he began bluntly. "You lead a sheltered life. How do you know what a criminal thinks? What do you know about street life?"

We had to agree with him.

"Look at you," he waved his hand over the four of us. "You're Mennonites. Have you ever been to prison?"

We shook our heads. "No, not even to visit."

"You don't know anything. I've served nine years."

Our hearts stopped. That would explain the difference. He was right; compared to his knowledge, we must have seemed ignorant.

Everything about him should have alarmed me, and I think I was on my guard to some degree—all of us were—but I also remember liking him. There was something about his honesty, his directness, that appealed to me.

We encouraged him to continue.

"Maybe I have something you need. I know how a criminal thinks."

Never in my life had I thought that nine years behind bars might be an asset, a kind of specialization. The search committee had been put together with a special consideration for different expertise: there was someone with media know-how and another with administrative skills; the others had political contacts, investigative minds, business experience, money sense, a mother's heart. But no one had thought it necessary to have someone on the committee with an understanding of the criminal mind.

Our visitor assured us that he was now living straight. He told us about his family and a bit of his history. He told us that he had worked as a bouncer after his stay in prison but was now in maintenance work. "Come with me in my van," he offered. "I'll show you what kind of a neighborhood you live in."

"Why don't you go to the police?" I asked. "Why come to us?"

"With my record, if I showed interest they'd lock me away."

I could tell by a glance at Cliff's and his parents' faces that they were thinking the same thing I was. It was one thing to feel secure in our own living room, but it was an entirely different thing to go out and drive around with this man.

"Come on, I'll drive you around. You—" he said, pointing at Cliff, "and your father here."

"But maybe Candace isn't in this neighborhood," I stalled. "Why do you want to concentrate on this neighborhood? Personally, I think she was probably picked up by a car. She could be out of the city by now."

"That's where you are wrong," he countered. "They don't do things like that. They stay where they are; they don't travel around much." He stood up. "Come on, I'll show you."

Cliff stood up, shrugged his shoulders, and said, "It won't hurt. Come on, Dad."

The man had a black van parked outside. I watched from behind the curtain as they got into it. A black van, of all things. What if . . . ? What were we doing?

Cliff's mother and I were distracted the entire time they were gone. We kept trying to comfort each other. "They'll be back," we must have said to each other a hundred times.

They did come back—late.

"The black van wasn't the worst," Cliff said as we debriefed. "I nearly didn't go with him when I saw the old freezer in the back. The man said it was in there for traction."

We laughed, probably more out of relief than anything else.

The man had taken Cliff and Dad around the entire community on the most enlightening tour they had ever had. He revealed how to identify drug pushers' houses, and he pointed out the homes of Bravo motorcycle club members. He also pointed out many shelters, camper trailers, sheds, and heated garages that should be searched. What was most frightening was the high ratio of these kinds of homes, garages, and sheds in our area.

But what were we to do? Even if we believed him—and I think we did—how could we get into those suspicious houses? How could we interview those people? We had no authority. What were we to do with this new insight? How could we ever feel safe again?

Right from the first search committee meeting, the members had talked about the importance of a public appeal. Three weeks into the search, they asked that I go on television again and plead with the public for them to help me find Candace.

I hated the idea and fought it. But finally there was no choice. We were desperate again. A press conference was called for December 20, twenty days after Candace had disappeared and five days before Christmas.

The press conference was held at the Mennonite college next to MBCI. We arrived early, so I went to the ladies' washroom at the far end of the building and read my prepared statement over and over again. I couldn't stop crying. What would I do? I needed to gain control. I remembered our first interview. I had found strength in the thought that we were doing this for Candace.

I took a deep breath. I could do this for Candace. I washed my eyes and reapplied my makeup. As soon as I entered the room, we were ushered to the table.

"Candace," I read. I could feel my control slipping, and I looked up. There was a piece of fuzz on the microphone, waving in an imperceptible breeze. "If you are watching, we want you to know how much we love you. And no matter what has happened, nothing will change our love. We just want you to come home. We want to be a family again. Odia and Syras talk about you all the time, and even Percy the cat misses you."

I looked up. None of the reporters were looking at me. It seemed as if they were all sleeping.

"If someone is keeping you from coming home, I'd like to plead with that person to let you go. We're not seeking revenge or even justice; all we want is for Candace to come home."

All of this seemed so trite, so hokey.

I addressed the public. "The worst is not knowing. As long as we don't know what has happened to Candace, we are going to worry—Is she cold? Does she have enough to eat? Is she hurt?—that is why we are appealing to everyone."

How will they react to this later? I wondered. *I should have prepared something different.*

I continued as steadily as I could. "And for those of you who have backed us and cooked for us, prayed for us and informed us of what you have seen or what you know, we can't thank you enough. Your concern and love has offset the horror that we are feeling." I took a deep breath. "More than anything in the world, we want Candace home for Christmas."

It was deathly quiet when I finished. Dave asked the reporters if they had questions. Cliff answered some, I answered some.

I only remember one question: If Candace was just a runaway, weren't we at all worried that all of this publicity might be keeping her away rather than bringing her home?

No, we assured the reporter, we weren't concerned. We knew that this was serious. We were certain that Candace was being held against her will and this was the only way to find her.

Somehow I maintained my composure. The lights were turned off and the cameramen bundled up their equipment. I was finished. I stepped off the platform and broke into sobs.

The media took our message and portrayed it beautifully. One reporter caught our mixed feelings. "The Derksens, who were calm and relaxed through yesterday's news conference [little did they know], occasionally speak of Candace in the past tense, but they still speak of her with hope."

Juvenile Division Acting Staff Inspector Roman Giereck was quoted as saying that the police had received close to two hundred calls from members of the public, but that no evidence had been uncovered that would indicate foul play. "This is very strange that we haven't been able to come up with anything," he said.

With the press conference out of the way, the next obstacle loomed large. Christmas was only four days away. Christmas would come whether we ignored it or not.

Our families had called to say that some of them would come out for New Year's but that none of them could make it on Christmas—would we be with someone? Yes, we told them, friends had invited us over. But when it came down to giving our friends a definitive answer, we declined.

We did attend the Camp Arnes Christmas party, and everyone was wonderful to us. They didn't expect us to be the life of the party; they gave us space to be or do whatever we wanted. But in spite of their sensitivity, we found we had to be on our toes constantly. In our position, even small talk became treacherous. It's amazing how glibly we talk about killing. "I could have murdered him" doesn't mean a thing—usually—but with us standing there it took on real meaning. The speaker turned three shades of red, and we jumped in quickly and smoothed the situation over so he wouldn't be totally mortified.

One couple started talking about their great plans for their kids—and then remembered us and paused. Someone else inadvertently mentioned Candace, and then glanced over at us wondering how we would take it.

It seemed as if we were constantly bending over backwards, and I'm sure everyone else felt the same way. We weren't going to put anyone else through that on Christmas day.

We certainly hadn't been neglected. Everyone had done their part to bring the Christmas spirit to us. We had been lovingly overwhelmed with Christmas cards, Christmas cake, and Christmas gifts. Complete strangers had come to give us their best Christmas decorations. I remember one woman coming to the door and giving us a complete Christmas train display on silver foil. It was the cutest little engine and caboose made with goodies and covered with Froot Loops, popcorn, and gingerbread cookies. It had a little fence of pretzels enclosing a menagerie of animal cookies. It must have taken hours to put it together.

One of Candace's friends, a young boy who had played with Candace at Star Lake for three summers, asked his mother if they could cut a Christmas tree for us. He and his mother brought it over. We hadn't even thought of putting one up.

It certainly wasn't anyone's fault, then, that we spent Christmas alone. We had received many invitations, but we decided the best thing to do would be to withdraw and be alone. We weren't even sure what would be an appropriate way to commemorate Christmas without celebrating it.

We tried to have a traditional Christmas Eve by ourselves. In the evening after church we had our usual Christmas story reading, and then we opened gifts. I tried to shelve my feelings, but I couldn't. I'd laugh, enjoying the gifts, but the tears kept rolling down my cheeks.

"That's it," I told Cliff. "Tradition—doing the things the way we did them when Candace was here—is just too painful. The only way to deal with this is to do something that doesn't feel like Christmas."

So we didn't go to church Christmas morning. We let the kids play with their gifts while we cleaned up and tried to read. When it came time to eat our Christmas dinner, we hopped into the car to look for a place to eat. It was an unbearably cold and windy day. We had purposely not made any reservations, because we didn't want to go to a "good" restaurant. We weren't celebrating; we were just eating out. We wanted a nice, ho-hum family restaurant. But we had never been out on a holiday before, so we were totally surprised to find that all the family restaurants were closed. We decided that even McDonald's would do, but it was closed, too. We drove down Portage Avenue. Everything was closed.

To lighten the moment, Cliff said, "This is probably the most authentic Christmas we will ever have—just like Joseph and Mary looking for a place to settle and finding nothing open."

We eventually found a small, greasy-spoon cafe that was open. It seemed especially designed to let the bitter cold wind howl right through the front entrance and out the back. We fit right in with all the leftover people who obviously had no place to go. Without talking to any of them, we seemed to know each one's story.

I'm sure their head cook was having his Christmas at home, because the food was the worst I've ever eaten. None of us could finish our plates.

Next we went to see *Pinocchio*, an old Walt Disney classic. It was a safe choice, we thought; the kids would enjoy it and so would we. But not far into the movie, we found ourselves watching a heartbroken Geppetto out looking for his lost, abducted son.

Cliff and I looked at each other over the kids' heads. In the dim light, barely able to see his eyes, I knew what he was thinking. *There is no escape. There is no relief, not even in a simple Walt Disney movie.* We couldn't go around it, under it, or over it; we had to go through it.

I still think we came home that day feeling as good as the day could have allowed. We had suffered. We had fashioned an experience that matched the way we felt inside and it had been good to do that. I think the kids were a little baffled by it all.

The only thing that kept us going was the knowledge that my sister Sophie, her husband, Clare, and their two children, Donna and Gene, were coming for New Year's. The police had also mentioned something about organizing another search around that time.

CHAPTER 9

Looking for an End

New Year's Day is about new beginnings. We were still looking for an ending.

My sister Sophie and her family arrived on Sunday, December 30, the day the police had decided to do another thorough search of the area.

The police couldn't have picked a worse day. The temperature hovered between fifteen and thirty degrees below zero. The whole city was still digging itself out of a snowstorm, and the sun was shining down mercilessly on the bright white snow. The glare was enough to blind anyone.

This search was to be much more comprehensive than any search the police had done yet. During the first days of Candace's disappearance, the police had retraced her route with dogs, had searched the river-banks, and had made an aerial search of the area. A few days later, they had stopped cars and questioned all the people who used Talbot to go home on Friday after-noons. But this search was to be different. This search was to be a full-fledged ground search that would include private property. I understood that many of the officers were volunteering their time. Candace's school was to be the headquarters, and the search committee provided coffee and donuts.

Cliff and my brother-in-law Clare went to help and observe. Sophie and I watched from the window as the searchers combed the area.

At the end of the day, they all reported back that they had found nothing.

New Year's Eve is usually a time when everyone looks both backwards and forwards—two things we couldn't do. We didn't dare let ourselves. So again we planned an untraditional holiday. Cliff hooked up video games for our niece and nephew, and we rented some videos. But we were careful this time: no violence, no abduc-tions, no murders, no sex, no intense emotions. With those restrictions, it was almost impossible to find a movie. The few we chose were pathetic.

On New Year's Day, when everyone else in the family seemed absorbed and happy, Sophie and I slipped out of the house for a drive. We both needed to find an answer for ourselves as to why, with all the searches, someone hadn't uncovered something. We backtracked down Talbot, driving slowly, and then took the first side street, counting sheds and empty build-ings—anything that looked abandoned. At one point, we even got out and looked in a few windows. But there were so many sheds, so many suspicious-looking build-ings, and they all were on private property. Slowly we began to understand what the searchers had been up against. There was no possible way that we could even begin to do a thorough search of even one city block. A city block probably has more uncharted, forbidden terri-tory than a mountainside.

We went home. Just as we opened the door, we heard Syras shrieking, "The table is falling down! The table is falling down!" We could hear the rest of the fam-ily downstairs playing games, totally unaware of what was happening upstairs. Sophie and I ran into the dining room. The tablecloth was slipping off the table, the cen-terpiece balancing precariously on the edge, and there sat Percy with a mischievous cat-grin on her ugly face.

I scooped Syras into my arms, Sophie rescued the flower arrangement, and Percy disappeared upstairs. It was a small thing, a minor crisis—something that hap-pens regularly in a house with a recently-turned-three-year-old and a high-spirited cat. There hadn't been any danger of Syras getting hurt, but I was shaking. All of life suddenly seemed so precarious. My children seemed so vulnerable.

When my sister and her family left, they told us that my sister Luella was planning to come visit in a few weeks. I sensed that my family was organizing a support system.

The new year started with a call from the police. They wondered if it would be possible for me to track down Candace's dental records. "Not that we'll need them," the voice said. "Actually, I don't know why we need them now. It's just nice to have on hand."

I knew why, but I wasn't going to talk about it either.

Right after that call I got a call from a sixty-seven-year-old lady with a mysterious voice. She sounded confident and efficient as she described a scenario that she felt explained how Candace had disappeared. She sounded like an old-fashioned Agatha Christie sleuth. "I help find people," she said. "I've had fifty years of experience."

She had developed a method of tracing people through obituaries. "I have this bag full of obituaries," she told me. Did I know so-and-so who had died a few years ago? No? Well, perhaps I knew this other person.

She told me a little about her husband—not a nice person, I learned—and some stories about the people she had found. She wanted to know a few facts about Candace, and I answered her questions. I sensed that in some ways this was just another mystery to her—a game, a puzzle.

The search committee declared the sixth of January to be a national church prayer day dedicated to Candace. The previous efforts to contact churches had been a local effort. This time a letter was going to be sent to two hundred churches nationwide.

Early that morning, Cliff received a call from Robert Jessop, the father of a girl who had been missing for three months and had recently been found, strangled. Mrs. Jessop and I got on extension lines so that we all could talk. We empathized with them and talked about the hurt, the pain, the fears, and the loss familiar to both of our cases. This was the first time we had really shared with someone whose case closely paralleled ours, and we easily exchanged similar stories about searches, psychics, and rewards.

"We hoped for the best and expected the worst," Robert said. He told us how he had been asked to take a polygraph test because he was the main suspect in the case. We wondered out loud if it had been difficult to be considered a suspect. "Yes," he answered. "I took the test, though, because it's the only thing the police understand. I'm just glad I passed. The polygraph can be unreliable." We understood what he was saying. They had been willing to do anything for their daughter.

At least we won't have to go through that. Cliff has an ironclad alibi, I thought.

Again and again, the Jessops told us what a difference it made to them to have found their daughter's body and to know the truth of what had happened. Her body had been found on New Year's Eve, only seven days earlier. They were still raw in their grief, but already they were saying that anything was better than not knowing.

And you know, we understood. Their daughter had been strangled; that must have been extremely difficult to accept, but at least they knew.

Later, as we sat down for breakfast, I asked Cliff, "Everyone is praying today. Do you think this will be the day?" We had heard from quite a few people that they believed God might use this prayer day to reveal where Candace was and so prove to everyone that he was sovereign. Even some of the media had suggested that.

Cliff shrugged his shoulders. "It could be. What about you? What do you think?"

I thought about it for awhile, then answered, "I think this is the day we can relax completely. She won't be found today."

His eyebrows went up in surprise. "Why?" he asked tentatively. I could tell that he wasn't sure he wanted to know.

"I don't believe God needs to prove himself. In fact, I think God avoids any hint of a showdown."

"Oh?" said Cliff, putting down his coffee cup and

wearing that funny smile he has when he listens to what he calls my "homespun theology."

But my thinking was based on my understanding that faith, the ability to believe in the unknown and unproved, is essential to having a relationship with God. Throughout the Bible, God is looking for people of faith with whom he can relate. If faith is so essential to our relationship with God, God would never do anything to threaten our need for faith. God would never allow anyone or anything to prove, without a doubt, that he existed. Evidence and proof would negate the need for faith. God loves us too much to ever eliminate the necessity of faith.

I didn't convince Cliff on the subject, though. He just shook his head, shrugged his shoulders, and said. "It really doesn't matter whether she is found today or not. If she isn't, it doesn't mean God hasn't answered. The answer is simply no or wait."

At two o'clock that afternoon, CBC came to interview us about the prayer day. Trying to explain to a camera how we felt about prayer was a unique experience. *The Free Press* also checked in to ask us a few questions, and the police called. Still, the day passed like any other. I had been right—Candace wasn't found that day. But Cliff had been right, too. And if the others who so strongly believed that Candace would be found that day had been right, we certainly wouldn't have quarreled with the outcome.

Besides working with the police, we were working with the Child Find organization. They had distributed our daughter's picture throughout their Canadian network and had also submitted it internationally. We were pleased with their advice and concern, and we had started to make inquiries into starting a chapter in Manitoba.

We found ourselves wishing there had been a Child Find branch in Manitoba when Candace first disappeared. We met with a few other people interested in beginning a chapter. Cliff and I decided that since he was caught up with Camp Arnes and the search committee, I would put my efforts into this new organization.

The search committee was looking into hiring a private investigator. Cliff and I thought it was a good idea until we heard the cost. It would cost $10,000 just to bring him in for a preliminary investigation, the total possibly running up to $100,000. It wasn't a question of whether there would be money for this or where we would get it, but it didn't seem fair to spend that kind of money carelessly.

All of this was taking place during the time the news of the Ethiopian drought was hitting the Canadian press. Daily we were shown the dreadful suffering of starving people. Mothers were losing their entire families. Money was needed to help relieve the suffering.

Dave Loewen was leaving on a trip west to recruit counselors for summer camp. He stopped by the house to pick something up, and we asked if he had a few minutes to talk. He didn't, of course, but he sat down anyway.

Cliff and I sat on the sofa, and Dave relaxed in the armchair. I think that's when it hit all of us: throughout the whole six weeks the three of us had never really sat down and talked. Cliff had attended all the search committee meetings, and I had started to attend the meetings after Christmas, so we had always been involved in the decisions right from the beginning, but the three of us had never been alone to discuss how we were really feeling.

Dave had been doing triple duty. He had covered for Cliff in the office, kept up with his own work, and chaired all the search committee meetings. We knew the camp was far behind schedule in their summer promotions and summer staff recruitment, the key factors to the success of the summer. Dave had sacrificed much, so it was good to be able to relax for a few moments and tell Dave in person how much we appreciated his work. We also told Dave that we had some reservations about spending so much money on a trail that was continually leading to dead ends. Wouldn't it be a waste? Wouldn't it be better perhaps if we had some concrete leads to go on before we started? Could a private investigator really find something that the police hadn't been able to uncover? Should we wait? Could we find someone less expensive? Dave nodded. He understood.

Two hours later, Dave got up to leave. "We'll wait until I get back, and then we'll talk about this again," he said.

This time we knew that things were officially being put on hold. Most of the committee members who had worked with us in December had to get back to their work. Our pastor was leaving for a conference, Dave would be gone for two weeks, and we, too, felt we had to start working on our own lives again.

Suspended animation is what my husband called it, living in suspense the way we were.

As far as we could tell, Odia was carrying on as she always did: calm, steady, and practical. Whenever we discussed our plans, she would join in or just accept what we had to say. We felt comfortable about our conversations and felt that we had a pretty good idea of how she was coping.

But how this trauma was affecting our three-year-old, we didn't know. We had no idea what was going through Syras's mind. Often we didn't take the time to explain things to him because we didn't think he understood or we just didn't have the right words in our vocabulary or in his. But then something would pop out, and we'd realize he understood more than we gave him credit for.

We found out he had his own theories. The thirteenth of January, forty-four days after Candace's disappearance, we all went out for a quick lunch after church at a nearby fast-food place. As we began to eat, four teenage girls plopped themselves down at the table next to ours. Pillows, duffel bags, and huge black rings under their eyes made it obvious they had just had a slumber party. They ordered soft drinks while they waited for their parents.

The girls were all attractive and slim, with hairstyles so similar to what Candace wore. Laughing, giggling, talking loudly—they were confident of their youth and totally unaware that they were making a spectacle of themselves. We all watched them, hungry for our own teenager. Syras was watching them with interest too. He turned to us, and in his three-year-old lisp he said matter-of-factly, "Candace is lost. Someone shot her with a gun." Then he turned back to sipping on the straw of his Coke.

Cliff and I looked across the table at each other in alarm. Where had he picked that up? We took turns trying to explain to him that, yes, Candace was lost, but we didn't know if she had been shot with a gun. We didn't know what had happened to her; that's why we were still looking for her. We said it over and over again in as many ways as we knew how.

Syras watched our concern with interest, but his eyes had glazed over. We had the distinct impression he liked his own version much better than ours. His at least had an ending; obviously we didn't have one.

Finally we gave up. We would let it be.

But in his own little way, Syras had raised the issue. How long is it possible to go on with no ending? Would we eventually fashion our own version too? Had we done that already?

CHAPTER 10

The Hard Answer

Seven weeks into the search, we once again decided we needed to accept what we could not change. We knew that there are many children who disappear and are never found again; we knew it was entirely possible that we might have to live the rest of our lives not knowing. We had two other children who demanded that we continue to live. We had a mortgage, bills, and responsibilities that demanded we pay attention to life.

Cliff had gone back to work a few hours each day shortly after Candace disappeared. He complained that it was difficult to concentrate and that he tired easily, but I could see that just the effort was doing him good. So, when I heard that Camp Arnes needed someone to come in to the office a few hours a day to type the summer camp registrations into the new computer, I jumped at the chance. And Cliff was right; it was extremely difficult to concentrate those first few days. But I knew that with effort, if I persevered, it could be done. Those two hours of diversion, away from the ringing phone at home, became a badly needed break.

But the search for Candace never left us. We were always conscious of our first priority. After a morning at the office, I often found it just as difficult to concentrate on household chores. One Wednesday afternoon, as I was staring out the window trying to pull my thoughts together, I noticed a neighbor doing something that was uncharacteristic. He saw me watching him, and he disappeared nervously. Ordinarily I would have thought it was none of my business, but now anything that looked remotely unusual became highly significant.

We had been told over and over again that in all probability we knew Candace's abductor, that the person was probably within our community. We watched everyone closely, including our circle of friends and acquaintances. But there was only one person of whom Cliff and I weren't sure. He was the only person with unexplained mysteries and shadows in his life. And here he was. . . .

As I withdrew from the window, I remembered some unusual comments he had made about Candace. I remembered how she had never wanted to be near him and how disgusted she had looked whenever we even mentioned his name. I also remembered that he didn't have an alibi and that he had admitted to being in the vicinity that night. My list of suspicions quickly built an airtight case against him. He could be our prime suspect!

We had mentioned our suspicions to the police, and they said they had questioned him, but was questioning good enough? Had he been thoroughly investigated? All Wednesday evening I was preoccupied with the thought.

The next morning at the office, I couldn't shove my suspicions out of my mind. Every hour on the hour I could see his guilty face on my computer screen. Finally, I gave up. The only way to get rid of this suspicion was to do something about it. But what? How could we possibly make the police take us seriously? How could we investigate? The only thing to do was to go right down to the police station. Maybe, if we marched in and sat down in their office, maybe they'd listen. If they cooperated, maybe we could set a trap that would flush out the truth once and for all. We could have this man over, present some kind of evidence, and watch his reaction—maybe even confront him directly. Anything was worth some peace of mind.

Cliff wasn't quite as convinced as I was, but he had always thought this person suspicious too, and it was our only lead. We didn't expect it to take us very long since we were going during the noon hour, so we picked up Syras from the baby-sitter's on our way to the station.

There was an eerie silence that seemed to follow us through the station corridors. It was as if everyone recognized us. The receptionist seemed surprised when we introduced ourselves, and she hurried away to alert the supervisor. After a few minutes, the two sergeants assigned to the case greeted us. They, too, seem unusually nervous. Had we done something wrong? Weren't we supposed to come to the station?

We tried to tell them that we had something to report and that it would only take a few minutes of their time, but they didn't want to listen to us. They told us it could wait; they had something much more important to tell us. They asked if I would stay with Syras in the reception area while they talked to Cliff alone. I didn't like the idea. We had come together. It had been my idea. What was up?

I was hoping Cliff wouldn't let them separate us, but in his own bewilderment, he just shrugged his shoulders. "It won't take long," he whispered to me as he turned to follow them into a big office.

I didn't have a choice, so I sat down in a chair and looked for something to distract Syras—and me. I could see the officers talking to Cliff through the office window. Whatever they were discussing was grim.

I paced the waiting room. Syras seemed as fidgety as I was and started to whimper. I tried to interest him in some car pictures in a magazine, but nothing held our interest. I felt a rising sense of irritation. What could possibly be going on? Didn't they trust me? Was Cliff telling them about our suspicions? Were they planning a trap without me? Did they think I was too stupid to understand any plans that they had? If I was a man, would they dare to do something like this to me?

Just when I thought I would explode, the two officers came out. They asked the receptionist to look after Syras and ushered me into the room where Cliff was waiting. They told me that Cliff had something to tell me and then left the room, closing the door behind them. It didn't make sense to me. What could he have to say that couldn't wait till we were home?

I sat down on a chair and Cliff sat on the edge of the desk. I watched him carefully for some sign as to what was going on. He leaned back casually, too casually. I knew something was wrong. He waited for one long moment, and I knew he was choosing his words carefully.

"Wilma, they've found Candace. They've found her body. . . . She's dead."

I was furious. Had the police brainwashed my husband into thinking that I'd believe a line like that? What stunt were they trying to pull? "Cliff, don't joke about this."

Cliff's eyes didn't flinch. "I'm not joking, Wilma."

"You don't come to the police station on your own and then hear this. It's too outlandish," I said evenly.

"They've been trying to get ahold of us."

"We were at the Camp Arnes office. They know the number," I reminded him curtly.

"Well, actually, they've been trying to get ahold of Dave Loewen or Pastor Epp. They didn't want to tell us alone."

I hesitated. That could be true. Both men were out of the province.

"Dead?" I asked cautiously. Maybe if I played along he'd stop playing their games and level with me sooner.

"Yes," he nodded, looking relieved that the confrontation seemed to be over.

"She was found in a shack by the Nairn overpass."

"That close?"

He nodded.

"When did they find her?"

"This morning."

"Who all knows?"

"Everyone, it seems. The media have been sitting on it until we're notified."

"How . . . did she die?"

"They don't know yet. Her hands and feet were tied. It looks like she froze to death."

It was too unreal. "Her hands and feet were tied." The words swirled through my mind. It didn't sound like a formula murder scene. I looked at Cliff; I would know if he was lying. He looked so miserable. His eyes were pleading, and I could read volumes in them. He was really saying, "Wilma, please believe me. Candace is dead. Hang on to your pain. Just believe me so we can get out of here."

Oh, my darling little daughter! The tears started to slip out and I turned away. My tiny percent of hope was disappearing. It was dying. I could feel Cliff's nearness, but we stood apart. If we had hugged, both of us would have fallen apart.

We went over the sparse details again. Cliff waited patiently as I groped for understanding. "Then it's all over." I said finally. We could leave. We no longer had to talk to the police. Everything had changed. The whole search was over. We could go home.

But there was one more question. "How do they know it's Candace?" I asked.

"They want me to identify her."

"I'm going with you. Can I?"

He nodded.

We turned to the door, and the officers moved away from the window. Why had we come here? It wasn't supposed to happen like this. It was supposed to be a call in the middle of the night or two policemen coming up the walk with our pastor; I had been prepared for every possibility except this one. What a dreadful place to find out—a cold police station with two sergeants pacing outside the door.

When we opened the door, the officers looked back and forth at each of us, obviously trying to assess the trauma. I was annoyed with them, but I masked my feelings. They offered to take Syras and me home while Cliff went to identify Candace. Once again, they were professional and firm. The car was waiting for me downstairs, they said. It would be no problem.

They were going to shut me out again! But this time I was ready for them. I wasn't going to let them separate us again. We needed to go through this together. No matter how bad the scene might be, I had to see for myself. I had to see Candace, and it would be best if Cliff and I did it together.

"I'm going with Cliff," I said firmly.

They looked at Cliff. He nodded his head.

"Should we drive you there, the both of you?"

We said we were quite capable of driving ourselves and our car was just outside. Syras would come with us.

"Are you sure?" they asked.

Syras clung to my hand. I needed him. He'd be okay if I was okay; I'd be okay if he was there; we both would be okay because Cliff was with us. Couldn't they understand that? We needed to be together.

"Yes, we're sure."

They let us go.

Candace's body was at Seven Oaks Hospital, northwest of where we lived. The officers told us that we would be expected. We would just have to enter the front doors and there would be someone there to meet us.

As we climbed into the car, I half expected Cliff to drive on home and tell me that it had all been a lie, but he didn't. He turned left onto Main Street and headed toward the hospital. He drove slowly, dreading each yard we covered.

"Don't you think we should hurry a little more? They might be waiting for us."

"Let them wait," he said. "We can take all the time we want." And that's when I knew, without a doubt, that it was indeed over. The tears rolled down my cheeks and nothing would stop them.

"I'm scared, Cliff."

He nodded.

"Cliff, how are we going to go through with it? What if it's too horrible to bear?" The officers had told Cliff that she hadn't been hurt, but could we believe them?

"It's all over," Cliff reminded me. "We have to remember that she isn't suffering anymore."

He was right. It was only her body that we would see. She was safe in heaven. And though I was scared and dreaded going, I knew that I needed to see Candace. I knew that if I didn't, I'd forever have to live with my imagination. And my imagination was always worse than reality. No scene was as bad as the one I had in my mind's eye that very moment.

At the hospital, we pushed the big doors open. The medical examiner slipped her arm around me, and we were taken into a private lounge and introduced to an officer from the homicide department.

"She doesn't look pretty," they said, starting to prepare us. "The blotches on her skin are from the cold. They aren't bruises." They gave us two Polaroid pictures, and my fingers trembled as I took them. It was Candace.

They were right; it wasn't a pretty picture. The horror of facing her own death was etched into Candace's face.

"I'm sorry," the medical examiner continued gently, "but we thought showing pictures would help to prepare you."

I wanted to tell her how grateful we were that they were being so considerate, but the tears wouldn't stop.

They then briefed us on the details. They told us

the body would be allowed to thaw and that even though she might have died on the evening she disappeared, her death certificate would record January 17, 1985, as the date of her death.

We nodded mechanically.

"How did she die?" I kept asking. No one gave me a straight answer.

Finally, the officer said, "We can't be sure until after the autopsy, but her hands and feet were tied. Right now it looks as if she might have frozen to death."

"That doesn't make sense. What would be the motive? Who would take her and just tie her up and leave her to die? She didn't have any real enemies."

"It could have been sex. Tying . . . bondage . . . it's sexual," he said slowly.

Of course. I nodded. "All of this is a little hard to believe."

"I know."

They took us down an endless corridor, and someone held Syras while we went into a little white room. A tiny figure lay draped with a white sheet on what appeared to be an operating table.

It wasn't Candace. In real life Candace was so much bigger. This was just a little corpse. But I forced myself to look closer. Yes, it *was* Candace. Candace minus her personality was so small, so terribly small, just a shell. Frozen, she looked like a grotesque, dusty mannequin, and I drew back in horror. I didn't feel any attachment to what lay there. It was Candace's body, but it wasn't Candace.

They asked us if she looked the same as the day she disappeared. Was her hair the same? Her clothes? They wanted to determine how long she had been in the shack.

Yes, the clothes were the same; her hair was the

same. Everything, as far as we could determine, verified that she had died that first night.

We left the room.

"Are you going to be all right?" the medical examiner asked.

I nodded numbly. "Yes. We'll be all right. We were expecting something like this. It's good to know. It's good to know that she wasn't physically abused." But there was no controlling the tears that kept rolling down their well-worn path on my face. It seemed contradictory to say that I would be okay and yet not to be able to stop crying.

"When you get home . . . ?" her question continued.

"We have friends," I said quickly.

"Yes, I know. You have a wonderful community."

I nodded. "They'll be there," I said. I wasn't really sure if they actually would be; in fact, I doubted it. How would anyone know? But it didn't matter; I just wanted to go home and be alone.

All the way home, we swung dizzily between the sense of relief that we had found Candace and the plummeting depths of the realization that she was dead, that we would never be a complete family again. Back and forth, up and down, around and around—we hardly had time to think of what would happen next.

I was amazed our house was still standing just as we had left it. As we came through the back door, the front doorbell rang. It was a reporter.

"I hate to bother you, but now that you know what has happened to Candace, how are you feeling?" she asked.

I'm not sure who I had expected—a friend, the postman, anyone but the media. She looked like she hated her job at the moment. A photographer paced the sidewalk behind her, looking almost as miserable.

"We're relieved," I said automatically. "We're glad it's over."

Cliff, who was right behind me, said, "In many ways it is over." His voice sank lower. "But in many ways it is just beginning."

"Could we talk with you? . . . take a picture?"

We hadn't said no to the media yet, but I couldn't pose today. "Not today," I said. "Give us a little time."

She nodded, and I closed the door.

"Cliff, what did you mean 'it isn't over yet'?"

"We have to find the killer now."

I looked at him in amazement. I hadn't even thought of that.

Things began to happen fast. Other media vans pulled up, and Cliff left to get Odia out of school. He didn't want her to hear the news from anyone but us. The front doorbell rang after he left, and I hesitated to answer it. I didn't want to talk to the media, but what if it was someone else? I opened the door.

It was a friend. He stepped into the room, sobbing. "I just didn't think it was going to end this way," he repeated over and over again, and I was shocked. Then I remembered he had been extremely optimistic about one particular lead. Had he thought all along that Candace was just a runaway? Had he put in all those hours for a runaway? There wasn't time to talk about it—the back doorbell was ringing—so I tucked the thought away.

Ester came in bringing the cold air with her. "I've been sitting out there sending all the media away. The nerve!" she sputtered. Other friends were spilling into the house, and we had a quick caucus about what to do with the media.

"You don't have to talk to them," said Jantz.

"Honey," added Ester, a touch of her southern drawl coming out, "you can do anything you want. You don't need them now." She grimaced.

It was good to hear them say that, because we really didn't want to meet with the press then, yet we couldn't dismiss them that easily. They had been there when we needed them, and I felt we owed them something. When he got home, Cliff agreed. "We don't want to talk to them now, but can we make it for another day?"

"I'll handle them," Jantz offered. "When?"

After some discussion, it was agreed that it would have to be Saturday. Today we needed time to mourn; tomorrow we'd need to make arrangements. "Can they wait that long?"

Ester jumped in. "You can do anything you want."

Jantz nodded his head. "I'll tell them."

It was such a relief not to have to worry about it.

I had always imagined that we would need to call a list of people, beginning with the search committee, when we found Candace, but now I realized that we wouldn't need to. The media was alerting everyone.

It was a spontaneous open house. Some friends left and others came—red-nosed, wild-eyed, and disheveled, but none of that mattered. The kitchen began to fill up with food again, and some of the women took over keeping it organized.

Ester was screening our calls, answering the door, and walking around pouring hot tea with our old, cracked teapot. Our house seemed so cold. I wasn't sure if it was because the door kept opening or because we were all in some kind of shock. Ester went upstairs and found Cliff's old stocking slippers and continued to shuffle around in them, raging like a bull one minute and smiling and making everyone comfortable the next. Ester told me later, "When I heard the news over my car radio, I was so mad I just tore my nylons." There were huge runs up and down her legs. It seemed so uncharacteristic; she was always so careful about her appearance, but today she wore them like medals. It was good to see her anger, her energy. I felt more like a wounded bird that just wanted to hide under a bush and bleed to death.

At ten o'clock that night, the house slowly began to empty. Dave, Fran, and Heidi had come in from Camp Arnes the minute they had heard the news, and everyone agreed that it would be good for them to stay with us for the night.

Some friends, Anne and Gilbert Sperling, had sent along a freshly baked, still-warm cherry pie with Dave and Fran. After everyone left, we sat around the kitchen table to eat it and to wind down.

The doorbell rang. I got up to answer it, thinking it must be one of the guests coming back for something forgotten. People were always leaving boots, mittens, and hats behind. But it wasn't a friend. It was a total stranger. He was dressed in black—or maybe it just appeared that way because of the dark. He looked vaguely familiar, but I couldn't place him. I asked him inside, and he introduced himself.

I knew the name, but I still couldn't place him.

"I'm the father of the girl who was murdered at the donut shop."

My heart stopped. I felt the blood drain from my face. I remembered the case. The police had charged a suspect, and the trial had been in the news on and off for the last two years. I had never paid much attention to murder cases before, so I hadn't followed it closely;

but even from the headlines, I had sensed that there was deep hatred and anger involved in the case.

I stared at him in horror. He was the parent of a murdered child. And now he had come to our home because we belonged! I shuddered. What a gruesome identity!

I invited him into the kitchen and introduced him to the others, inviting him to join us for a piece of cherry pie. It was then that he told us the purpose of his visit. "I have come to tell you what to expect. I know all about it."

And he did. He had a fantastic memory for every graphic detail from the events of the last two years. He retold the story of his daughter's murder, beginning with the moment when he had learned of the murder and the history of the suspect. He was convinced that the accused man was guilty, and he went on and on about the frustration of not being able to prove guilt without a shadow of a doubt. He said that he was still taking meticulous notes of everything that happened in court.

We had all stopped eating our pieces of pie, and we listened in horror as our guest continued to nibble at his and describe the pain, anguish, and hopelessness of his life. I kept thinking, *Lord, why now? Why do we have to listen to this now?* And if he was some kind of messenger, why did God have to send someone so graphic, so descriptive? I wanted to leave, to give an excuse to check the kids upstairs, but I was glued to my seat.

He told us how the murder had destroyed his life, his health, his ability to work and to concentrate. He listed the medication he was taking, and I wondered how he could survive. I glanced at Cliff, and I could tell he was thinking the same things I was. *What if this man has a heart attack right here in our kitchen!* He looked so pale and worn. "I'm telling you this to let you know what lies ahead," he said over and over again like a prophet of doom.

It was two hours later, well after twelve o'clock midnight, when he finally finished his piece of pie and took his leave.

We were all exhausted. The last two hours had seemed like three days. We made Dave and Fran as comfortable as we could downstairs, and Heidi slept in Odia's room.

Cliff and I whispered softly to each other as we got ready for bed.

"Cliff, do you think we're going to lose everything?" I was remembering the statistics for marriages breaking up after the death of a child.

Cliff was quiet for a moment, deep in thought. He looked as miserable as I felt.

I continued. "There has to be a way around this. I don't want to lose everything."

"We won't," he said to comfort me.

"But how can we be certain? Cliff, I don't want to lose you, the kids, my health, or my sanity. We've made it this far; we have to make it."

He nodded. He's not at his best at night, and I knew he was tired, but I needed to find one little part of the answer before I could even think of sleep. I needed him to process it with me.

I went to brush my teeth. Surely others had survived a crisis like this. How had they done it?

My grandfather had survived the atrocities of Russia. He had lost his job as a promising businessman; he had seen his village plundered, women raped, and relatives disappear—some of them murdered. But he had survived. He had more than survived.

I had known him at the end of his life. I had followed him around as a child and watched him prune his garden of roses, at peace with himself and nature. He was always in search of the perfect rose, and he would call me over when he found one. It would be a bud just about to open up. "This is when I love them the most," he used to say.

Our church was full of older people with "stories" too. Some of them remained haunted; some of them had found a resolution. One could see the difference. I knew that my grandfather had found the way through, and now I was sorry I never asked him how he had done it.

I came out of the washroom. So much of life is still theory. It is one thing to theorize about a problem; it is something totally different to go through it experientially. Suddenly I knew what my answer was for tonight.

"Cliff, I don't know why we had to have that visit tonight, but I think the man came with a special message for us."

Cliff looked up from pulling off his socks. He was used to my strange ideas and probably was wondering what was coming next.

"I think he came to tell us that if we look for justice, it will destroy us."

I remembered Cliff's earlier comment that this was just the beginning, that now we needed to find the murderer. I wondered if he would find it harder than I to give up the thought of actively pursuing justice.

"Cliff," I said slowly, watching him, "I don't think we are ever going to find a justice that will satisfy us by trying to find the murderer or seeing that he gets what he deserves. I think we have to find it another way."

A veil dropped over Cliff's eyes, and I knew that he wasn't sure of what I was saying.

"We will have to wait for true justice; we won't find it here on earth."

He nodded. "We won't be able to figure it all out tonight, sweets," he said softly, and we turned out the lights.

He was right. But I felt better having said what I had.

Suddenly the justice issue seemed such a small thing compared to the events of the day. All the pictures of the day started to roll before my eyes like some silent movie. The police station, the faces of the officers, Candace's silent, bleak face etched with the hideous red blotches of that night's horrors.

I opened my eyes. *I'll never be able to sleep again*, I thought. *I'll never be able to close my eyes again.*

Cliff was lying very still.

"Do you see her, too?" I asked, ". . . just lying there?"

"Yes. I can't get her face out of my mind."

"What do we do now?"

We lay in absolute silence for a long time. We were exhausted. We had only a few hours before we needed to get up and go to the funeral home. But our minds wouldn't stop whirling.

We had refused to take sleeping pills. I hadn't taken any drugs when my children were born; I'd had them by natural childbirth, and I was determined that I was going to experience their death naturally as well. But now I wasn't so sure if I had made the right decision. The physical pain of delivering Candace didn't compare with the pain of losing her.

Finally, I had an idea. "Let's remember pictures of Candace when she was a baby." Maybe memories would dislodge the pain. I began. "I remember her in a yellow snowsuit, just learning to walk."

"Candace in a dark navy pantsuit," Cliff joined in, "in the autumn leaves."

"The birthday picture where she put the spoon in her mouth and wouldn't take a bite because the movie camera was running."

"The one with the cats . . . the black cats."

"Candace with the horses and Heidi."

It was like a slide show: beautiful pictures with warm memories. But the minute we paused, there on the screen of our minds was the last picture. We could never erase it, but somehow in the series of happier days, it had lost some of its power.

"With Tracy and their bikes . . ."

"As a flower girl . . ."

"Suntanning . . . swimming . . . playing with Syras . . ."

And on and on until we were too tired to remember anymore. We slipped away. After all, sleep wasn't our enemy.

At an unearthly early hour the next morning, we drove to a hastily arranged appointment at Klassen's Funeral Home. We tried to keep it businesslike. We had never planned a funeral before, so the funeral director led us through the items that we would need to think about. Cliff started making a list.

The date?

We had been told it might take up to five days before they could release Candace's body. The director, Walter Klassen, said he'd find out and get in touch with us to let us know when the body arrived.

A memorial card?

He showed us two samples, and we chose the one decorated with a shaft of wheat on it.

He reminded us that we would need bulletins for the program, and we told him we'd pick them up on our way home.

Which church did we want?

Our own.

Who were we going to invite?

Invite to a funeral? Anyone who wanted to come.

Maybe we should think of a bigger church then, he suggested. And which cemetery did we want?

We didn't know. Should we buy a family plot?

Not necessarily, he said. We were young; we could decide that later.

We decided on Glen Eden, the cemetery on Highway 9 on the way to Camp Arnes.

Coffin?

We went into a room filled with coffins. *This is unreal*, I thought. *This can't be happening.*

A white coffin caught our attention almost immediately, one with a little pink bud embedded in ribboned material. It was feminine . . . young.

We went back into the office.

What about a cement vault?

What?

Would we like the coffin to be put into a cement vault? It would protect the coffin. It would keep the ground from caving in.

How much would that cost?

He gave us an estimate.

We couldn't afford it. "Besides," I said, "we don't believe in putting a lot of money into a death. It isn't Candace we're burying, it's only a body. It's only a body," I repeated, trying to believe it.

Suddenly Cliff put his hand on my arm. I looked at him, but he couldn't speak. He was choked with tears.

"I want the vault," he said slowly.

"But Cliff," I said, a little annoyed and a little bewildered, "we can't afford it."

"I couldn't protect her during life," he whispered in pure anguish. "I want to protect her now."

Oh, Cliff! I felt as if my throat would close. I looked up at Walter Klassen and saw that he was struggling with his emotions too. We sat in silence for a long time. No one could speak. There was no question; we would buy a vault no matter what it cost.

I think it was right there in that office that Candace's death took on yet another shade of reality. Every decision, every choice became increasingly more difficult. We fumbled with our words, with our tears, and with an endless supply of Kleenex.

I was amazed that Walter cried with us. "It often happens here," he said, understanding. "I never really get used to it."

He waited till we were ready to continue. To whom or what would we like money gifts to be donated? Gideon Bibles? Another charity?

We hadn't given it much thought. Maybe in our case it wouldn't be necessary to set up a memorial. People wouldn't give now; they had given so much already.

No, the director told us, people like to be able to express their sympathy.

We asked how much people usually gave, and he told us it might be anywhere between two and seven thousand dollars—more if the person was well known.

We asked ourselves what Candace would have wanted, and we both immediately thought of Camp Arnes.

We left with a list of things to do. On the way home, we discussed what charity we would choose. We both envisioned something at Camp Arnes. I loved the idea of a swimming pool. "Camp Arnes has a swimming pool in their plans; I've seen it in their blueprints. I don't think Gideon Bibles is right for Candace. It's too old somehow. [Don't ask me to explain that kind of reasoning.] I can't think of anything else. . . . Candace loved to swim."

Cliff mulled it over. I could see him weighing the idea against his own values.

"Our happiest moments with Candace this last year were when we went swimming every Friday."

I'm sure the same pictures flashed through Cliff's mind that were going through mine: Candace diving into the deep water behind her father and then hovering near the bottom, beckoning for me to follow, knowing that I couldn't. My whole winter's ambition had been to swim underwater—to stay underwater with them—but I just couldn't. I'd plunge in on top of them, and they'd reach out to help pull me to the bottom, teasing me, but I couldn't even sink far enough to grab hold of their hands. I'd just bob to the top like a cork, and they'd follow me, laughing. The younger kids had loved seeing Candace do something that I couldn't.

Finally Cliff nodded. "It's not a bad idea."

I was excited. It fit so perfectly. We could start the fund for a swimming pool. It would be a place where people could go and have fun as families, just as we had. It would symbolize youth, life, and hope.

"I'll talk to Dave," Cliff promised.

After lunch, Cliff went upstairs to get ready to go out again, but I lingered at the table, drinking my coffee. There was so much to do, so much to think about. The first evening of Candace's disappearance, I had confronted God with the question why. Now that we knew she had been murdered, the question kept coming back in different forms. Why had Candace died? She was so young. She had so much to offer. Why her? Of all the young girls that had walked home from school that day, why Candace?

I could feel the weight of life's thousands of hard

questions settle into my thoughts, and I knew that it wasn't going to be easy to find the answers. As I sat there, I mentally thumbed through some of the answers, especially the ones I remembered discussing with Candace. I remembered one particular evening.

Candace had gone to baby-sit at a neighbor's house across the back alley. Around ten she had called me. "Mom, the kids are in bed. I'm playing video games. Can you come? I'm scared."

Ever since she had inadvertently watched a horror movie at a friend's house she had begun to express fear more and more. So I went over and sat down on the rug beside her. She beat me at a few video games, we munched on some peanuts, and I eventually broached the subject. I first questioned her to see if her fears were grounded in reality. Did she have something of which to be afraid?

"No," she assured me. It had just been a fear sparked by the movie. She had described the movie in detail—it had been about murder.

After listening and talking about her dreams, her fears, and other things, I remember saying, "Candace, you can't let fear rule your life. When you are afraid, pray that God will protect you."

I'll never forget how she looked at me with her big blue eyes and asked, "Mom, can you tell me, honestly, that if I pray to God to protect me, that nothing will ever hurt me again?" So much for Sunday school answers. My daughter had grown up.

I had asked the same question when we lived in a northern Indian reserve and our lives were threatened. For an entire evening, Cliff had been held at knife point. At the time, we couldn't resolve the question of God's protection. We felt so vulnerable.

Later, when we met a relative in ministry with the

natives and we saw that he had come to terms with danger and threats to his life, we asked him what had helped him. He told us of his assurance that should God cut off his life in a premature and violent way, his death, then, would have more of an impact than the rest of his life would have had.

I told Candace the story. I told her that death was not the worst option. To live a life with no value and no meaning was far more tragic. I told her that if her life was committed to God and she died a violent death, God would use her death to have more of an impact than her life. Oh, how glibly we speak!

She didn't answer me right away.

Finally I asked, "Are you okay, Candace?"

She looked up, and there were tears in her eyes. "Yes, Mom."

Her fears were never as prominent again.

Now the incident created its own set of questions in my mind. Did I have the right to promise my daughter those things? Had she taken my words at face value? Had God been listening? Would he honor her commitment? Did he really mean it when he said that when a kernel of wheat falls into the ground and dies, it will produce many seeds? That was the verse we had chosen for her memorial card.

What was meant by *seed?* What did I mean when I said *impact?* Candace had asked me that once, too. We had been talking about values in life, how what we chose to value shaped our lives. She had asked me what I thought was most valuable.

Love, I had told her—not money, not fame, not position. She looked doubtful, so I told her about a funeral I had attended. The woman had been at the bottom of life's totem pole. In the world's eyes, she'd had absolutely no status. She had been living on her retirement pension plan; she had been divorced in a highly religious and unforgiving community; she had a retarded child and a heavy German accent; she had never been a great housekeeper or cook; she was uneducated and poor; she was attractive, but not beautiful. "But when she died, there were more genuine tears at her funeral than at any other I have ever attended," I told Candace. "And I wondered why, until I listened to the story of her life. She knew how to love."

For me, her life was a verification of the biblical teaching that it is only love that endures. Only love has eternal value. Not the Hollywood "love" that mixes love with desire, but rather the kind of love that is sacrificial. The kind of love that will give up rights, needs, and even life for another person. Very little of what we give is truly void of self-interest. But if an act does transcend human selfishness, then that act—even if it is as small as giving someone a cup of cold water—becomes memorable, becomes eternal. And whether that means the act lives on in the form of human memories or actual heavenly reward doesn't really matter. We have been promised, and I've seen it over and over again, that sacrificial love outlives the donor. It has a life of its own, and it creates its own impact.

I had tried to tell Candace this in different ways. I told her that most people never really remember what you've accomplished or what you've become except maybe with envy. People are really only touched by the love you give to them. This woman, I remembered, had never really thought she was all that important. But her gift to others was to make them feel important, and she was remembered for it. Being a "people person," Candace had quickly understood and liked the idea of there being power in love. I had seen her exercise that gift. I couldn't help but wonder if her love would seed. Would it be memorable? Had I steered her in the right direction? Had she lived long enough, invested enough of herself? I would watch, wait, and hope.

My questions also turned around to stare me in the face. Candace's murder would now also be our test. Could we continue to care, to be gracious, to give, to forgive? Or would we, having lost something so precious, now withdraw, lose faith, and become bitter, self-pitying, and miserly? Did we really believe that the only important thing in life is love?

My pathetic, frightened, shriveled soul could only whisper, "God help us."

When Cliff came down he found me still sitting in thought. He remembered the incidents I described to him as clearly as I did, and he shook his head in amazement as it all came together for him.

"What do we do now?" I asked.

"Maybe we can nurture her love," he offered.

"How do we do that?"

"Tell her story . . . and try to be loving," he answered with a shrug.

"But what can we *do?*" I needed action.

"We just have to let it take its course. We can't control it."

Cliff soon left for the office to get ahold of Dave Loewen, who was at Three Hills, Alberta, and hadn't yet been told that Candace had been found. Cliff called him to let him know and to discuss a memorial contribution for a swimming pool. Dave needed to check with the board, so he said he'd call back.

It wasn't long before he called. No, the swimming pool hadn't been approved; could we think of something else? The pool had always been a source of contention in the Society. There were many members who thought there were more important things to do at Camp Arnes.

But by now my heart was set on the swimming pool. "Cliff," I begged when he told me, "does he know why we want the swimming pool? It isn't only our choice. It's because of Candace. She loved swimming. All the other ideas just don't suit Candace. This one suits perfectly. It's a symbol of life. We're not asking them to build it, just to let us start the fund." I really couldn't understand why we couldn't give money where we wanted.

We called Dave again and listed our reasons. We told him of Candace's love for swimming, how last winter we had started swimming every weekend as a family, how we had talked about a swimming pool for Camp Arnes, how it was a symbol of life, and how this contribution was only to be used as seed money—it would hardly be enough to build a pool.

Dave listened to our plea, then cleared his throat. "Well, listening to your story makes a difference." There was a long silence on the other end of the line.

"We need an answer by tomorrow."

"The board can't meet."

"It's just seed money."

"It's not that easy. This would mean a commitment on our part to build a pool."

"We'll call Dave DeFehr ourselves."

We called and Dave called. It took a lot of calls, and I'm afraid we twisted their arms. They couldn't say no to us. I think we sobbed our way into convincing them.

Eventually the answer came back: if we phrased it as a "dream" then it wouldn't be as much of a contract, and Camp Arnes wouldn't be committed to building immediately. It would give the board space to present the idea to the Society at the annual meeting.

As soon as it was approved, we decided we would announce the swimming pool fund at the press conference the next day as well as at the funeral. But I had second thoughts as soon as it was settled. I wondered if we had done the right thing. Would Camp Arnes be stuck with a commitment that was all wrong for them? Were we creating a white elephant?

Ever since Candace had disappeared, I felt like we had been shoved on a runaway train and were racing toward some destination, out of control. I had thought that once we found Candace, the train would pull into some kind of a station. Now I knew that whatever journey we were on wasn't over.

CHAPTER 11

Saying Good-bye

The feeling that we were on a train racing out of control toward a destination not of our own choosing stayed with us that entire week as we prepared for the funeral. The journey itself was terrifying. The speed with which things were happening and the choices we had to make on the spur of the moment were unnerving. The train tracks twisted and turned through strange new terrain where flashes of good and hints of evil colored everything.

On Friday, the day after Candace's body was discovered, we found out that the shed she had been found in was only about five hundred yards away from our house. It was at the end of the railway tracks that led off of Talbot Avenue. She probably had taken her usual route home and was forced off the road at the point where Talbot and the railway tracks intersect. The shack was on private property, off in a desolate corner of a brick and lumber yard. Apparently the shed had been built fifty years earlier to house a piece of machinery used to haul sand, but it hadn't been used for a long time. No one from the company had entered the building for the last two years until a company foreman went into the shed looking for a machinery part. He said he had seen the body immediately.

After the body was removed, the shed was guarded for the first day, but eventually the police moved the small, eight-by-twelve-foot structure to their station.

Our first question was whether the police had checked the building during their local search; and if they had, how had they missed seeing the body if it had been so obvious to the foreman.

The police admitted that they had looked in the building but they hadn't seen the body. Their only explanation was that the weather had been extremely cold that day and the sun had been bright. The officer could have been suffering from snow blindness when he peered into the tiny, dark, windowless shed.

Those were the facts, fairly easy to accept, but the feelings weren't that easy to sort out. She had been so close to us the whole time we searched. Why hadn't we just walked over to that shed? How could we not have known?

Dave Loewen called from Three Hills, Alberta, to say that he wouldn't be able to make it back until the evening before the funeral. It would be the responsibility of the rest of the search committee to help us with the funeral preparations.

At the next meeting, when the committee heard that we were going to open the funeral service to the public, they warned us that we might have a huge crowd attending. They explained that the search had become a public event and that many people in the city had begun to identify with us. Strangers had felt along with us and now felt that they knew Candace. Were we sure that we were ready for that kind of crowd? We thought about it, but it only convinced us more that if the people of Winnipeg felt that close to Candace, they also had a right to say good-bye.

The committee caught their collective breath. "You'll need help," someone said. They suggested that we should hold the funeral at Portage Avenue Mennonite Brethren Church, the largest Mennonite church in the city. It could seat two thousand people. Our church would provide a lunch afterwards.

Harold Jantz had already contacted the media to set up a press conference for Saturday. Together we outlined our purposes for the press conference: to respond to the media as we had promised the first day, to thank them for their help in their coverage of the search, to thank the public and invite them to the funeral, and to announce that anyone wanting to express their sympathy could donate money to the dream of building a swimming pool at Camp Arnes.

The runaway train stopped for an unscheduled pit stop that Friday night. The last thing we did that day was to watch the news to see if there was an update on our case and reacquaint ourselves with what was happening in the rest of the world.

But after our story, the evening news carried the story of the trial of a man who had gone on a shooting rampage. Then they profiled the murderer's boyhood, telling a pathetic story of a young boy abused again and again by a tyrannical father. Cliff and I were glued to the set. Time stood still. The train stood still.

All murder cases were now appendages of our own. I found myself questioning from my new perspective. Was this man a typical murderer? In this case, was the man's father also guilty of the final act? If so, shouldn't the father be held accountable for what his son had become? How do you evaluate violence? Is a death by gunshot a worse crime than a life of abuse?

Cliff read my mind. "It doesn't look as if there is ever only one person guilty of a crime," he said.

Does that apply to our case, too? I wondered. *Could anyone who felt good about himself have forced Candace off the road and tied her up in a shack? Surely only someone who was driven by hurt, guilt, rejection, or uncontrolled needs would do something like that!*

Cliff and I both had such healthy, normal backgrounds. In comparison to the tormented perpetrator, we had so much.

Maybe this man was, in some way, a victim, too. In fact, maybe it wasn't we who were victims at all. Victims are helpless; were we really helpless?

Slowly it dawned on both Cliff and me that our faith in God gave us resources, gave us options. We didn't need to remain victims. We could free ourselves.

There's a wonderful yet simple verse in the Bible that says, "Do not be overcome by evil, but overcome evil with good" (Romans 12:21). We realized that we did not have to be overcome and destroyed. We could emerge victorious. But how to do this remained the question. To overcome small evils was fairly simple— but murder?

This was where our heritage and our education came to help us. We knew there was an alternative to vengeance: forgiveness. We both knew that in order to be truly free we would have to turn what was meant for evil into good. We would have to forgive. Instead of focusing on the evil done to us and seeking vengeance, we needed to look at the full picture of justice. Without justifying the evil act, we needed to see the picture that God sees: we are all guilty, and we are all forgiven.

Forgiveness is a widely misunderstood concept, and I'm not even sure we fully understood it at the time. Cliff had preached sermons on the subject, and we had discussed it at length, but it was something totally different to actually have to forgive. All the head knowledge in the world wasn't good enough at that point. We needed to process the concept with our hearts.

And we didn't have all the answers. At that moment we would have lost every debate on the subject. But by faith—a step totally in the dark—we had come to the simple conclusion that in order to be free to live again, we needed to forgive. We decided we wanted to forgive.

I think in all of this it's important to remember that we were essentially seven weeks into our grief. To this day I'm amazed at how real my intuitive feeling was that Candace had died the first night. All through the search we had operated on our 10 percent hope that she was alive, but deep down we had known the truth. Finding the body was only a confirmation of what we had known all along. Our ability to begin to distance ourselves at this stage was due to the fact that we had to some degree grieved for seven weeks already.

We stood up to go to bed, and the spell of that moment was broken. That's when we noticed that the train had stopped, waiting for us to reach this conclusion. But the minute we got up, we were back in motion, and we could feel the train gaining speed again.

There were so many things to think about. There were so many terrifying moments ahead of us: the press conference, the funeral, the emotional journey. It was only because we were so entirely exhausted that we managed to sleep on that swaying train.

The next day, Len DeFehr picked us up to go to the press conference. Harold Jantz chaired the conference, and Cliff read his statement. Then we allowed time for questions.

The first question was about our emotional reaction, and we told the reporters we were tremendously relieved that Candace had been found, but now we were trying to accept her death. Then they wanted to know how we felt about the perpetrator, and Cliff and I paused. Should we be honest? Would they understand? We had no choice; our only strategy throughout the ordeal had been to be honest, so we tried to convey to them that we felt compassion for this person, that we had chosen to forgive.

Cliff, always sure of himself, was able to say that he had already forgiven. I think for him just making that choice was somehow conclusive. It went with his nature. He lives in the present.

I'm a little different. I tend to live in the past and the future; I only dip down into the present occasionally. For me it would take longer to process, and I would never be sure if I had forgiven entirely. I told the reporters that I had chosen to forgive. I wasn't sure if I actually had—yet.

In hindsight I can see how strange our answer must have seemed to them. They had no idea of the grief we had experienced for seven weeks or of the intense spiritual journey we had been on during the last two days.

One reporter immediately wondered how we felt about capital punishment, and we didn't trust ourselves to give an answer. Intellectually, it shouldn't have been a question. But we weren't following our minds, we were following our hearts; and frankly, we weren't sure where we were going to come out on the issue. We were looking at life from a totally new perspective, and we hadn't explored it enough to commit ourselves yet. We told the reporters this, and they accepted it.

The lights went down, but the reporters stayed seated and asked questions informally. It was almost as if they wanted to know what made us tick. I would have loved to tell them, but I didn't know myself. We tried to describe our faith, but it was a pitiful attempt.

I didn't know what they were thinking, but for a minute I forgot they were the press and felt we were among friends. I felt that in some way they had been with us on our journey for the last month and that they had a right to continue with us to the end. We invited the media to the funeral.

We rested on Sunday and mapped out the next week's activities. Our families were all coming at different times; they all needed places to stay, and there were many details to care for. Usually I hated details. In fact, during the search, I hadn't been able to concentrate on whether we needed one or two scoops of coffee in the coffee pot. But with Candace found, I started to find a bit of relief in details. It saved me from the bigger questions.

On Tuesday our families started to arrive, and because the funeral was going to be so public, we had a private viewing of the body that evening.

I know it would have been much more civilized to have closed the coffin and had her picture set on it, but

there is nothing civilized about death. I knew our families and close friends needed to see her as much as we
did. My mother said over and over, "It's a miracle that
after six weeks we can still see her one last time. It's
truly a gift."

Candace looked lovely lying there so still, so calm,
and I was glad to see her once more with the horror
removed artificially from her face.

The day before the funeral, the police called to say that
they needed to take a statement from both Cliff and me
and that they would like us to come to the station.

Our first response was, "Can't it wait till after the
funeral? Our families are in from British Columbia and
Saskatchewan, and there are so many details to look
after."

"No."

"Can you come to the house? It would make
things easier."

"No."

"What is so important?"

"Nothing. We'd just like to take a statement as
soon as possible," they insisted.

When we arrived at the station, the sergeants
wanted to question me first. I didn't mind particularly.
At least I wouldn't have to pace in their dreadful reception room again.

The two sergeants ushered me into a small office
without windows. Pen in hand, they began to ask me
questions. They wanted to know the details of the day
Candace had disappeared. Most importantly, they
wanted to know how often Cliff had gone to look for
Candace.

I felt as if the train was picking up speed and
careening through the Fraser Canyon. I couldn't

remember how often Cliff had gone out looking for Candace.

"Try," they prodded.

"Was it once . . . twice . . . three times?" I wondered out loud. "At least twice."

"For how long?"

"Not long." I couldn't remember exactly. I hadn't been watching Cliff during that time; I had been worried about Candace. "No, maybe he went once again. He must have gone three times." I didn't have my notes along. I just couldn't remember!

The train was swaying dangerously around the curves. We were flashing through black tunnels where the darkness was as overpowering as the bright sun.

I had always told myself over and over again that even if Candace was found right next door, I shouldn't blame myself. But now the questions lurked in the dark valleys. Why hadn't we checked that shack? Why hadn't Cliff gone along the railway track? Why had he turned around?

"What times did he leave?" "When did he return?" I couldn't focus outside my own horror. I thought that maybe they were evaluating and documenting our movements to make sure that we had been responsible parents and had done everything we should have done to find Candace. But why now? Why couldn't they have waited a few days?

It seemed as if they asked the same questions a million times.

Finally, they were finished, and they fashioned a statement out of what I had said and read it back to me. I listened. It was as truthful as I could remember. I hesitated a moment before signing it. I hated being under such pressure, inside and out. I reviewed the details in the statement; the most it could do was incriminate us as irresponsible parents. If that's what we were, then we would have to deal with that reality, that blame. I signed the statement.

When I emerged from the office, Cliff took one look at me and grew furious. "I'm taking her home," he said, his eyes flashing. "I'll come back after I've taken her home and then you can question me."

The officers took another look at me and nodded. "We'll take her home."

An officer drove me home. The train had leveled off and was racing through a valley. But I was frightened that the officer driving me home might start interrogating me too, so I started rattling on and on about the weather and about all sorts of little things. I asked about his family, his children, and he told me. We had a nice conversation, though I caught him staring at me with the biggest question mark in his eyes. He must have wondered how I could be interested in his family at a time like this. He didn't know that I was only seeking relief in someone else's life; there was no relief in mine.

The day of the funeral was fittingly cold. In the morning, the thermometer registered a reasonable ten degrees Fahrenheit, but the weatherman promised that it would dip as low as minus eleven by evening. The temperature wouldn't test our endurance as much as the windchill would, though. At least the elements seemed to be consistent with the mood of the whole tragedy.

I don't think any of us dared to think about what might happen that day. We had never been at a public funeral, and we had no idea how it would go.

The two detectives who were going to stay at our house during the ceremonies arrived early. We showed them where they could get coffee and something to eat

and apologized for the state of the house. The men were
a reminder that this was not going to be an ordinary
funeral. We had been told that murderers often attend
the funerals of their victims, so plainclothes detectives
would be watching the crowd. To top it all off, we heard
that there was a woman who objected strongly to the
way the whole situation had been handled and that she
was planning a protest in front of the church.

We were all braced for the very worst. Our only
comfort was that it couldn't be worse than what we had
already experienced.

The funeral home's limousine pulled up in front
of the house right on time. Cliff, Odia, and I, as well as
our parents, rode in the first car. The rest of the family
followed in another. The sun was bright and a haze of
snow drifted about us as we started from the house.

As we approached the church, the traffic thick-
ened, and for a minute I wondered if we might even be
late. It was an unusual place for a traffic jam. But the
traffic parted mysteriously to let us through, and slowly
I realized as we approached the overflowing parking lot
that it was the funeral that was creating the traffic jam.

We were already accustomed to the sensation of a
train moving out of control, and it seemed as if we were
now being moved from one car to another. We were
ushered to a private room, then to the foyer, and then
we were walking slowly down the aisle following Candace's white coffin covered with red roses and with a
banner, reading "Friends Are Friends Forever," draped
over the front. The blurred faces along the aisle were
drawn, white, and silent. We sat down on the front
bench, and the program began.

The MBCI choir was sitting in the choir loft, and
we tried to smile at the students we recognized. David
was in the choir, in the last row right at the end. The

media had found their place to the left of us, much closer than I had expected. I wondered uncomfortably why we hadn't confined them to the back.

Keith Poysti, our assistant pastor, led the congregation in the first hymn, "We Praise Thee, O God," but I couldn't sing. If I had uttered a sound, it would have ended in a sob. I mouthed the words.

Keith then introduced Dave Loewen. Dave had been asked to officially represent the search committee and to thank the public, the police, and the media for their help.

"By God's hand, Candace has become a sacrificial lamb," he said. "This event has brought into focus both the worst and the best of Winnipeg. While evil has run its course, good has triumphed."

The choir, directed by Peter Braun, stood up to sing. It was too much for me. The train was again picking up speed. It seemed totally absurd to be sitting there calmly while Candace's body was imprisoned in a casket.

I knew that there were close to two thousand people in the building, and I was told later that many people had been turned away at the door. I was surrounded by people who had come to support us in our grief, yet it was the loneliest moment of my life.

I couldn't stay in the sanctuary. I had to get out, but I couldn't. I, too, was imprisoned. But there was a way; I would rely on my own way of escaping. I went back in time . . . down memory lane.

It was a perfect summer day in the Fraser Valley. I was in fourth grade. A new boy had moved onto our street—a tall, lanky Dutch boy in fifth grade. He had a great throwing arm and joined us for evening baseball games in our cow pasture. A few hits, a few catches, a few throws, and he was an instant hero.

After one evening's play, he invited me to come to see his family's farm. They had made a few changes. . . .

It was a beautiful farm. It must have been late spring because I remember how absolutely enthralled I was with light lime green weeping willow tree and all the mother hens that were scratching for grain with their little broods of chicks following them around the yard. I scooped one up, and it felt like a cotton ball against my cheek.

When my friend saw my delight with the chicks, he asked me to follow him into a shed, and in a dim corner he pointed to a nest where the eggs were just beginning to hatch. It was like being invited to a drama on opening night. We watched, enchanted, as the eggs cracked open and exposed scrawny little creatures that didn't look anything like the fluffy things running around the yard.

We noticed that there was one egg with a large crack that didn't seem to be making much progress.

"I'll help," I offered as I bent over to pick it up.

"No, don't touch," he said, standing up to lean against the wall. "They need to do it all by themselves. Let's go."

"No. Look. Can't you see it needs our help? If I help it, I'll give it a head start. It's already late."

He shook his head. "It will die if you help it too soon."

"Helping never hurts anything. Please," I pleaded, waiting for his permission. "I promise I'll be careful."

He shrugged his shoulders. "Okay. Find out for yourself."

I cracked the egg and the chick flopped out. It looked just like all the rest of them as it struggled to find its legs.

"See," I said. "It's not going to die."

We watched for a while as it flopped around, but when it seemed to be okay, we went to explore the rest of the farm.

Just before it was time to go home, we checked in on the chicks again. Through a crack in the wall, a shaft of light spotlighted the nest. My chick had been shoved to the side of the nest, and it wasn't moving. It was dead.

I was aghast. "You really knew all along that it would die?"

"Yes."

"Then why did you let me do it?"

"You wouldn't listen."

"You could have stopped me if you had really wanted to." He was twice as big as I was.

He looked away. "You'll believe me next time."

He was right about that. "Your dad will be furious," I said.

He shrugged his shoulders. "He'll never notice. We have so many."

"What do we do with it? Where can we bury it?" I was imagining a tiny grave with a pansy or two and a sprig of weeping willow.

"You don't bury a chick," he said and picked it up. He walked to the back door, and with his powerful throwing arm, he heaved the tiny body clear over the huge barn and I heard it hit the manure pile with a faint splat.

The whole afternoon had been spoiled. "You shouldn't have done that."

"It's life on the farm," he struggled to explain.

"I'm going home." I bolted for the front door and out of the shed.

My sister had always insisted that I not pollute the world with ugly words. If I really was angry and needed to spit out a word, I should use pretty words like names of flowers. But this time daffodils, crocuses, and gladiolus didn't suit the occasion. I groped for a word—this-tle, stinging nettle, . . . "Skunk cabbage," I hollered as I ran down the road. "You're nothing but skunk cab-bage!" But I don't think he heard me; he had already started his evening chores.

A few days later he came by, bought me a choco-late bar and a Coke, and all was forgiven. And he was right. I never doubted his word again.

A lot had changed since then, but some things hadn't. The little girl who went running down the road screaming "skunk cabbage" was still alive in me. I wanted to scream. But there was another reason I had recalled the story. As I looked at all the people who had come to support us, I knew that no one really could. We were alone. We were encased in the shell of our grief. And even though to others it might seem as frag-ile as an eggshell, to us it was as formidable as a brick wall. Still, we had to peck our own way out of it. Our attempts might seem pitiful to those watching, but we needed to do it for ourselves.

Life begins that way; it ends that way. That's why God stands beside us, watching but choosing not to help the way we might want him to, knowing that if we don't meet the present challenge, we won't be ready for the next.

We each have our own timing for the events of life, and grief is no different. Some seem to move through the stages without effort. Some of us struggle every inch of the way.

Ruth Balzer cut through my thoughts as she stood up and began to tell Candace's story. We had chosen Ruth because she had known Candace through the Camp Arnes Follow-up Program, a winter program designed to give the kids spiritual support throughout the winter. Ruth had picked Candace up every Tuesday.

In sixth grade, Candace had often left for the evening in a vague kind of mood. But she had always come home renewed, and we knew that a large part of it was due to Ruth's influence on Candace. I don't think Ruth ever knew what a model she was for Candace, but we did, and it was important to us to include Candace's favorite people in the program.

We hadn't wanted an obituary or eulogy. Candace was too young for something so staid and formal. Besides, she didn't have many accomplishments. We wanted Ruth to give a simple, descriptive story about who Candace was, what she was like, and how Ruth herself had felt about her.

I looked up at Ruth standing so calmly behind the pulpit. She was saying, "To know Candace was to love her, not because she was more special than anyone else, but because she knew how to love." She described how Candace loved to swim, run, play basketball, and ride horses. "I often saw her draw out a shy person or make a newcomer feel welcome."

She described Candace as a gentle spirit, cheerful, enthusiastic, and real, and as having a giving faith. One of her stories brought out a laugh, which Candace would have loved.

The choir got up to sing. At first, I hadn't wanted a choir, and I had said as much to Dave Teigrob when we were discussing the funeral arrangements. "We'll have taped music. It must be torture to sing at a funeral, and I'm not going to ask anyone to do that."

"But people like to sing," Dave said very gently.

"Even at funerals?"

He nodded. "The concert choir sang at Daryl's funeral." Earlier that year a twelfth-grade boy had been killed in a train-car accident. "It was something they could do for Daryl and his parents."

"Would they want to do it for Candace?"

"Yes," he answered. "I know they would. In fact, I think if they weren't asked, they would wonder why since they did it for Daryl."

Young faces in the choir loft; beautiful singers who would soothe raw nerves and reflect the hope of youth in the midst of despair—I could see its appropriateness, but I still found it hard to believe that those young people would actually want to do it.

"I could ask for you," Dave offered.

I had looked at Cliff, he had nodded.

And now they were singing . . . beautifully.

So much care had been taken in choosing the music. After that conversation with Dave, Katie Epp, our pastor's wife, had reminded me of congregational singing. Had I thought of favorite hymns? What songs would I like?

I didn't know anything about music, so I had finally given all the responsibility of selecting and coordinating the music to her. She had put time and thought into it, and now we were reaping the benefit of her expertise. The songs matched the mood; the words expressed the sentiments of the moment.

Cliff then announced the swimming pool fund. Again, this was probably highly unusual for a funeral, but it was part of the story.

And then Candace's song . . .

Cliff introduced the song and told the congregation how Candace had played this song every night for the last year and a half, how the words were her gift to us now.

I tried to brace myself. The media were right there.

In a way, this funeral wasn't for me as a mother. Before we arrived, I had bundled up my emotions and put them in a straight jacket. A funeral is for friends and acquaintances, for people who want to say their last farewells and need to shed a tear. My grief as a mother was too raw, too big, and too unexplored for such a setting. I can understand the need for "wailers" at a funeral; with paid wailers, I could have allowed myself to wail. But in the quietness of the church, with the formality, I kept a good grip on my emotions.

But that song had been so much a part of Candace that when the melody floated through the loudspeakers, it was as if her presence walked softly down the aisle. The tears began to slip. Even if I couldn't grieve as a mother, I could grieve as a friend. We had been friends. We had just recently reached the stage in our relationship where we wanted to go out shopping together, wanted to do things together, wanted to talk. I had never lost my position as mother; I had just acquired a new role as an older friend. Now the song reminded me of all that.

With the faith and love God's given
Springing from the hope we know
We will pray the joy you live in
Is the strength that now you show

But we'll keep you close as always
It won't even seem you've gone
'Cause our hearts in big and small ways
Will keep the love that keeps us strong

The chorus:

And friends are friends forever
If the Lord's the Lord of them
And a friend will not say "never"

> *'Cause the welcome will not end*
> *Though it's hard to let you go . . .*

All through the weeks of searching, Odia had never shown any sign of emotion. I hadn't expected her to—at her age it's so hard to understand everything. My grief was different from hers. She was losing a sister, I was losing a child. But now I could feel her trembling beside me. She knew all the words, and she sang with the song as the tears rolled down her cheeks.

I hated to see her pain and held her close. *That's what funerals are for*, I reminded myself, *to say good-bye*.

I've been told that there wasn't a dry eye in the place. Even though it was painful to cry, all of us needed to do it.

The song continued:

> *In the Father's hands we know*
> *That a lifetime's not too long to live as friends*

Candace was telling us all that though we had to say good-bye, we could still hold each other close.

Prior to coming to Winnipeg, we had lived in North Battleford, Saskatchewan, for almost five years, and Candace had developed a very special relationship with Tracy Vickers, who lived across the street, two houses down. The two had been inseparable. They were the same size and had the same interests. Even their differences—Tracy was more reserved, Candace more outgoing—were complementary. They could entertain themselves together for hours.

When we moved to Manitoba, it was heartbreaking to watch Candace mourn her best friend. As a going-away present, Tracy had bought Candace a goldtone locket. Candace treasured that locket and wore it all the time. Even after it began to tarnish, she still wore it.

This worried me a little. I wondered if she was making the necessary adjustment to our move, or if, for some reason, she still needed Tracy emotionally. I thought that when she met Heidi at Camp Arnes and they started to become good friends the necklace would come off, but it hadn't.

One time, when we were traveling through Saskatoon, we made a special effort to revisit North Battleford so that Candace could see Tracy. I thought that if everything had gone as life usually does, the two girls— now almost young ladies—would have changed so much that the bond wouldn't be as strong. The memories would be replaced, and Candace would put the necklace away.

I was secretly a little happy when we arrived at her house to find that Tracy had another friend visiting her. Just as I suspected, Tracy had changed. I felt a little sorry for Candace as I watched the two girls, once so close, now stand awkwardly apart, assessing each other. We spent the afternoon with them, and by the time we left the girls were enjoying themselves. Still, there was a noticeable distance between them. The good-byes were warm, but not tearful.

Driving back, I gently prodded her.

"Tracy has changed?"

"Yes."

"You've changed?"

"Yes."

"It's not quite the same?"

Cliff gave me a warning look telling me that I should leave the girl alone, but the question was already in the air.

Her voice was quiet but steady. "No, it wasn't the same."

There was a pause. I hoped she'd continue.

She did. But she had second-guessed me. "Mom?"

I glanced back. She was looking out the window fingering her necklace as she said, "It doesn't matter how much we change." She turned to look at me. "When we walked to the store, I saw the old Tracy. She'll always be my friend." And she continued to wear that necklace for another two years.

She was wearing that necklace the day she disappeared.

Pastor Epp stepped to the pulpit as the last notes of the song faded and began his meditation. "Whatever evil befell Candace, it will not have the last word in her life. God's peace is the last word," he began.

He was echoing our hope. His words were a comfort to us, and I hoped they were a comfort to all those who had come, to all those who were listening. CBC radio was broadcasting most of the funeral live.

And then it was over, and we were following the white casket down the long aisle. Another of Candace's songs, "Great Is the Lord," accompanied our procession.

Candace had once told me, "Mom, my favorite song is 'Friends Are Friends Forever,' and I wanted to tape only that one, but I accidently taped 'Great Is the Lord' as well, and now I keep listening to it, too. I like it almost as much. 'Friends' makes me a little sad. 'Great Is the Lord' picks me up and leaves me with a good feeling."

I had forgotten the effect that song could have. We had chosen it because it was one of Candace's songs, but it had its effect as we walked out. It gave us a good feeling.

We stepped outside. The sun had disappeared, and the force of a blizzard swirled around us. Just as I was stepping into the car, a strange man broke through the crowd and grabbed me. He only wanted to give me a little Bible and to wish us well, but it reminded us again that this wasn't an ordinary funeral. The person who killed Candace could easily have come as a guest.

The funeral procession pulled out onto Portage Avenue. Three patrol cars led the procession, but we could hardly see them because the blizzard was so strong. I knew we were in a sad parade, but for a few moments the blizzard mercifully curtained us from public scrutiny.

Once out of the city limits, the storm was even more intense. We could barely see a car-length ahead of us. Just visible in the blanket of white, we noticed three police officers standing at the gate of the Glen Eden Memorial Gardens, saluting, paying their last respects to Candace as we entered.

I had often wondered how people could bear the sadness of seeing a body go down into the ground. But as we drove into the cemetery, I was glad for that tradition. I had read somewhere that it's important to go all the way to the end with those you love, and now I knew it was true.

The force of the wind nearly swept us off our feet as we got out of the cars. My brother, Wes, was wearing only a light jacket and was visibly trembling with the cold as he struggled with the coffin, trying to be as gentle with it as possible, as if she could still feel the pain.

I was grateful for the storm. It was a gift. It would have been so much harder if it had been a nice day with the birds singing in the trees. Somehow this strange storm was a reflection of our inner turmoil: no one has the right to take another person's life; the world is a cruel unfriendly place where innocent children have to absorb the pain; since the creation, everything has gone wrong; we are spinning out of control.

I felt bad that I had on a prairie coat. I wanted to take it off and suffer with my shivering family; I wanted to feel the last cold that Candace had felt.

Suddenly the little ceremony was over and we were supposed to move to the car, leaving Candace behind.

It couldn't be over yet! I hadn't said good-bye! I hadn't insisted that everyone leave me alone with Candace so that I could say good-bye. I hadn't held her.

The director gave each of us a flower from a spray of flowers. I stepped up to the coffin suspended over the grave and bent down to touch it. It was cold. "'Bye, Candace. I love you," I whispered, glad that the strong wind would grab my words and whisk them away before anyone could hear. Maybe, just maybe, it would carry them to where she could hear.

We went to our church for lunch. The public guests had left and it was only friends and family who stayed with us. Some of them started to tell us what Candace had meant to them.

One young man, who had been in Candace's class and about whom Candace had always talked so admiringly, told us what their friendship had meant to him. I wish Candace could have been with us to hear all those wonderful things being said about her. I was amazed that, young as she was, she had already left a legacy of love.

After a service and a light lunch, Dave Loewen invited everyone to surround our table in one massive hug. Someone said a simple prayer. Then we went home, emotionally exhausted, yet somehow encouraged.

The officers who had stayed at the house to guard it had left, and on the dining room table was a small cut-flower bouquet. A boy down the street—another of Candace's friends—had left it for us, and a neighborhood store had brought over large plates of cold cuts for those who came to stay with us.

It wasn't until that evening that we realized how much strain we all had been under. We were sitting in the overflowing living room, relaxing. We all had hit the depths of grief during the day and now were almost celebrating, relieved that the event of the day was over. It felt good. The mood became lighter and lighter. Even though some hadn't met before, we all seemed comfortable with each other. Our Winnipeg friends and our two families from out of province had been brought together and bonded by a common tragedy. It was good to see that kind of interaction.

As we got tired, people started describing the different beds everyone was going to sleep in that night. The Wiebes had a water bed, and they were trying to persuade my parents to try it out for the night. To help reassure them, Mary Wiebe described their first nights on their water bed.

Mary is a good storyteller and a delightful person, and her story about sloshing around in this huge bed brought out hysterical laughter that surprised all of us. We promptly felt guilty, uneasy, as if we had betrayed Candace, and I wish we hadn't. It was good to laugh. It was healing to laugh. Crying and laughing are actually the flip side of the same emotion, and we needed it. We shoved the guilt aside and laughed some more.

My parents were going home by train the next morning, so we left the children at home with my sisters and took advantage of the moment to have breakfast with Mom and Dad before they left.

We were all struggling with a heavy sadness, a quietness. We ate at a nondescript restaurant and covered the moment with small talk. Cliff went to a coin-operated paper machine and bought the city's papers.

We were shocked as the headlines—both papers, front page—jumped out at us. "Peace Triumphs!" said *The Winnipeg Sun* and devoted the first four pages to our story. The story in *The Free Press* centered on Candace. Both were excellent stories, and both suggested that somehow, in all of this tragedy, good had triumphed.

Dad had been unusually quiet during this second trip, and I hadn't been sure if it was just the hustle and bustle of things or if he was troubled. I watched his reactions carefully as he read the stories. When he laid the paper down there was a new peace on his face. "Now I understand," he said quietly. "On the train trip here, I was so puzzled. I wondered how God could allow something like this to happen. But now I know."

He didn't elaborate, and he didn't have to. All of our lives we had been drilled to believe Romans 8:28, which says that "all things work together for good to them that love God" (KJV). He was wondering where the good was in this tragedy. Where was God in this?

I looked at the headlines, but somehow they weren't enough for me. The pain was still too raw. I needed so much more good to equalize this pain. I wondered if there was ever going to be enough good to satisfy me.

I could feel the train speeding out onto the prairie, too fast for us and still towards an unknown destination. But some of the fear was gone now. Maybe there was an engineer in the front of this train. Maybe there was a destination.

My father, who always showed such remarkable restraint in most things, bought all the newspapers he could find.

CHAPTER 12

Changing Expectations

We felt empty and disoriented right after the funeral. It wasn't easy to change focus. For six and a half weeks we had channeled all of our energy into looking for Candace, and now we had to do a complete about-face and turn our attention to trying to live without her, to getting back to our lives.

In the process of our search, we had wanted something more. We wanted to turn the tragedy—the whole dreadful nightmare—into something good. We wanted to find some value in it so we could eventually live with it. Child Find and the swimming pool were two causes that seemed to fit this need.

But the hardest, most frightening goal was to be

able to forgive, to vaccinate ourselves with forgiveness as an antidote against bitterness and the subsequent spiral of losses that seemed to be inevitable after a homicide.

Our problem was that we had no idea what forgiveness meant in this kind of situation. Forgiveness isn't an easy concept to understand at the best of times. Did we know what we were committing ourselves to? Even the initial decision to try to forgive had already left us feeling as if we didn't care. It seemed as if we were abandoning Candace—twice.

The most difficult part of even beginning to think about forgiveness was that we had no idea who the murderer really was. Was he a friend or foe? male or female? young or old? respectable or vagrant? We didn't even know the motive. We decided that we would have to wait for the autopsy results before we could really deal with the issue.

The first afternoon after the funeral, my sisters Luella and Pat asked me what they could do for me. They believed I would go through a really tough emotional low soon after they were gone, and they wanted to help prepare me for that time. Was there anything that I dreaded doing, something I couldn't do? They asked over and over again in their gentle ways, but I resisted their help. I wanted them to sit down and relax, but they insisted. I thought about everything that needed doing. Yes, there was one thing that needed immediate attention, though I dreaded even thinking about it. It was all that unanswered mail that had taken up residence in the basement. I brought up the first big box and set it on the dining room table.

They groaned.

"What do you want to do with these?" my oldest sister, Luella, asked.

"To answer the whole lot of them."

Always ready for a challenge, she started to sort them into cards and letters. "I can answer the cards."

I had memorial thank-you cards to use to respond to the cards and stationery for the letters.

"Here." Luella held out the first answered card. "Is this the way you want them?"

I recognized the name. "You can also thank that family for the casserole they sent over . . . the letter, the call, and I don't know what else."

"You mean—"

I nodded. Some people had first responded to the disappearance of Candace seven weeks earlier with a note, then they had checked in after a few weeks with a casserole; some had sent us a card at Christmastime and then again at the news of Candace's death, also sending a check for the memorial fund. Even though the money was being handled by Camp Arnes, the office was forwarding the accompanying notes to us so we could respond to them if we wanted. If we didn't coordinate the process, responding to each piece of mail individually—each gift, each gesture of kindness—would mean that some people might get five thank-you notes.

"Is this the only box?" Luella asked.

I shook my head.

"We'll never be able to sort them out by memory." I agreed.

Meanwhile my younger sister, Pat, who had been reading some of the letters, sighed softly. "This good friend of yours has written you a lovely letter which only you can answer." She handed me the letter.

"I know. But I don't know them any more than you do, so it really won't make much difference who answers it."

"You mean, you don't know who they are?"

"I've never met them. We just had a nice conversation over the telephone."

She picked up another letter. "This one seems so private, too. I can't answer it."

Luella began to gather her notes and put them back into the box. "This can wait. Everyone knows how busy you are. Besides, you already gave a public thank-you at the funeral."

Pat agreed. "Wilma, you have gone through so much already. People wouldn't want this also to be a burden for you."

Soon we had talked ourselves out of the responsibility of answering all the letters—at least right then. My sisters were right. The letters could wait. I would buy index cards and record each letter or note. Once they were all tabulated, I could send out thank-you cards. Maybe my friends could help at that point. My sisters agreed. I packed up the box and took it downstairs again.

By the time I came up, they had found dust rags and the mop and were battling the dust, Percy's black hairs, and loads of wash. They had decided that the least they could do was to leave my house clean.

I had always been the poorest housekeeper of the lot, and my sisters couldn't get over the way I did things. As they discovered all my dreadful housekeeping habits, we laughed, joked, and had a wonderful time.

During all of this, a distant relative dropped by to pay his condolences. He visited with Cliff in the living room, and at one point, I looked up and noticed him watching us. I knew immediately that he didn't understand our joviality and that he disapproved of it. I knew that he would go back to his family and tell them that I didn't care, that he had actually seen me laughing.

The temptation was to sober up quickly, to play

the role, to bend myself into the "we really care" posture so that everyone would be satisfied. It sometimes seems that the big question occupying a community after a death is whether those left behind really cared. I had seen that question surface during the search for Candace. I could see it in this relative's eyes now. I suppose the question itself wasn't what bothered me, it was the misinterpretation of our actions.

Our guest couldn't see past the veneer of hilarity to the deeper desperation that we were feeling. He couldn't see that we had just chosen another form of emotional relief because, at the moment, we had used up all our tears. He didn't realize that he was seeing us seven weeks into our grief.

I was just thankful that my sisters didn't condemn me or each other. It was because we knew each other. They were the ones who had been in touch with me the seven weeks, who had walked with me for the last five days, who had cried with me, and who were now signaling to me that it was okay to laugh, okay to clean the house, okay to have a few moments of relief before another wave of grief.

I could put on a dour face and a black dress and mope for the next ten years, but would that convince anyone that I cared? No. Then people would probably condemn me for not being able to forgive and to cope. I remembered my mother's words: *Be true to yourself.*

She was right. I would never be able to please everyone all the time. People around us wanted to put us into safe boxes that they could understand. But those same boxes would confine us, hamper us, and eventually destroy us. I had to decide whose opinion was most important to me: the public's, my family's, my own . . . or God's. I was extremely fortunate that those important to me were so understanding. But even they might not understand some day. Would I then allow them to box me into their expectations? As important as they were to me, I couldn't allow them that liberty.

In the end, I really could answer only to myself, though I would add Mom's unspoken words, . . . *and to God.* God and I knew exactly what had happened in my life; we knew the depths of my pain, the depths of my loss. We had walked together through the dark nights. We had cried together. I had nothing to hide. I didn't have to put on a face for God; he had created me.

Even then I knew that the hardest image to keep centered, to deal honestly with, was my own reflection in the mirror of my soul. What was important was to keep peace with myself and with God. If I could do that, I didn't need to worry about public opinion.

Much later, just as I had suspected, we heard that our relative had indeed gone back and reported to his community, friends, and family that I had been totally unfeeling, that the day after the funeral he had seen me laughing.

It wasn't only the murderer that we needed to forgive. We had to begin by forgiving all the little misunderstandings that surrounded us. Often, at the end of the day, Cliff and I found ourselves saying to each other, "Let it be. They didn't know what they were doing. If they truly understood, they would see it differently. Let it be. Let it go."

During the next few days as each one of my family members left, we made it a point to go out alone with them for coffee before we delivered them to the airport, train station, or bus stop. Our collective grief was so easily lost in a full house, and it was during those coffee times that they could share what they had been going through during our crisis and we learned how it had affected their lives. None of us were ever going to be the same again. At those coffee times, we could share more intimately about our own grief, and they could ask those questions that were too private for open discussion. It amounted to about one good talk and farewell a day. It worked out perfectly, because we needed one good processing time daily.

After the last person had left, it was back to work. The search committee met again four days after the funeral. The preliminary discussion was about where the committee should go from that point. Was it all over? Was their mandate finished? They decided there was still an agenda. MBCI was involved with helping the police organization, Crime Stoppers, reenact some scenes to be aired at the end of February and early in March. There were leftover business and financial considerations from the funeral and the search. And many of the organizations involved—Glen Eden, Klassen's Funeral Home, River East Mennonite Brethren Church, and Portage Avenue Mennonite Brethren Church—had donated heavily and needed to be thanked both informally and formally. We were overwhelmed by their generosity.

We found out that the manufacturer Winnipeg Wilbert Limited had decided to donate their Monarch vault to encase the coffin. We had expected to pay for this—to sacrifice for this—for Cliff's emotional satisfaction that Candace was now finally protected. When we heard the news, I glanced at Cliff. He bit his lip, and I knew that he was fighting his emotions, overwhelmed with gratitude.

I did a quick calculation of the expenses of the funeral and compared it with all the gifts and donations. We balanced. We hadn't benefited one penny from Candace's death, but, miraculously, we also hadn't lost.

Len DeFehr reported that approximately six thousand dollars had been received for the memorial fund for the swimming pool and that there was still four thousand dollars left over from the search committee's funds. We also learned that the man who found Candace's body had declined the two thousand dollars reward money and the police were in the process of deciding where this money should go. Most likely it would go towards the memorial fund.

The last statement in the minutes of the meeting was probably the most revealing. "The perpetrators are not a priority project for us at present." We had chosen other goals.

We were surprised to find ourselves just as busy after the funeral as before it. Our goals were different, the work was different, but the activity was much the same.

On January 29, ten of us met together and formally organized an interim board to start working on establishing a Child Find chapter in Manitoba. We decided that the most logical first step would be to attend the annual Child Find conference to be held in Calgary, Alberta. We chose five people to go to the conference.

Every time Cliff and I thought things were getting back to normal, something would come up. On a Sunday evening early in February, two detectives came to our door to give us the final results of the autopsy. After we had made sure the children were occupied, we sat down with the detectives in the living room. Very carefully they set the scene. Candace had died of exposure— hypothermia, they said. The toxicology tests indicated that she had not been drugged or poisoned. All they knew was that her hands and feet had been tied and that she had been abandoned in the shack to die in the freezing temperatures. The crime scene was disorganized; it looked as if someone had attempted to bury some of her belongings, and it did look as if this person had spent some time with her.

I couldn't believe it. Even as we sat there listening, the whole situation seemed so unreal, so totally illogical. This couldn't have happened to our family. This wasn't the kind of thing that happened to peace-loving Mennonites living in Winnipeg.

My need to know dragged me back to reality. "Was she sexually assaulted?" I asked.

"No."

"Was she hurt in any way?"

"No."

But why? We asked over and over. None of it made sense. Why would anyone take a young girl and tie her up and leave her to die? What could the motive have been?

They shrugged their shoulders and watched our reaction as if they were waiting for something. They gave us a few more details about how they had found her belongings and how they had found her body. Candace's vocal chords hadn't been swollen, they told us. She hadn't tried to scream.

Oh, God! She hadn't screamed! Who had terrorized her so completely that she hadn't even screamed for help? I could feel my heart twist painfully as I visualized the possibilities.

"It doesn't look as if she struggled much," they said, and they continued giving us details.

No struggle could only mean that she had been too scared, too terrified. She had been totally overpowered! She must have thought it too hopeless or too dangerous to try.

They finally came to their conclusion. "We feel because of this evidence that she was probably with someone she knew."

I couldn't believe it. With the same details they had given us, the police had arrived at a totally different conclusion than I had. No struggle and no screaming spelled terror to me, but the police thought it meant a lack of fear. I tried to explain my point of view, but they couldn't seem to fathom anyone not fighting back—a perspective probably based on the difference between being a woman and being a tall, well-built male, I realized. There was no convincing them.

As they were leaving, one of them turned to me. "She was a virgin," he said. I couldn't read his eyes. Their whole presentation that evening had been strange. There had been no sympathy, no understanding of what this was doing to us, just cold hard facts and that slight edge of . . . I couldn't put my finger on it.

The words kept repeating themselves in my mind. "She was a virgin." Part of me, the part that had known all along that it was an abduction, said, "I know. I knew it all along. I didn't need that information." Another part of me, the 10 percent that doubted everything and had been hurt by the accusations that she had run away and had wondered about all the sightings and all the different interpretations, that part needed that bit of information. It laid all doubts aside. It was conclusive evidence that we had known our daughter. She really had been an innocent little girl—half woman, half child—who had been lured or forced off the street that night and terrorized. We had known Candace, and it was wonderful to have her memory secured.

But those stark words, "She was a virgin," drove home the reality that Candace had died before she could even begin to live. Instead of a beautiful white wedding dress, we had been forced to buy a cold, white coffin. Would I ever be able to accept the injustice of that?

Just before the detectives left, they assured us

again that they would be doing their utmost to find the guilty party and that they were positive that they would find him. I wasn't so sure. They didn't always find their man. The police in Edmonton had never found Jake Plett's wife's murderer. How could they be so sure they would find this one? It seemed as if there was even less evidence in our case.

As we closed the door behind them, I looked at Cliff; he looked drawn, torn . . . and old. We had changed. Both of us must have aged ten years in a space of two months. I had lost fifteen pounds. Cliff had grayed.

"The police are different," I said.

Cliff nodded.

"What is it?"

"We're dealing with a more serious division— homicide. I think there are different men, different approaches."

I wasn't so sure that was the entire explanation. For one thing, our feelings toward them were different. At first, their appearance on our doorstep had signaled help and information; even when their suspicious questions were difficult, we had always looked to them to solve our mystery. Whenever they had come, whenever they had called, that first moment had always been one of expectation. But now . . . now that we had the answer, we didn't need them. We didn't want them intruding on our lives anymore. Our feelings had changed.

I also wondered if part of the explanation was that they might still suspect us. If they did, it would mean that their suspicions had changed. It's one thing to be suspected of being an unkind or an inept parent; it's another thing completely to be suspected of murder. Were we now murder suspects? Was that the change we were feeling? I shoved the thought aside. That was ridiculous. We had good alibis: I had been home with the kids; Cliff had been at the office. There was no way that we could have been involved. I decided that the evening's discussion had left me paranoid.

The autopsy report had unsettled us more than we wanted to admit. After the detectives left, we paced the floor. We went through every detail of the whole case from beginning to end. Actually, there had been few surprises. We had known most of it. It wasn't the information that bothered us as much as the lack of information. The lack of conclusive information only meant that the mystery would continue. The different conclusions at which the police and I had arrived were just one example of how the whole matter would invite speculation. As long as there was a continuing mystery, most of the suspicion would focus on us. If there wasn't a clear motive, the police would center the investigation on those they knew best—us. Even if the police weren't suspicious of us, someone down the line would be. People need answers, and if they don't have them, they'll make them up.

I couldn't really blame anyone. Here I was a trained journalist with my own mystery. My whole training had been to continually look for answers, to find answers, and then to expose the answers. I hated unsolvable mysteries. But, I asked myself, would it have been better if Candace had been sexually assaulted so that we would have more answers? I had prayed that first night for Candace's protection. I had laid out all my personal fears and wishes and begged God not to allow her to be abused. I had said that I could accept her death as long as she hadn't suffered. I had heard that death by hypothermia is supposed to be one of the most painless ways to die. Why wasn't that the comfort to me that I had anticipated it would be?

There were so many possible scenarios. Had

someone intended to sexually assault Candace but, because of my prayers, suddenly decided not to do it? Had there been a noise outside the shed that had frightened him off? Had Candace said something that miraculously turned him off? And even if the person had only intended to tie her up and get his jollies that way— wasn't that still an answer to prayer?

Was I the kind of person who wouldn't take total responsibility for my request if the answer to my prayer was not all that I had wanted? I swallowed hard. I decided I would never complain about the continuing mystery and the suspicions, because the most important thing was that Candace had not been physically abused. I had no choice. I had asked for that. Now I had to learn to live with the mystery.

But I still had to deal with what had happened. The horror of those torturous hours that Candace must have spent in the shack—the freezing cold, the fear, the hopelessness, the ropes, the emotional abuse—I would have to learn to live with that . . . somehow. I wasn't sure if I could. I wasn't even sure if I could confront it yet, if I could allow myself to absorb the full impact of the experience.

Late at night, I paced the floors again. There was only one comfort: Candace had gone through the experience only once. It was all over for her. What had happened had ended. She was safe now. Clutching that thought, I could slowly replace some of those images of her terror with living pictures of happier days.

I knew that this would not be the last time I would make this journey—remembering the horror and replacing the pictures. Thankfully, Candace had lived it only once. I would live it a thousand times.

As I looked out the window, I again thought of the person who had done this. He (or she) was out there somewhere. Whether this person realized it or not, he was part of our family now. This person held the last moments of Candace's life in his hands. We were inextricably linked in a relationship of sorts, and I wanted to know, to see, to talk to the person. There were times when I just didn't think we could go on unless we could find that person and confront him. Then I'd remember what Jake Plett had said. This person, whoever he was, had taken enough from us already. He wasn't going to take any more. Very gently, I removed myself from the questions, from my desperation. We didn't need to know.

And that day, as I had done so many times before—with much struggle, with much weariness—I relinquished my frustration to the safest place I knew—into God's hands.

I wondered if this was forgiving. I suspected we hadn't even scratched the surface of our own anger and emotions, but at this point I wasn't responsible for them. Maybe forgiveness wasn't so much about the end result as about our attitude at each moment—constantly releasing our justice issues into God's hands; finding comfort at the end of each day in the fact that we didn't need to have all the answers.

About this time, we heard that there was a psychic who had predicted where Candace would be found. Gordon Sinclair, a local columnist in the city's daily paper, had been in contact with a woman who had seen a vision, and he wrote about it in his column a few days after Candace was found. Sinclair is the kind of columnist who has the courage to pick up the news that is as close to gossip as you can get without being totally tacky. He's the kind of columnist that no one admits to reading, yet everyone always remembers exactly what he wrote. At times, we heard more reactions to what he wrote about us in his column than to the stories about us that hit the front page.

A woman named Dorothy had called Sinclair on the eleventh of December, eleven days after Candace had disappeared. She had said she was thirty-one years old and had two small children, a husband, and a dog. She told him that she had seen in a vision where Candace was. According to her, Candace was in "a very large packing crate near a railway, close to a bridge, near Nairn and Highway 59." Sinclair had told the police this, and the police had checked the area but hadn't found any packing crates.

After Candace was found, Sinclair remembered the similarities. The newspaper described the shed Candace was in as "a bunch of plywood nailed together to cover a piece of machinery and sitting on skids"—much like a packing crate.

The prediction did sound close to the real thing. I read it a few times, wondering how we could have missed that clue. Then I remembered that there was a catch. Highway 59 was about as far from where Candace was found as the school was. Nairn overpass was nowhere near Highway 59. Such a place didn't actually exist. As for being near a railway, we lived near a maze of railways. In fact, we had often joked that depending on where we looked we were on either the right side or wrong side of the tracks. For those of us who knew the area, this woman's prediction was no more accurate than those saying that Candace would be found close to the route she took home.

The police officer had been correct when he told us that psychics tend to predict the same thing: by a railway, by a bridge, in a dark place. Actually, it was the ex-convict, who had told us how a criminal thinks, who had given us the most accurate information. He had told us that she would be found in our community, telling us the reasons why. Good common sense and experience are still probably the most reliable sources of information.

Yet I think all of us wonder at times how powerful our minds can be. What were the powers that struggled that night? What was the answer to prayer? What was the reason? And my biggest question: why, from the moment she disappeared, had I been drawn to pray at the window overlooking the Nairn overpass? Why had it been so difficult to shut the drapes of that window?

For the most part, February was an extremely cold month with temperatures dipping down below minus twenty degrees Fahrenheit consistently.

The letters kept coming, and I kept trying to write out index cards for them to get some order into the mass of paper. People had put so much thought into them.

Many of the letters began with a similar theme, like a letter from southern Manitoba: "Although our paths have never crossed, we feel that we have known you people for some time." Someone else sent us a quote from Elisabeth Elliot: "Only by acceptance lies peace, not in forgetting, not in resignation, nor in busyness." And there were many who told us that they were amazed at our stand and our courage: "My deepest condolences to you and to your whole family. I must commend you for your bravery."

It was good to hear about others' struggles with our tragedy. A girl a few years older than Candace wrote, "During the time Candace was missing and after she was found, I seemed to be fighting with God. I couldn't see why he took her life away, why it had to be Candace. She was a Christian and a darn good one. How could he let this happen to her and us? But you just can't stay angry at God forever. He's God and he's forgiving. But I still wonder why?"

I was puzzled at some of the responses. A boy who had never met Candace or us wrote, "At first I wasn't sure exactly what this feeling was and maybe I'm still not. But you see, I believe that I love Candace. I love her as a fellow human being and I would like to aspire to be more like her —to be able to love and care as much as she did. I've cried a lot over this." It was hard to understand how people could be so affected by a tragedy of which they weren't a part, yet I hung onto the words "I aspire to be more like her."

Inmates at Stony Mountain Institution, a federal maximum- and medium-security penitentiary, wrote us notes. One wrote, "My greatest and deepest apology for your dear daughter. I'm a prisoner convicted of murder."

There were those who, in trying to comfort, said things in ways I don't think they meant to say them: "I thank the Lord that he did not test me the way he has tested you. No evil will befall those who trust the Lord. My heart reaches out to you."

There were homemade cards from children. One was about a child's idea of a heaven with "sun tables and umbrellas"— similar to Candace's concept of heaven. Classes of school children sent envelopes of little notes telling us that they were feeling our loss and remembering us.

Others told us horror stories: "Our only son, three and a half years old, was run over by a half-ton truck and instantly killed. Our second daughter was killed when she was fifteen." Another: "Our fourth son was stillborn and our four-year-old daughter was sexually assaulted by a young relative."And another: "I have a daughter who has been a problem on drugs and alcohol for the last four years. She has gone through many treatment centers all to no help. . . . Somehow through our experiences with our daughter I could almost associate with yourselves and your heartache."

Around Valentine's Day a poster-sized Valentine was delivered to our home from the Ridgeland Hutterite colony. About the same time, a very official letter came from Prime Minister Brian Mulroney and his wife, Mila, and another came from the federal health minister, Jake Epp, and his wife.

During the days that followed the funeral, we received approximately forty letters and cards a day. But by February, the number had dwindled to ten a day. I kept writing out little index cards and coding the different gifts, and once or twice I tried to answer letters. The official letters of thanks were easier; I could sign them "Cliff and Wilma Derksen." But when responding to the casual, personal letters—the ones that I would have ordinarily signed with all our names—I couldn't get past Candace's name. For thirteen years, I had been signing "Cliff, Wilma, Candace . . . ," and there was no way I could just stop that deeply ingrained habit now. Was it that I wasn't ready or didn't want to? I wasn't sure. But each effort left me in tears. It was much easier just to keep filing the index cards.

Here I have to apologize to all those who wrote those wonderful letters and cards and gave us gifts—each of whom deserves a wonderful, thoughtfully phrased thank-you—and to all those to whom I promised, in a *Winnipeg Free Press* article, an answer that I was never able to write. Maybe this book is one more attempt to say thank-you.

It was about this time that we started to get reactions to our statements of forgiveness.

A poem we received:

Candace,
I never met you
but the thought of your young body
placed in the frozen ground today
makes me despair—
an unforgivable sin, some say—
so ask God, while you are there,
to forgive me.

The person who wrote this poem added, "Although I'm supposed to be a mature adult and the mother of two children, I somehow cannot assimilate an evil this immense into my understanding. . . . Wishing you his peace—and hoping for some myself."

One letter put it directly:

I am unsure of your feelings exactly because I have not experienced the death of someone very close to me (knock on wood). All I can do is to send you and your family my deepest sympathies. I also hope, in time, your hurting stops.

I still do not understand how you can send out precious love for the killer of Candace. He/she has stolen something very precious from you and you send out love? In the Bible doesn't it say, "EYE FOR EYE, TOOTH FOR TOOTH"? I feel much hatred for that person and cannot forgive what he has done to a sweet, innocent, thirteen-year-old girl. I do not understand your feelings. . . .

I could feel the pain in those words. I understood the anger.

An article in *The Toronto Star*, February 16, 1985, also explored our feelings about forgiveness. A sociologist was quoted saying that "the 'turn the other cheek' belief is more deeply embedded in those whose religious convictions are strong, especially in the case of Mennonites.

"I understand the Mennonite religion quite well," he went on to say, "and I expect that this would be their reaction. But I sure wouldn't expect it from anyone else who didn't have those religious beliefs."

I was a little horrified with the article. I didn't think that it was any easier for us to forgive because we were Mennonite than it would be for anyone else. We didn't forgive *because* we were Mennonite. Forgiveness is a universal concept, a universal alternative. Granted, it's a difficult concept, a difficult choice, because it's something that goes completely against our human nature, but it is equally difficult for everyone.

Pope John Paul II isn't Mennonite, and yet he walked into the cell of Rebibbia prison outside of Rome to meet Mehmet Ali Agca. He took the hand of the man who had tried to kill him, and he forgave him.

Perhaps being Mennonite gave us the beginnings of an understanding of what forgiveness is. Our pacifistic traditions may have heightened our awareness that we did have a choice in this matter and clarified what that choice was, but I resist the idea that Mennonites and forgiveness are synonymous. We had chosen to forgive because we wanted to survive our tragedy. We wanted to remain loving, pliable, gracious, and optimistic people. And even though we didn't know all there was to know about forgiveness, we knew that it was a way to healing. And we were optimistic that someday we would be able to forgive fully—not because we were Mennonite, but because God first forgave us.

We thought the search committee meeting on the eleventh of February was going to be the last one.

We met in the Christian Press board room. I

looked around the table at Harold Jantz, Henry Wedel, Dave Teigrob, Dave Loewen, and Len DeFehr. We had all braved the subzero weather to meet together, but it was an awkward meeting. Before it had seemed as if the overwhelming need to find Candace always chaired the meetings, set the agenda, and moved the discussion at a fast pace through the allotted time. We had been driven, and now we weren't. Now we were all bogged down rounding up the details.

The tiny click of a stone against the window drew our attention to the frantically waving, almost-frozen figure of Ester, who had been locked out. We opened the door and she came storming in, giving her excuses. But even her presence didn't take away the gloom.

Perhaps no one else felt the gloom; maybe it was only Cliff and I. But Cliff and I were very aware the time was coming when we would be saying good-bye to this group of people who had supported us so well. We knew that no amount of money could have bought the services they had provided at the time of our greatest need. We never could have hired any others who could have acted so quickly on their own initiative, outguessing our wants, knowing what was best, and having the energy to do what was necessary so promptly.

Probably the biggest gift they had given us was the knowledge that, together, we had done everything possible to find Candace. They had given us the knowledge that the city of Winnipeg had never before seen such an extensive search. Candace's death would be easier to live with because of that.

Len reported that the memorial fund had risen to ten thousand dollars. I don't think any of us expected the memorial fund to grow much after the funeral day. Yet, a month later, the cards and letters were still finding their way to our house and the Camp Arnes office, with large and small amounts of money designated for the pool.

The committee decided that they wanted to support Child Find and advanced one thousand dollars to help start it in Winnipeg. And the police reported to us that they were going to issue a reward for five thousand dollars for information leading to the arrest of the perpetrator.

Cliff and I reported that our own personal agenda included a trip to Toronto to appear on the "100 Huntley Street" show again to try to thank the church audience.

The committee also expressed concern that the investigation had zeroed in on David Wiebe. He had been asked by the police to take a lie detector test, and we wondered why they were focusing on him. David had been taking a driver's lesson during the time Candace disappeared, so there was no way he could have abducted her. Other friends had also been questioned.

We decided we had to meet again.

We held our last committee meeting on March 5. By then the memorial fund had reached $16,200. One young girl had given her whole piggy bank of 2,887 pennies to the fund. There was indication that the giving had, in a sense, just begun. "When the public gives that much," someone said, "then the business community will also want to become involved." The swimming pool had received a beautiful vote of confidence from the community.

With many thanks, we disbanded.

Going home I remembered my conversation with Candace when I had told her that if she committed her life to God and she then died a violent death, God would use her death to have more of an impact than her life would have had. Was God going to honor that commitment now? Was a swimming pool going to be part of that impact? Would there actually be a swimming pool at Camp Arnes someday?

I had wondered when it would come, when my rage would surface and clash with my ideology. I don't remember what day it was. All I remember was that the room was warm and bright with the afternoon sun. The phone had finally stopped interrupting us as much. A friend had come to visit, I had made a pot of tea and pulled out a plate of delicious dainties from my still-overflowing freezer, and we had settled down to have a good talk.

We hadn't seen each other for a while, and she told me about a few of the things she had gone through as a spectator of our experience. She told me about her own questioning as to why this should happen to a friend, and I realized anew that our friends had gone through this with us. It was good to hear her anger, her perspective of the news coverage, and her theories about what might have happened. She told me how she admired my forgiving spirit. "I know that you have forgiven. I sense no vengeance in you."

I wasn't as sure as she was that we had come to that resolution, but I was grateful for her words. I thanked her for her confidence. "We're trying," I said.

She asked if we were sleeping, if we were having nightmares.

"We're sleeping. We're having dreams, but not nightmares," I told her.

Her next question caught me off guard. "If you could let yourself go, what would satisfy justice for you? Would it be execution?"

I had never allowed myself the question. I didn't think I was ready to face the complexity of it. But I felt safe with her, and her question was an interesting one. Perhaps it was time to think about it. I purposely loosened my controls and explored my inner feelings, my emotions. My friend waited in silence as I fell into deep thought.

"No," I finally answered, half to her and half to myself. "No, it wouldn't be enough. Execution, capital punishment, wouldn't completely satisfy me emotionally. If the offender were executed, he would be dying for something he did—he would deserve it. Candace was innocent. She died for no reason, for no fault of her own. She died young, in her prime, full of potential, full of anticipation, full of dreams—full of immediate plans of a good weekend. She would have contributed so much to our lives. Just to execute the offender would mean that he was being punished for what he had done. It would be removing a liability to society, a hopeless case. There's no equity in that."

I was shocked at my own answer. But I continued, "His death, one death, wouldn't satisfy me. . . ." I went deeper into myself, groping for the feeling of equity. "Ten child murderers would have to die." I paused, still groping for the satisfaction of justice. It was almost as if another voice answered for me, ". . . and I would have to pull the trigger myself."

Oh, the feeling was wonderful! In my mind's eye I saw ten hooded figures lined up against a brick wall. There was a gun in my hand, and, immediately, I took advantage of the moment and aimed and pulled the trigger ten times. The feeling was delicious. They deserved to die. The figures fell one by one.

If I had been able to preserve my reverie of that moment, I'd now be in favor of the death penalty. It felt good. It felt so right.

But I have a vivid imagination of which I'm not

always in control, and it had run away with me. As the camera of my imagination continued to roll, I saw the hoods fall loose and expose ten faces vulnerable in death. I saw the blood and the desecration. I looked up and saw their families mourning the loss of their sons. And being so close to my own grief, I could identify with them fully, and I felt their loss as keenly as I felt my own. And worse yet—when I thought of it—was the possibility that one man might not have a family, might not have love in his life, and I would have snuffed out his last opportunity.

I was devastated.

At that moment I couldn't describe what I had just seen to my friend who was waiting so patiently for me to fill in my long silence. "But that doesn't satisfy," I told her hoarsely. "I think our choice to forgive is the right one."

I was so grateful for her friendship. I really don't think I could have gone through that imaginary journey into my inner emotions if I hadn't known she was there to help out if I got into trouble.

I also knew I would never be the same. I had realized the depths of my rage. I realized that I could kill and that I could feel good doing it. It's not a pretty picture of oneself, and I was angry that someone had driven me so far into my dark side. I had seen a glimpse of the enormity of the anger that comes from losing a child to homicide. I understood now how it could take control and how it could grow, fester, and eventually destroy us. I had met the enemy, and he was, as Pogo says, inside of me. Still, I had taken another emotional step in forgiveness. It was a small one, but it was an important one.

Since then I have seen many others make that choice: "I want to kill him, but I won't because that would make me the same as he is." There's an ounce of forgiveness in that statement. A person who takes a life deserves to pay with his own. That is the perfect, complete law that, whether we want to admit it or not, is written on our heart. God acknowledges that law in the Old Testament when he allows that justice is an eye for an eye, a tooth for a tooth.

But choosing not to take the law into our own hands is a tiny bit of forgiveness. It is a small step, not all that generous, but it is a step, nonetheless. It puts us into the position of being able to free ourselves from what has happened, to gain control of our lives again, and to regain the ability to choose how we want to react to whatever has happened. By forgiving we can transcend the hurt and choose to be loving again.

So many times we think forgiving has to be done all at once—one giant leap from hate to love. I don't think it works that way. This step was simply deciding not to do what I desired to do—to react in kind. This decision didn't even include the offender. I had just changed the direction of my own heart.

I felt released. I felt clean. I felt that I had been victorious. I felt in control again.

As I refilled our cups with tea and we continued to enjoy a pleasant afternoon, I wondered what lay ahead. Where else would I encounter such rage? Would there always be someone with me? Would I always find my way through? I had a feeling that I had only just begun.

Cruel Suspicions

It had been four months since Candace's death, and one day Lily Loewen, the outdoor education coordinator at Camp Arnes, stopped by my desk and asked how we were doing. I assured her that we were doing fine. I confessed that it was a bit hard to concentrate, but otherwise things were going as well as could be expected.

But this time she wasn't satisfied with that answer.

"Wilma, how are you *really* doing?"

"Fine," I assured her again.

She cleared her throat. "There are vicious rumors," she said in a low voice.

I was a little surprised at her new concern. We

had talked about rumors before, and we had agreed that they were inconsequential. So I shrugged my shoulders. "What else is new?" I smiled. "We've heard them all by now. Have Cliff and I divorced again?"

"No."

"Candace was illegitimate, and I had an affair with the milkman. No, maybe this time it was the mailman."

"No . . ."

"Well then, what have we done now? Let me in on the gossip."

"I don't know if I should," she hedged.

Her caution aroused my curiosity. Lily had never had trouble being straightforward with us before.

"Lily," I said, trying not to appear overly alarmed, "we've been through the worst. It really doesn't matter what people are saying. It's never going to be as painful as losing Candace. You can tell me. I can deal with things I know, but I can't deal with something I don't know. Besides, rumors aren't true."

"I don't know about that. Rumors come from somewhere; often they have some kind of truth," she said.

I actually agreed with her. Though some of the rumors were absurd and untrue, like those about Candace not being our daughter and about my having an affair, I did like to keep my ear to the ground. Rumors revealed a lot about what people were thinking—their fears and sometimes their hopes. This one sounded serious, and I braced myself.

Lily needed more reassurance.

"Lily, whatever it is, it's better for us to know about it in advance so we can prepare ourselves. That's one thing we've always appreciated about you and Dave—your honesty. You've never protected us; please don't start now."

"Wilma," her eyes filled with pain and tears. "They are accusing Cliff of killing Candace."

I couldn't believe my ears. I couldn't believe that Lily was taking the rumor seriously. "Lily, it's just one of those off-the-wall rumors. We expected some of this. Don't take this seriously. People who know Cliff, who know anything about the case, know that Cliff couldn't possibly have done it. People have this need to find someone in the family to blame, because then it means they are safe. Don't take it seriously."

"No, Wilma. It's not coming from the public. The police suspect Cliff."

The impact was like a bomb exploding. "The police?"

She nodded.

"But they know Cliff was at the office. They couldn't possibly . . . if anyone has an alibi, it's Cliff. You all saw him. Why don't they suspect me? No one knows where I was."

She shrugged her shoulders. "They suspect him."

"How could he have?"

Her voice was low and deliberate. "They think it is entirely possible that after you picked up Cliff and he went looking for Candace, he might have found her in a compromising situation and taken her to the shack and left her there as punishment. Later he went back, and she was dead."

"But Cliff isn't like that."

"I know."

"When he went looking the first time, we were already scared that she might have been raped. To find her in any kind of situation would have been a relief."

"I know."

"That still means there would have to be someone else involved. Why hasn't that person come forward?"

"I know."

"It doesn't make sense. The crucial time between four and five is still unaccounted for. Besides, Cliff wasn't gone that long. They said the person who tied Candace up apparently spent some time in the shack."

"Maybe you lost track of the time."

"I did—but, no, I didn't. I was aware of the time. We were constantly looking at the clock. I was upset with Cliff for not looking harder. It seemed he'd go out and in no time he'd be back."

"I know. I know. But the police don't know that."

"Well, I'll tell them!" I said angrily.

I could tell that she was taken aback at my outburst.

"I'm sorry, Lily. I'm so sorry. This just took me by surprise. I'm so glad you told me."

She nodded.

My husband was being accused of murdering my child! And I had thought the police lacked imagination! Surely this wouldn't come to anything. Were we being followed? Was our phone bugged? What did it mean to be investigated? By now they might know more about us than we knew about ourselves.

I remembered something that suddenly made sense.

Coming home late one evening from a Child Find meeting, I had noticed that the front door was slightly ajar. My first thought as I dashed up the front steps was, *He's back for the whole family!* I rushed into the house expecting the worst.

A police officer was standing in our living room. Cliff was on the phone. The air was tense. Cliff's face was white.

The officer stepped over to me. "He's on the line

with someone who says he's the one who murdered Candace."

I glanced at Cliff again. He was asking, "You said you did it. What did you do? How did you get her to go to the shack?"

"There's a telephone downstairs," I said to the officer, and immediately he went down.

I hovered beside Cliff. "Did she say anything?" he asked the caller. I glanced at the notes he was taking. The person's answers were vague, and he had been on the telephone for a long time.

Finally Cliff cupped the receiver and whispered, "I don't think this is the guy. He doesn't know anything." I could see his disappointment—or was it my own? As horrible and painful as it would be, we wanted to find the killer; we wanted to know what Candace had said, what she had done that night.

Another police officer came through the front door without knocking. "We've got it. We can go pick him up." And both of them left.

Cliff assured the caller that he was glad that he had called and we were thankful for any information regarding Candace, then he hung up the phone and sat down.

"What a feeling! In the beginning, when I first thought that this was the guy—that I was actually talking to the guy—what a feeling it was! But he didn't know anything. Why would anyone want to call up and say he did it when he didn't?"

We were totally baffled. We had heard of another person who also had confessed to the murder, but it was found that he hadn't even been in the city at the time. Strange.

"How did the police know about it?"

Cliff hesitated. "I don't know. They walked in during the call."

I had thought it was a weird coincidence.

The next day the police had called to let us know that the caller hadn't been able to give any straight answers. They were sure it was a false alarm.

Now the incident made sense. Our telephone and our lives were being monitored. How would I tell Cliff that he was a suspect? Should I tell him?

It took me two days to convince myself that this bit of news wouldn't bother Cliff, that he would just laugh at it. He could be like that sometimes. A lot of things didn't bother him. The things that I considered amusing he often would take seriously, and the things that I took seriously he often thought were funny. Maybe this was one of those times.

I told him in the evening when the kids were in bed and we were having tea. I tried to put it into bite-size pieces. I tried to prepare him, but I didn't do very well. He paled. He didn't laugh.

Cliff asked the same questions I had asked, and I tried to use Lily's calm voice. I tried to reassure him that their suspicions were totally unfounded and that they'd realize that soon. Eventually, somehow, we managed to convince ourselves that nothing would come of it.

But we weren't surprised a few days later when Cliff had a call to ask if he would come to the police station and take a polygraph test. The police said that they would like to test me later as well.

Both of us knew more or less what a polygraph test was all about. We had seen an extensive documentary on TV about it; and since the investigation, we had read about it. We knew that it would be a risk, and we discussed it as such. But the weight of our discussion was not on the risk of it, but on how it could help the case.

Right from the beginning, we had been frustrated by the way the investigation had always centered on us. It was now April, five months after the fact, and they were still looking at us. By this time, there had been suicides in the community, our neighbors had moved—the whole face of the community had changed. The trail was cold. On the other hand, is it ever too late? Maybe, just maybe, if Cliff took the test, then they would finally look somewhere else.

Even though we knew the polygraph would not hold up as evidence in court and probably didn't have much credibility with a majority of people, we also knew the police put a lot of stock in it. It spoke their language. Christine Jessop's parents from Queenston, Ontario, had said the same thing. When Christine's father had been accused of killing his daughter, he had taken the polygraph to convince the police.

I don't remember being full of fear. We knew the risks, but I think at that stage we would have done anything—even sat in jail—to help clear up the case.

Two hours after Cliff left for the station, the possible implications hit me full force. If Cliff, for some strange reason, failed the test or the machine miscued, he wouldn't be coming home. He would be arrested for suspicion of murder! I no longer felt as if something that dreadful couldn't happen to us. Something dreadful and unimaginable had already happened to us, and I knew now that absolutely anything was possible.

I had admit to myself that it hurt that the police were accusing Cliff of murder. It is always hard to see the people you love misunderstood. That's why it had hurt so much when we heard that the police had called the whole episode a prank. By that very word, they had somehow minimized what had happened to Candace and at the same time incriminated her as a willing participant.

The reporter had called me in March. "Have you heard what they are saying happened to Candace?"

"No," I had answered. Sometimes it seemed as if we were the last to hear.

The reporter summarized the press conference. During the announcement of the police force's five-thousand-dollar reward for any clue leading to the arrest of Candace's murderer, the Sergeant Inspector had said that they suspected "the motive didn't start off as murder. This offense may have started out as an innocent event. However, due to unknown circumstances, the victim was left in the shed, and, as a result, died of hypothermia."

When he was asked if the tragedy may have been the fallout of a childish prank gone awry, he said, "That's what I'm leading to."

He had gone on to say that murder motives usually include revenge or hate, as well as personal, sexual, or financial gain. "The usual motives have been ruled out at this point in the investigation."

It was the word *innocent* that knocked the wind out of me.

"What do you think, Mrs. Derksen?" the reporter asked.

Of course I couldn't agree with the police. Why had they put us in this awkward situation? We had been so careful to cooperate with them, to work as a team, and now they were purposely saying things without warning, not even giving us time to think through a gracious reply.

Innocent. The word kept hammering through my attempts to think logically. How dare they call it innocent! They were the ones who had first said that tying someone up was a sexual act. Cliff had been reading a lot about serial killers and murderers (to my horror, till I realized this was his way of trying to understand and of coming to terms with Candace's death), and over and over again he had pointed out passages stating that some victims had been tied and then abandoned. The books said that sometimes serial murderers began by only tying their victims; but the next time it was tying and raping; and the next time, raping and killing. This was a documented progression. It wasn't that we thought Candace had been victimized by a serial killer, but maybe this person had that kind of inclination. How could the police now quickly dismiss any sexual motive?

And I knew it wasn't innocent. I could feel myself starting to tremble. How did I know? How could I feel so strongly the terror that she must have gone through? Why did I identify so strongly? Then I remembered.

It had happened when I was in seventh grade. The day had been beautiful, the perfect temperature. My parents had gone to attend my older sister's graduation, and I had been left to look after my younger brother. To pass the evening, I set up our high-jumping stand and began to practice. I felt light on my feet—not enough to break any records, but light enough to really enjoy jumping over the makeshift bar.

I was thrilled when two neighbor boys passed the house on their bikes a few times and then finally had enough courage to stop. I had grown up with the younger boy and had a sister/brother relationship with him. But the other boy was fifteen and relatively new to the neighborhood, and he had the longest, darkest eyelashes I had ever seen. I thought he was wonderful.

I invited them to join me, but they couldn't jump. I don't remember exactly how it started, but as the evening shadows lengthened romantically, they threatened to kiss me. When I resisted, they started to chase me.

I was probably more confused than afraid at first. After all, it was only the love of my heart and a child-hood chum.

I remember running barefoot through the garden, screaming and jumping with the greatest of ease over Mom's enormous potato plants as the boys lumbered after me. It took little effort to elude their grasp. At one point, I dashed into the house, but they followed me. I ran into the washroom and locked the door behind me. But the younger one knew where we conveniently hung the key, and he started to open the door. I had no choice. I squirmed through the laundry chute into the laundry room and out the clothesline door.

Half of me wanted them to catch me; the other half—the idealistic part—wanted them to leave me alone and keep it friendship until I was much older. Then I could talk about love. My ideal was that I would kiss only one man—the man I would marry.

I was quicker than both of them, but I was outnumbered. As one chased me around the garage, the other one waited. I didn't stand a chance. I ran right into his arms. Together, they tied me to an apple tree.

I wasn't screaming anymore. The minute they overpowered me, they had ceased to be friends. I was scared.

After conferring, they turned to me. "If you kiss us, we'll set you free. If you don't, we'll dunk your head in the ditch until you say yes."

By *ditch* they meant the sewer canals that ran along the houses and road. We loved to catch minnows in the ditches, but there were suspicious-looking brown-ish globs that accumulated along the edges. To have my head stuck in that —! But the choice was easy. I would never kiss them now. Never.

"I don't care," I told them. "You can drown me, and I'll never kiss you." I think that's when they realized they had gone too far and I would never voluntarily give in. Unbeknownst to them, I had wiggled my hands until the ropes were free, and I ran into the house and locked all the doors.

That was an incident that had started off as an innocent prank but could have gotten out of hand. And even as innocent as it had been, there had been sexual overtones. The minute they overpowered me, it had lost its innocence, it had ceased to be a prank, it had ceased to be fun. And the minute it lost its innocence, I had stopped screaming and struggling; I had become frightened. Whatever feelings I'd had for the older boy had died instantly.

So I knew what the police meant when they said it could have started innocently. But that's exactly what was different in Candace's case. The timing was wrong, Candace's frame of mind was all wrong, and the placing of her friends just didn't fit into an innocent prank gone wrong. The day had been too uncomfortable for anything to have just developed lazily on its own. There had to have been a strong motive already in place before Candace came on the scene. She wouldn't have hung around for any kind of nonsense; she knew we were waiting for her, and none of the people who mattered to her were even in the vicinity. Whatever had happened never had any shred of innocence about it.

I wanted to scream! Candace had been forcibly taken to a strange place. The dynamics were different than those of a prank. Couldn't the police see the difference? She had been forced! They were trying to say, as they always did, that the victim was in some way responsible.

"Mrs. Derksen?" The reporter was waiting for an answer.

I took a deep breath. "We can't make light of the fact that she was tied up and left to die. It does look like something went wrong, but I still believe it was a malicious prank." The word *prank* was my one concession to the police's statement as I tried to minimize the distance between our opinions.

The next day the paper's headline had read, "Prank Turned Ugly, Candace's Killer Likely Didn't Mean It." Under another sidebar headline, they had written, "Vicious rumors put to rest. Wilma Derksen still believes someone's malice claimed her daughter's life."

I hated being shoved into a corner and forced to defend Candace, attributing motivation when I didn't know why Candace had been abducted any more than anyone else did. I also couldn't understand how the same evidence they had used to call it a prank could now be used to build a case against my husband. How could they make such conclusive statements when I knew they didn't have conclusive evidence?

Thoughts still churning, I tried to busy myself with housework while I waited for Cliff to return, but I couldn't seem to function. Even the beds couldn't hold my attention, so I roamed around the house. None of it was important.

First someone off the street had taken my daughter; now the "justice" system threatened to take my husband. There was no safe place! What if Cliff was booked? What would I do? What would happen to us?

And lurking in the recesses of my mind another question emerged. Had I fingered him somehow?

During the initial panic, in my attempt to paint a picture of our family relationships, I had told the police and everyone else that Candace had a wonderful relationship with her father. I had described the way they teased each other in the morning and swam together. I had wanted to let them know that even though I hadn't picked up Candace—that even if she might have been angry with me—she wouldn't have been angry with her father. I never thought or suspected that something so innocent could be misconstrued and could hint at something incestuous.

I also remembered the police interrogation right before the funeral. They had asked again and again about that first evening. Over and over they had asked how many times Cliff had gone out, and I hadn't been able to remember. Why hadn't I been able to remember? I had remembered everything else so vividly. Had they sensed my hesitation? Had they interpreted it as some desire to protect him? I would never do that. If he had killed Candace, I would have been the first person to turn him in. Though I loved him, I knew he was not above the law.

But they were wrong about Cliff. He was the kindest, gentlest man I knew. That was why I had married him.

I found myself going back in time, going over every detail of our married life, back to the first time we met and got to know each other. It had been sixteen years earlier.

I'm not sure when I first saw Cliff. He sort of emerged out of the sea of students in our first-year class at Bethany Bible Institute. He was different. He was an artist, and it seemed as if we were always working together on the same committee. The first project was a missions display for which the committee had decided to create a globe and make all sorts of little dolls to represent the different peoples.

As an artist, Cliff had no trouble turning a big round ball into a model of the Earth and making the dolls, but I didn't find any of it easy. My dolls were pathetic. They all were crooked, grimy, and disabled. I was ready to discard them when Cliff casually sauntered over, and as we talked and joked he transformed my little dolls into works of art and never took the credit for it. He never embarrassed me.

I was intrigued by his creative hands. They moved so confidently, steadily, and lovingly over the dolls—twisting, turning, creating. They reminded me of my grandfather's hands. I had spent hours as a little girl watching my grandfather, intrigued with his huge, gentle hands. I could still see in my mind's eye how he softly nudged the little blueberries so they would fall into his cupped hands, how he massaged the udders on the cows, and how he plucked the wilted roses and caressed the rose buds.

"Someday, Cliff, you're going to make a wonderful grandfather," I blurted out as I tried to thank him.

He didn't know how to answer me. It was an odd thing to say, and I wasn't even sure why I said it. For a moment, I wondered if he might think that I was in some way trying to insult him. I thought I should explain, but how does one explain that kind of statement?

After a moment of surprise, a twinkle floated into his eyes, "I guess you'll make a good grandmother someday." Was that somehow prophetic?

We continued to work together. In our second year, Cliff and I were on the yearbook committee—he as president, I as secretary. I would design a page, laboring to get the edges and lines straight; but no matter how much I worked at it, everything was still slightly off balance until Cliff would happen by and, with the tiniest adjustments, make the whole page suddenly fit.

I thought him a miracle worker. Sometimes, during the class break, I would watch him draw caricatures of the teachers. It was almost as if he could see the picture on the plain white page before he even started to draw. I tested him. I asked him to draw a face beginning at the collar and he drew a perfect, symmetrically balanced face. I asked him to start from the cuff on a wrist, and again the picture that appeared was perfect.

Even though he never asked why I asked him to jump through these artistic hoops, I knew he was wondering what I was trying to prove. "You can see the picture before you start, can't you?" I asked. He just laughed. He never let me in on his secret.

There wasn't a lot of social time in our friendship. I moved in different circles than he did. I tended to be with the less responsible crowd from the West Coast, and he was closely knit with the more serious Prairie crowd. Still, it took us an unusually long time to put that yearbook together that year; I remember the fun that we had.

Then, one day towards the end of that second year, as we passed each other in the hall, he whispered, "Can I meet you in the museum after supper?"

Museum? I wondered what Cliff would want to talk to me about in the museum.

The museum was an old building on the campus used mostly for music practice. Each empty classroom was equipped with a piano. Why would Cliff choose to meet me there alone? Neither one of us had any musical ability; if we met there and were seen there together, we'd be romantically linked forever, and he was already going with someone else.

Probably unfinished yearbook business, I surmised. I slipped out of the dining room as soon as possible and went to the museum. I sat down at an old piano and nervously played the one hymn I knew. Cliff came in warily, and I broke off the song in the middle of the chorus.

And that's where he told me that he loved me. The word he used was that he thought I was "special." It was a total surprise. I really thought he loved the other girl, and I begged for time. I needed to think. I really had never considered him romantically, and there were some other fellows. . . .

It was the end of the school year, and Cliff went back to his home in Saskatoon and I went back to my home in British Columbia—to think. The conclusion I arrived at was that I didn't want to belong to anyone. I wanted to go to Africa and be a missionary. I wrote Cliff to give him my answer.

The following winter, I returned to Bethany for my third year. This time I was president of the yearbook committee and Cliff was president of the student council.

Some of our classmates came to meet the train from British Columbia and Cliff was one of them, but he didn't so much as look at me. It was his studied indifference that unsettled me the most. I realized that I couldn't have it both ways. I couldn't enjoy his friendship without a commitment.

I was miserable. Life wasn't much fun without him. I realized how much of my school life had been part of his: the missions committee, the banquet decorating committee, the yearbook committee. He had always been there, helping me, believing in me, making the long, hard hours of work fun. He was always calm in a crisis, always creative at the dead ends, always honest, always trustworthy. I let him know I was sorry.

Sixteen years later, I was still convinced I had made the right decision to marry him.

I was still convinced he would make a wonderful grandfather after we had our own children. In fact, I was even more convinced than I had been in college. I had always known that Cliff was talented. During our school years, he had been known for his public speaking abilities, his art, his guitar playing, his acting, his athletic skills—there just didn't seem to be anything he couldn't do once he put his mind to it.

But it had been only in the last five years that his talent with children had emerged. His work in camping ministries had helped him develop a new awareness of the needs of children. To entertain them, he had become an illusionist, making little red balls disappear, making scarves appear, and magically mending ropes that had been cut in two. He loved children, and the love was mutual. Children took to him. We rarely went anywhere where some kid wouldn't recognize him from camp and call out hi. The hands that had always been gentle and creative were becoming, with time and maturity, even more gentle, more creative, and more loving. Before my very eyes, he was becoming the perfect grandfather, to my children, to all children.

Accusing Cliff of murder was something like accusing Santa Claus of murder.

Cliff walked through the door at noon, white, drawn, and a touch grayer.

"How was it?" I asked.

"You're not taking that test."

He described the process in detail. The worst moment for him had been when they laid out the accusations and he realized that this was no game, no routine exercise. They were deadly serious.

But once it was over and just as he was about to

leave, the polygraph technician had told him, "You are an honest man." He had then taken a thick, oversized file and dropped it onto the desk. "We can throw this away now."

We had been right. They had been spending valuable time investigating us. Even knowing the risks, in the clarity of hindsight, we were still convinced that it was worth the risk. They could now get on with the investigation.

They never did call me to take the polygraph, and I never spent time waiting.

With that, I thought the chapter on our relationship with the police was over. And it was, to some degree. They didn't come around; they didn't call. It appeared as if we all were returning to normal.

But it had left a residue.

I didn't know what it was at first, but when I saw the dark pants, the stripe up the side of the leg, and the shiny black shoes through the glass of the office door, I reacted strongly. I ducked into the washroom under the pretense of brushing my hair.

What was he doing here? It was after hours in the Richardson office building, and no one was expected except the Child Find board members for the evening meeting. Was he coming to the meeting? Then I remembered that someone had mentioned cultivating a police liaison.

I brushed my hair, took a deep breath, and walked in. They had all moved to the board table and we were all introduced.

He seemed friendly enough, eager and competent. Obviously he was the right choice for our advisory committee. But throughout his whole presentation and our questions, I could barely look at him. I just wanted him gone. I was puzzled at the intensity of my reaction.

On the way home, I had time to think. What had that been about? We'd had many uniforms in our house, and I had never reacted that way before. It wasn't fear. And I hadn't done anything, so it wasn't a guilty conscience.

I turned off of Henderson onto Talbot, the route Candace had taken. It seemed that no matter how often we traveled it, I couldn't help but remember. But it was when I saw the railway tracks and the 7-Eleven that I suddenly knew. I hated them. I hated the police force— the whole shooting lot of them!

All this time I had focused my attention on dealing with my dark feelings towards the *perpetrator*—the term I insisted on calling the murderer—but I had never thought that I might be developing a lot of anger toward the police. Now it was all out in the open.

It was as if I had been careful to keep the front yard of my life manicured, but had ignored the backyard. I had pulled out every strange-looking plant in the front lawn, making sure it wasn't anger. I had trimmed the lawn weekly and checked the hedges constantly, though sometimes I thought my careful inspection was too much. I pulled up the plants and inspected the roots so often that even the good plants were afraid to grow. But at least it was under control, and eventually, as I relaxed, it would take shape again. Now I had entered the backyard and found it full of rage, a jungle of black emotions against the police.

But no wonder, I told myself. They had done nothing but insult us. At first, they had treated us as if we were the abusers. By their insinuations they had called us religious fanatics, unfit parents, and alarmists. While Candace had been freezing to death in that shack, they had called her a runaway. If only they had believed us and gotten out the dogs that night, all of this could have been stopped. It was their fault. Their ignorance had prevented us from finding her. When they should have been reassuring us, they had instead put unnecessary doubts in our minds.

It was personal. They had never listened to me. I had always been treated like an unstable mother, a brainless woman. The day they had found Candace's body, they had kept me waiting in the reception area. They had told my husband before me.

Even worse, they had accused my daughter, who had suffered so much, of being half-responsible for what had happened to her. And they had accused my husband of being a murderer. They had suspected all the friends that we loved, sometimes even harassed them. We had tried to be so gracious, and they had shoved it back into our faces.

We were law-abiding citizens who had looked to them for help, and they hadn't done one thing to help us. Every initiative they had taken had been in reaction to the search committee's efforts. Our response had been to give them space. "They need to be suspicious," we had said over and over again to our friends. But none of those excuses held water anymore.

My backyard was so filled with ugly vines and tree trunks that it was pitch dark, and I knew I couldn't possibly cut my way through. I had hit an emotional wall. I didn't have the energy to try to forgive. I didn't even want to. *But what about our pact with God?* I asked myself. *What about our promise to forgive?*

As I turned into the back lane of our house, I whispered, "Lord, I can't forgive. And I'll be honest about it, too. No more speaking engagements, because I can't say we are victorious when we aren't. I can't get through this one. I just can't. If this is to be cleared away, you'll have to do it."

I felt totally dead inside. I didn't tell Cliff. Actually, I didn't say much of anything. There was nothing to say. How does one describe empty despair?

At the Child Find board meetings we were always given assignments, and mine for the week was to visit a Mennonite family on the north end who had called in about their runaway seventeen-year-old daughter, asking us if we could help.

I checked in on them the next day. Only the distraught father was home.

My first question was, "Are you sure that she ran away?"

"She left a note."

"Would she have a place to stay?"

She had been seen by friends, so she was in the community. It seemed as if everyone had a pretty good idea of what her next move would be: she would be coming home soon for more supplies. I helped the parents work through a plan on how they would contact her and let her know that they wanted to work things out.

As we were talking, I wondered why she had left if they were such good parents. I wondered if there had been any abuse. I wondered if they might be too religious or were imposing their style of living on the child. Had they forced her out?

As I drove home from that meeting and approached the railway tracks and the 7-Eleven store, I remembered my feelings the previous night and made the connection. I couldn't believe what I had just experienced. I could have been wearing shiny black shoes, dark pants with a stripe down the side, a blue shirt, and a revolver on my hip. I had reacted the same way any policeman would have reacted. I had suspected them of being the same things that I had been suspected of being.

Tears started to roll down my cheeks. I could feel

my deadness become alive again. By being forced to step into their shoes for a few hours, I could again understand. I had felt their emotions; I had asked their questions; I had seen the world through their eyes. I could almost visibly see the backyard being cleared out to let the healing sun shine through.

It felt so good, so warm, so free. I could love again. Even God had moved in close again. I had just been given a miracle. I don't believe in expecting miracles. I don't even believe miracles are good for us. But when they are given as gifts—like this one was—I am grateful.

It was amazing how everything had changed. From this new angle, I suddenly remembered that not everything the police had done was bad. There had been a lot of excellent officers who had come to our house, who had been polite, who had tried to reassure us over and over again that she was okay. I had seen some of them with tears in their eyes, and I knew some of them had worked long shifts and overtime, braving the cold to search for her. They had gone the second mile a thousand times. They were human beings who needed love just as much as I did.

Those vines had a force of their own, and I shuddered at how close I had come to being entwined and strangled, to succumbing. We had been right: anger has the power to destroy.

Driving to Saskatoon two weeks later, we stopped to eat at a restaurant filled with many of the local people. I saw two uniformed policemen enter, choose a table, and scan their menus.

I probably observed my own reactions as keenly as I watched the officers. The miracle had really happened. I watched them with no sense of irritation. In fact, we lingered over coffee and watched with amusement at the prompt service the two distinguished gentlemen received. We watched the different reactions of the customers to them—some friendly, some nervous, some flirtatious. It was just an interesting side dish, and I knew that even though the anger might surface again—I might have to deal with it over and over again—at least, for the moment, it was gone.

CHAPTER 14

Learning to Adjust

Adjusting. I think that is what they call one of the stages of grief where, whether you want to or not, you realize that you have to continue to live, so you do.

Every minute, every second of every day, we were reminded of Candace. Every time I laid out five plates instead of four, I had to put that fifth plate back into the cupboard. And every time I returned that plate, I knew that in a tiny way I was cutting more of Candace out of our lives.

Every time I needed to run to the store and wanted to ask her to watch the children while I was gone, the words stuck in my throat. Every time I saw something in a store that she would have liked (every aisle seemed to have something), I had to consciously remove the desire to buy it for her.

Whenever I saw her in a crowd coming towards me, I had to caution myself not to get overjoyed, knowing that the likeness wasn't Candace's. It was my desire to see her that was projecting her likeness onto a stranger.

I had never realized before how much a part of our lives she was, how much a part of our subconscious, until we tried to live without her. It was like amputating my right arm without any anesthetic. I think it was doubly difficult because this was the time when we wanted to preserve her memory, we wanted to keep part of her alive forever. And yet we found that in order to function normally, we were removing her little by little from our lives. It seemed so unfair.

The grieving process took time and emotional energy. We were constantly exhausted.

I thought it would be easier working in the Camp Arnes office, which was fairly free of Candace's presence. We had lived as a family on the campsite, but we had rarely been in the office together, so I relished the job of entering the registrations into the computer.

The job was fairly simple. I would take a registration card and enter all the data about the camper into the computer. There were a lot of names that began with *B* and *C*, so it took me few days to get to *D*. But suddenly there it was—her registration card: Candace Wynne Derksen; Birthday, July 6, 1971; 623 H——— Avenue, Winnipeg, Manitoba.

My heart lurched. What was I to do with it? Part of my job was to weed out any cards that weren't current. The usual categories included "No longer interested," "Moved away," and "Too old for the program." But this card had a different category.

There was a place on the card for counselor comments.

"Candace was a great girl, her attitude was superb."

That was the daughter I remembered.

The second counselor had written, "Spiritually, I could see that she took her faith very seriously."

I hung onto the words.

The third had written, "Strong Christian . . . she interacts well with her peer group, and she does her work well and with enthusiasm."

There was healing in those words.

The third counselor had gone on to write, "She had lots of knowledge about the Bible and participated. She was helpful. . . . She hardly mentioned the fact that her parents were at camp."

Good for Candace. We had tried to teach our children to carve out their own path, to find their own importance, and not to ask for special favors because their father was the summer program director.

They just say nice things about every child, I thought, and I thumbed through some of the other cards. But, no, the counselors had been amazingly honest.

I couldn't just throw the card away. I wanted to stuff it into my pocket, but it was the camp's property. I didn't dare mention it to anyone else in the office; I'd cry, everyone else would cry, and no one would get any work done. So I painstakingly wrote down all the information from the card into my notebook. Then, swallowing the boulder that kept growing in my throat and threatening to explode in my chest, I forced myself to cross out the card with a light pencil and write the word *DECEASED* on it as calmly as I could so that no one would notice how my hands had been trembling.

"This is good for me," I kept telling myself. "This is forcing me to face reality."

We were having to adjust our values, our dreams. My dream had been shattered.

When I was younger, I had thought my dream was to travel and to create, but I had learned that it wasn't what I really wanted.

When we were living in North Battleford, I won a trip to continental Europe. In fourteen days we were to take in Austria, Germany, France, and Spain. While making our plans, the travel agent—apologizing profusely—informed us that because of a difficulty in the scheduling we might have to make a twelve-hour stopover in London at the end of our trip. I was ecstatic. To see London, the center of drama and literature, had been a lifelong dream.

The whole trip I looked forward to being in London for one evening, night, and morning. To make the most of it, we chose to stay at a hotel near Buckingham Palace and we bought tickets for an Agatha Christie mystery drama. The whole time I expected something to go wrong because it was just too good to be true. No one gets his dream on a silver platter. But nothing went wrong. It didn't even rain. We were treated to the most perfect weather, the most perfect tours, the most perfect drama, and the most perfect late evening dinner.

But when we went back to the hotel after the most perfect night of my life, I wasn't perfectly happy. I was lonesome for my kids, whom we had left with their grandparents in a little prairie town in Saskatchewan. And then I understood what Dad had meant when he told us that our family times—around the campfire, taking a Sunday drive, or in the evening around the dining room table—were the most important times to him.

Now my dream for a complete family of three children was gone, and there was no one who could help us fill that emptiness. At one point, I tried to

change Odia into Candace. To some degree, she cooperated, but thankfully I quickly recognized what I was trying to do and realized that Odia could never duplicate
Candace, as Candace would never have been able to
duplicate Odia. Besides, I knew that if I tried to change
Odia into Candace, I would fail; I'd be left with an
unhealthy hybrid of the two. And then I would be left
with another loss—Odia. How could I replace Odia?

I had to find a way of becoming content with a
family of two children.

Losing her older sister was a huge adjustment for
Odia, too. It was interesting and painful to watch her
take over her new role.

One particularly hard day, we decided that we
needed to get out of the house and have a break from
our memories and pain. We decided to try out a new
Mexican restaurant. Just as we were leaving, Odia
dashed back into her room and came back with a book.
She always had a book with her, so we never even bothered to ask what she was doing. Once we were seated in
the restaurant, she pulled it out.

"Odia, you're not allowed to read at the table," I
reminded her.

"This is different, Mom," she said, holding it up.
It was a joke book.

All evening we were treated to wonderful groan-
ers like "Why did the chicken cross the street?"

Even Syras knew the answer: "To get to the other
side."

It worked. Some of the jokes were so bad that we
laughed at their ridiculousness, but that didn't matter.
We had a fun evening, and as I tucked Odia into bed
later that night, I saw the content look on her face. She
also knew it had worked. Candace had always enter-

tained us; now Odia, in her own way, had taken the leadership of the evening.

But I knew that her adjustments wouldn't be easy. I had friends who had experienced deaths in their families, and I had seen what it had done to the children. I wondered what Odia's adjustments would be and if I as a parent would even be able to help.

I watched for the questions. The first big question came as I was organizing some of Candace's things into a box and casually saying—again—how much we missed Candace.

It's a fine balancing act in grief. I didn't want to pay too much attention to Candace's memory so that the others would become jealous, and yet I wanted them to see my grief so that they would know that if something like this happened to them, I would grieve for them, too. I must have said something of that sort to Odia, and she was listening half-heartedly as she paged through a comic book. Then she looked straight through me. "This wouldn't have happened, Mom, if you had picked Candace up when she called."

It was said in her most casual voice, but I knew it wasn't just another casual remark. I was taken aback. I had never thought her anger would be directed at me. It seemed so misplaced. But I knew the minute she said it that it was real for her. She was having to make adjustments in her own life. The death of her sister had created havoc with her own feelings of safety and her belief in our ability as parents to keep her safe. It had to be dealt with. Momentarily I wondered if I was the right person to deal with it, but I hesitated for only a moment. You can't ignore questions and moments like these with children. Things have to be dealt with immediately.

I closed the box. I noticed that Odia was preparing to get up and leave the room. "Odia, sit here and let's talk about this."

She sat down but her eyes were averted.

"You're right. I should have picked Candace up."

She glanced up, a little surprised that I wasn't defending myself.

"Odia, if I could redo that day, I would pick her up. I'd sit outside that school all day just to make sure I didn't miss her. She was that important to us."

Odia looked down.

I searched for the right words.

"Odia, when there is a tragedy like this, we look for someone to blame. And the easiest thing to do is to take all of the blame, bundle it up, and lay it on one person—usually the person closest to us. But we can't do that. It's not fair. When something happens, there are usually a lot of people that are at fault. I should have picked her up. The police should have listened to us. Dad should have come home earlier that day. But none of us wanted to hurt Candace. I didn't tie Candace up and leave her in a shack to die. Most of the blame has to land on the person who actually did it. Candace should have been able to walk home from school safely."

Odia wanted to leave, but I stopped her.

"Next time you feel angry with me for not picking Candace up, remember that I'm sorry too. It's the one regret that I have to live with for the rest of my life."

When she finally looked up, the hardness had left her eyes. "I know that now, Mom."

I sensed that she needed to feel safe again. "And Odia, we'll never let this happen again."

She looked relieved. "Can I please go play now?"

I was left wondering if I had promised something I couldn't deliver. I had just learned the hard way that we can't always keep our children safe, yet here I was promising my children protection. Had I answered her questions adequately? I didn't know.

The second question came one evening when I was tucking Odia into bed after prayers.

"Mom, couldn't God have stopped the person?" She didn't have to explain to whom she was referring.

I took a deep breath. It was a question we had asked ourselves many times, and I'd had to adjust and revise my theology many times because of such a question. I dreaded the question. It's one of those questions that defies a definitive answer. I could only hope to begin to explore it, to perhaps redirect it and give it a beginning foundation—I wasn't sure what. I just didn't want her to blame or become angry with God.

I climbed onto her bed. "We have to talk." She groaned. I pulled the blanket over both of us and leaned up against the wall.

"Odia, I want you always to remember that God loved Candace and he loves us; he never meant for us to suffer. When he created the earth, he created a perfect world. Imagine no thistles, no mosquitoes, and no death. That's what he wanted for us. We always have to remember that."

"But the human race wasn't satisfied with that. Adam and Eve wanted more, and if we'd been there, we would have wanted more, too. So now we live in a fallen world. Nothing is perfect anymore."

I paused and then plunged into my theology. I walked through the Old Testament and the New Testament and tried to unravel all of God's truths for Odia, but she fell asleep before I was half through. In the end, I got all tangled up in the mysteries myself.

I sat there for a long time puzzling over the question.

How can we really know where God's control

begins and where it ends? Where was he the night Candace died? How come some children are saved miraculously and some aren't? What is God's responsibility and what is ours?

I have always come back to the thought that it wasn't God's intention to have Candace suffer. But when he gave us that beautiful gift of choice, he allowed good and evil to exist together. Today we're still allowed to choose between the two, and we still have to suffer the consequences of our choices.

As a parent, I can understand God better. I know that children learn best by their own mistakes, but allowing them to suffer the consequences of those mistakes is extremely difficult. It can be heartbreaking.

It is doubly difficult when some of their wrong choices affect not only their own life, but the lives of those around them as well. Still, that is what life is all about: to learn that what we sow is what we will reap. If God were to deny us this, he would be denying us the very freedom that he has promised us in Christ.

But what must God be feeling as he watches an entire world make wrong choices and collectively suffer for those choices? It must break his heart.

For we do suffer.

There are many different dimensions of suffering, and we often confuse them all as being one. One kind of suffering is the suffering we bring on ourselves. We make wrong choices and suffer the consequences.

But there is also the kind of suffering that is good for us. We need suffering to survive. It strengthens us. It gives us character. We need to suffer to prepare for the bigger trials in life that could destroy us if we aren't ready for them, much like the way we have to acclimatize plants. It's like we have to fight fire with fire. It seems the only antidote for suffering *is* suffering. We have to be vaccinated with suffering to be able to create an immune system. God can't take our suffering away because we need it to survive. We need to experience pain.

I'm not sure if it is even necessary to always know whether the suffering we experience is the result of our own choices or preparing us for something else. The most important truth here is that God has promised that he will never leave us. Our faith in God enables us to take all of our suffering and turn it around to benefit ourselves and God's work; God shows us how to do that. That is the challenge that faces all of us. It's the challenge that can lift even a boring, mundane experience into the extraordinary.

I would even take all of this one step further to say that it isn't enough just to wait and find God's will in whatever happens to us. Yes, there is a time to wait, but there is also a time to venture out and be more than a passive Christian. In the Bible we have enough direction to know what God has in mind. We are always to love, to create justice, to help the poor, and to be ambassadors for his cause. We don't have to wonder about these. We can begin to create good in a bad situation before we even know the scope of our problems. We can be proactive.

I like the image in Isaiah 30:21: "Whether you turn to the right or to the left, your ears will hear a voice behind you saying, 'This is the way; walk in it.'" As we move forward, we can be confident that God is right behind us letting us know his will. He doesn't let us stray far . . . as long as we continue to listen.

I climbed off the bed and switched off the light. Obviously I had needed to process my own understanding of God more than Odia did. And that was alright. I was sure the question would resurface some other time, and I'd have another chance to explain it to her and to Syras. Actually, it is one of those questions that can be answered best through living. That was going to be the hard part.

The third question came as another surprise.

Cliff came home one evening and announced at dinner that someone had given another substantial donation towards the swimming pool. Later, Odia asked, "Mom, if I died, would you build a swimming pool for me?"

Again, I recognized her innocent question as one of those questions that might have long-lasting implications. This one needed total honesty.

"No," I told her.

She looked startled.

"We would put the same effort into finding you as we did for Candace. We would hurt and grieve for you in just the same way. But I think we would pick a different project. You are different than Candace was. You have different interests than Candace had, and we would want to choose something that you are interested in. You've always had good marks. Maybe we would choose to help MBCI. They want to build an auditorium; maybe we would help them."

She seemed satisfied with that, but for me it was a warning that I had to be more alert to making sure that the attention shown to Candace's memory wasn't a threat to the other two children. Even though she wasn't with us anymore, there was still, to some extent, a sibling rivalry between the three of them.

Odia did adjust well. Her marks never floundered. She seemed to maintain her friendships, and her teachers reassured her that she was coping well. Still, just when we thought we had nothing to worry about, we had another glimpse of some of the things with which she had to cope.

Odia had a friend over one evening. Cliff and I were sipping our after-dinner coffee when Odia's friend casually commented on the jokes about Candace circulating in the school. When we asked them what kind of jokes they were, both girls shot out of the house.

Later we asked Odia again. She stalled and bit her lip.

"How many jokes are there?"

"Two."

"Are they about us?"

"No."

"Are they about you?"

"No."

"Are they about Candace?"

She looked away.

"Would they hurt Candace?"

She continued to look at the wall.

"Would they hurt us?"

She nodded.

"Do they hurt you?"

"Yes."

I would have loved to leave it at that. But just by her guarded response, I knew that whatever it was, it was too big a burden for a little girl. She needed to share it with us to lighten the load.

"Does the joke make fun of Candace?"

Odia nodded.

"Please, Odia, tell us," I begged. "We'll let you have a sleep over." I know bribery isn't good. . . .

She took a deep breath. "It's a stupid joke. The joke is: What did the Derksens get for Christmas?"

We shrugged our shoulders and waited.

"Candy in a box."

I felt the edge of a cold stainless steel blade slit my heart—not so much for myself but for the young face in front of us putting on such a brave fight for control. She told us the other joke, and it was much the same. Odia looked shredded after she had told us.

I looked at Cliff for a response, but I could tell he was groping for words. We were shocked. Yet we had to give her something, some kind of inner strength to face those kids again.

But first I wanted to use the moment. "Odia, there are always going to be people around who enjoy hurting other people. Someone very cruel hurt Candace."

She lowered her eyes and nodded.

Cliff's eyes were saying, "For Pete's sake, Wilma, hasn't she been through enough? Don't push her over the edge."

But I continued, "Candace was hurt, and we are being hurt, too. We have to be kind to everyone, even those who hurt us. But I also want you to be careful around people who like to hurt others. You can't take them seriously."

She nodded. She understood.

Cliff was wondering where I was going, and so was I. I wanted to give her some kind of courage, but it wasn't easy trying to turn this one around.

Suddenly I had an idea. "You know, of course, that people make those kinds of jokes about people in the news, about important people like Brian Mulroney, Trudeau, Elizabeth Taylor, and Reagan. Maybe Candace is important. Maybe Candace is famous now. This is just the result of all the attention we've been getting in the media. Let's think of Candace as a star."

Odia smiled. The door bell rang. She knew it was a friend. "Can I go play now?"

Cliff nodded, and Odia ran outside—so much lighter than she had been minutes earlier. It had worked.

Cliff didn't say anything. We just looked at each other for a long time. Why couldn't we protect Odia from pain? What kind of parents were we that we couldn't protect our children? Why didn't the words that seemed to give Odia courage leave some comfort for us?

After the search committee had disbanded, Ester began to play a different role in our lives. She took a special interest in Odia and often took her out for lunch or shopping, and Odia loved the attention. Knowing Ester, I guessed that she was also keeping her finger on Odia's emotional pulse.

After one of their outings, Ester stayed for a cup of tea while Odia went out to play with her friends.

I was curious. "How do you think Odia is adjusting?" I asked.

"Great. She's a really good kid."

I waited for more.

"She did say something," Ester began, then paused.

I nodded encouragingly.

"She said that she wished that she could have her old mom back again. I suppose you know what that means?"

It was hard to hear those words. I knew then that I hadn't fooled my family for a minute with my smiles. Odia wanted me to be myself again.

Couldn't I at least have one year to mourn? One year to be sad? But a year is a long time in a child's life, and my children couldn't wait.

Ester and Odia together were reminding me that adjusting meant giving up grief. It's difficult to give up being sad. Grief can become a substitute for the lost life; just the simple act of being sad kept Candace close.

I also wondered if, behind the veil of sadness and aloofness that I had maintained over the last months, I was also harboring a fear of loving as intensely as I had before. It was much easier not to become too involved again. Now it was apparent that Odia instinctively sensed that my attention wasn't on the family as it had been before. She was simply craving my love—a love that she needed and deserved.

I talked it over with Cliff, and we decided together that we had to make a symbolic effort to do something for our children that was fun and slightly extravagant. We decided to go to a circus.

Even this simple act wasn't easy. Leaving the house that evening was tough. I dawdled and delayed the process until I was the last to leave the house. I felt I was betraying Candace all over again. Our purpose for going out was solely to forget and to laugh.

They were waiting in the car. I had one moment. I leaned against the wall, torn by a thousand emotions. I felt I needed to explain. "Candace, we're not leaving you. We still love you. But we have to do this for the kids."

There was silence, but I felt she understood. I felt better. It was good to explain. There were several times during those first few months when I took the time to explain. Though I never presumed for a moment that it made any difference to Candace, it made me feel better.

The kids loved the circus. They couldn't believe their good fortune. And Cliff enjoyed it just as much as they did, if not more. There were moments during the circus when I, too, was able to forget about being sad. But when I did, I paid heavily. Forgetting even for a few seconds exacted its price in a strong, sharp pain when I remembered again.

I really hadn't needed to worry about forgetting. It was going to be a long, deliberate process before I would find my way back to simply being happy again.

Our emotions and our tears were a new factor in our lives. It seemed there was a certain quota of tears that needed to be cried, at first every day, then every other day, and then once a week. We had to deal with the issue of when it was appropriate to cry and when it wasn't. Was it even possible to control our emotions to the extent that we could choose when, where, and how we wanted to release them? We didn't know.

At first I fought to control them.

After the funeral, we heard that by a strange coincidence Michael W. Smith, the singer of Candace's favorite song, was scheduled to appear at the concert hall on March 3. He called late one night saying that he had heard our story and wanted to give Heidi and our family complimentary tickets to the concert. He also made arrangements for us to go backstage later to meet him. Odia, of course, thought this was pure heaven, but I dreaded it. More than that, I was afraid.

We still weren't in control of our emotions. We were never sure when the tears would overwhelm us. Because of this, we found ourselves trying to avoid anything that might upset that careful control. A concert by Michael W. Smith would only push us over the edge. How could I possibly bear hearing her song live when I couldn't even listen to a scratchy, faded, recorded version without falling apart?

There was only one way. First thing the morning of the concert, I put on the tape and forced myself to listen to "Friends Are Friends Forever." The song had not lost any of its ability to resurrect Candace's presence, and I could feel her come swaying into the room in time to the music with that bright smile that I had seen on her face every time she listened to her song.

I played it again, and again, and again, trying to substitute her memories with mine, hoping that by making it mine, her memory wouldn't be as painful. But I couldn't. It was her song. She had loved it so much, had played it so often that it was impossible for any of us to adopt it as our own. The hurt in that song would reach out and wrench my heart out of its cavity and squash it like mud.

I tried to treat it as background music as I dusted the house. But every time the chorus started, the dust would blur and I'd start sobbing.

Finally Cliff came home, took one look at me, and marched into the living room and turned it off. "What do you think you are doing?"

"I'm listening to it until I won't cry anymore."

He shook his head in total disbelief. "Don't you know that song will always make us cry? You'll never get over it. Doing this will make you sick, and you have to go tonight. You can't make yourself sick."

With that last remark, he probably unearthed my secret hope. I didn't want to go.

Actually, it was a wonderful concert. And when Michael W. Smith sang "Friends Are Friends Forever," I cried—and so did everyone else. But it was dark, there were no cameras on us, and it was so good to cry.

There was a place for tears; there always would be. We learned to become more comfortable and unapologetic about them.

As we were making the necessary adjustments to living on a day-to-day basis without Candace, we discovered that there was a good and normal way to keep her a part of our lives. The community around us was helping us to establish memorials.

Candace's school dedicated their annual yearbook to her and another student, Darcy Dyck, who had also died that school year.

The money for the swimming pool was still coming in, and the people who had donated to the fund were beginning to visit the camp and ask where the swimming pool was going to be. Dave Loewen felt that it would be appropriate to have a memorial for the people to see. He wondered if a plaque might serve as an intermediate memorial and asked if we would help in the design of it. We agreed. But a plaque seemed such a cold way to remember; Candace already had a tombstone. We wanted something that would be worth looking at, something that would tell her story.

We asked Dave if, instead of a plaque, we could design a permanent storyboard of the event, a collection of all the newspaper articles and a few pictures arranged in a durable historical marker–type frame. That way if people hadn't heard of Candace, didn't know her story, they would still find the memorial meaningful.

Dave agreed. The unveiling was held September 8, 1985, next to the proposed site of the swimming pool. It could have been an ending of sorts. But it wasn't.

We came home to hear that there had been another abduction attempt that weekend. A man had abducted a twelve-year-old girl on Friday and had taken her by car to the train tracks near our place and had left her tied up in an abandoned railway car. The girl was neither sexually or physically assaulted.

Was this our man or was he just a copycat? The police were unable to uncover any clues and were never been able to identify the assailant. It was frightening to think that the person might have struck again. It was more frightening to think that someone had actually wanted to copy the incident, that there might be two such people.

In discussing the incident with the police, one of the officers told us, "We asked the girl if she had screamed when she was with the man. She hadn't. She hadn't made a sound."

Candace hadn't screamed either.

My work for Child Find was important for meeting my needs to make a difference, to learn more about what had happened to us, and to keep busy.

We worked hard at establishing the organization, and by April 16 our chapter was officially incorporated. By June we had pulled together a full publicity package, and by summer we were beginning to hear from distraught parents.

At first I wondered if dealing with crisis calls would somehow remind me too much of our own crisis. But it wasn't like that. The more I became involved, the more I learned about missing children and the better I was able to put our own experience into perspective.

Child Find also helped alleviate some of our previous fears. I found out that the police had been correct in their statistics: most of the missing children in Winnipeg were runaways.

But not all our fears were alleviated. We were faced with a whole raft of irrational fears. Simple things in life suddenly took on mammoth proportions. One day Odia casually told me that she had been a little slow putting on her jacket and hadn't walked home with her friends. Not walked home with her friends? She had walked home alone! But nothing had happened, she reassured me over and over again.

The fears weren't consistent. Sometimes I was afraid and sometimes I wasn't. I had never been afraid of the dark before. But now, sometimes, when I came home from a late meeting, I would dash from the car to the house, and I'd be shaking by the time I got inside the door. The next time I wouldn't be afraid at all.

Sometimes I think I would have welcomed an intruder. Sometimes I wished that the person who had taken Candace would come into the house so I could confront him. When I was in that state of mind, I had no doubt who would win.

But we weren't dealing with our fears of the perpetrator only. We were suddenly aware of the total fragility of life and insecure about our own mortality. I'm still not sure if it was because we were now aware of death or because we felt that calamity has a pattern: when it happens, it happens in threes and fours. Do we fulfill our own fears? Does anxiety bring it on? I don't know. But the first year after Candace's death, it seemed as if death was stalking us.

One time Odia, Syras, and I were walking back from McDonald's on Nairn. It was a Saturday afternoon, and the street was exceptionally busy. I asked Odia a question above the roar of the cars, and suddenly, for no apparent reason, she stepped into the street into the path of an oncoming car. I grabbed her and pulled her back just in time.

"What did you do that for?" I screamed above the traffic, holding her close.

"I thought you said that we should cross the street."

"With this kind of traffic?"

"You said."

"Oh, sweetheart!" and I didn't let go of her hand until we were inside the house.

Then there was the time when we were swimming at a pool. Just as we were heading for the dressing rooms, Syras decided to run back and jump into the pool—right over his head—and he couldn't swim. I was quite a distance away when I saw his little head go under. In a matter of seconds someone reached over and pulled him out, but for that one brief moment when he was out of my control, I experienced all that horror again.

Soon after that Cliff came home to tell me that his allergy shot had been miscalculated. He had been over-dosed, and if they hadn't given him an antidote in time, if they hadn't noticed it, within seconds . . . !

This is it, I thought. *Death wants all of them*. Even when I was there watching protectively over my family, I couldn't seem to stop it. I just couldn't go through it again. I couldn't. I just couldn't lose another!

Very slowly, I had to put my fear back into per-spective. It could happen. Death is a part of life. To fear it is to fear life itself. I had to learn to walk with it, to live each moment knowing that death could happen again, and if it did, I would seek to find God's will in it, too.

I saw death differently for myself. I never actually contemplated ending my life, but it had become an option. Life after death was where Candace was. Death was actually the only thing that kept me from Candace, and I wanted so much, no, I needed so much to ask her if she was alright. I often wished that it had been me.

I noticed the change in my attitude when we passed cemeteries. They used to be places for the dead—lonely, sad places with only a small poetic value for the living. But now I envied those lying there. They weren't in pain anymore. They were with Candace.

There came a time when I had to choose which side I wanted to be on.

During that first summer, I took videos for Camp Arnes. It was a good job; it took me outdoors, challenged my skill, and kept me observant of the whole camp. One of my assignments was to videotape Camp Seton, their rugged ranch camp in the Carberry Hills, two hours west of Winnipeg.

I'm afraid of horses, so I managed to get Cliff to come with me for two days. It was decided that I would videotape and he would take slides with our 35mm camera. He should have been the one shooting the video; he was a much better, more experienced photographer than I was. But it was my summer assignment, and he didn't want to interfere other than to remind me to check my settings, suggest new camera angles, and help me carry the heavy equipment.

Camp Seton, exceptionally beautiful and situated along a river, was even more beautiful through a lens. We had a lot of fun experimenting and taking sunset shots on a cliff, appropriately called Inspiration Point, overlooking the river. We tried some trick photography in one spot where the campers looked as if they were jumping dangerously off a cliff into thin air—but landing safely on a pile of soft sand right below.

I especially liked the way the camp was laid out. The horses were fenced down in a valley, surrounded by the tents. No matter what we did, we could always see those gorgeous animals moving gracefully in their corral.

The camp director had planned a chuck wagon ride especially for us to photograph at the end of our second day. The lighting was perfect, and it promised to be even better with a full moon rising.

The director started harnessing the horses, but I didn't like the feel of it. The kids were hyper, and the monstrous draft horses were fidgety. I was fidgety.

It was taking them awhile to get set up, so Cliff and I went on ahead. The plan was that we would open the barbwire gate for them, videotape them as they came down the dusty trail, and then once they were through the gate we would get on and videotape from the wagon.

We went down the hill and wandered around looking for the perfect angle. The winding trail lent itself to the classic S-curve picture. Cliff wanted to stand right in the open and take a shot straight on; I wanted to find bushes to hide behind. I said it was because I wanted to frame the picture with some leaves, but in actuality, it was a precaution. I had stood in the open with the trail horses, and every time they had seen me and heard my video camera humming, they had shied away from me. I had a lot of video footage of horses shying away from the camera. But those were small horses compared to those pulling the wagon. I didn't want to spook them, and I wasn't about to put a whole wagon full of kids in jeopardy.

But the bushes I found didn't lend themselves to what I wanted. I was just about to look for some others when I heard a strange sound.

Cliff yelled a warning to me. "I think they're coming . . . and they're out of control!"

He was right. I glanced up just in time to see them come streaking over the hill. I ducked. I thought I was probably safe right where I was, hidden behind some bushes behind the fence. Surely they'd stay on the trail. They wouldn't run through the fence!

That was naive. They could run through a fence. I had heard stories. So just in case, I stood up slowly.

The team was veering off the road and heading right for me! I couldn't believe it. I was in a small ditch, and I could see those huge hooves pounding up the dust at eye level and the director desperately pulling at the reins. It was like a scene out of the Wild, Wild West.

I had seconds, but seconds can be a long time.

I didn't have flashes of my past cross my mind. I saw a bit of my present, but mostly I saw the future. If I stayed where I was, I could go to be with Candace.

The hooves were thundering towards me. I kept thinking, *This can't be happening. This only happens in the movies.* It would be over in a moment.

But I jumped—just in time. I felt the horses rush past me. Then I remembered the barbwire fence and raised my arms to protect my neck and face. I could feel the wire slash across my arms as I was hurled to the ground.

It was suddenly quiet. I lay twisted on the ground; I couldn't move because I was tangled up in a mess of video cords and barbwire. I heard Cliff yelling, and I wondered vaguely if he was angry because I hadn't taken pictures . . . or hadn't stopped the horses. Then I saw Cliff's face, his relief, and I knew that he hadn't been yelling out of anger. "Oh, thank God," he kept saying as he gently untangled me from my cords.

The video camera was fine except for one distinct souvenir scratch on the camera case. The director and the one camper in the wagon weren't hurt at all. The wagon had lodged behind two trees, and once the horses had shaken off their harnesses, they had begun to graze.

I was bruised and scratched. But the only casualty was my $3.99 watch from Zellers, which had been smashed by the barbwire slashing at my wrists.

I knew that I couldn't fool myself anymore. I

didn't want to die. I had just proven to myself and everyone else that I wanted to live very much. I had chosen to be with my family and not with Candace, and I felt guilty. Candace needed me, yet I had chosen life.

No, I knew I was wrong. Candace had needed me that winter night. She didn't need me anymore. My family needed me more. Whether I wanted it to or not, life would go on. I needed to adjust. I needed to learn how to live again.

CHAPTER 15

The Bottom Line: Forgiveness

I didn't know what to expect the day of the first anniversary of Candace's disappearance, November 30, 1985. I already knew from her birthday how difficult anniversary days were the first year.

Some of our friends guessed that it would be a difficult time for us and made all sorts of elaborate plans. We wondered about the wisdom of spending such an emotional day with friends, but we didn't say anything. Then, the day before, we discovered all the plans had fallen through. There wasn't enough time to make alternative plans.

The anniversary day fell on a Saturday, and when we got up that morning, it had all the markings of being just an ordinary day. I wondered if by ignoring it, just not talking about it, we might not really notice it.

But right from the beginning, even without any words, I could tell that a cloud had descended on us. Even the kids sensed it and seemed preoccupied.

By afternoon, I was desperate to escape from the heavy mood, and I tried to arouse Cliff into making some last-minute plans. Couldn't we at least go shopping?

Cliff had retreated to the basement to work on the computer, and he looked up from his swirl of papers, irritated. I suddenly knew that his absorption was his escape, and he was comfortable in it.

I prowled around the house a bit longer and then decided that maybe Cliff had the right idea. I needed to drown myself in work, in hard work. The hardest work I could think of was washing walls.

I should have known it wouldn't work. I'm never in the best of moods when I'm housecleaning as it is; why would it be any different this day of all days? I could tell that instead of losing myself in the scrubbing, I was just becoming more and more irritated. I stared at the hundreds and hundreds of little fingerprints. Did the kids touch the walls all the time? Were they blind? Did they find it impossible to walk down a hall or down the stairs without feeling where they were going?

As I worked my way down the stairwell, I glanced at my watch. It was getting closer and closer to four o'clock. I started to understand the importance of an anniversary. It is probably the closest to the original moment one ever gets.

Time seemed to stand still. Why was this moment so terrifying? What actually happened this time a year ago? Suddenly, I knew! This was not only the anniversary of the day that Candace disappeared; it was also the anniversary of my decision not to pick her up.

There were fingerprints on the wall above the bottom step, and I wondered how they had gotten there. Cliff and I never touched that section of wall, and Odia and Syras were too small. Only Candace, like every teen I knew, would hang onto the doorjamb and swing herself out over the main floor. I looked closer. They were her size. They were Candace's fingerprints!

Immobilized, I sat on the stairs looking up at them. I couldn't wash them off. So little of her was left. How could I remove one more evidence of her life?

Without looking at my watch, I knew what time it was. It was five minutes after four. The moment was heavy with expectation, as if Candace might call any minute and I would be able to get into the car and pick her up and save all of us from going through the year of pain. We would have Candace again.

The wishful moment didn't last long. Suddenly the expectations turned into accusations. Why hadn't I picked her up?

This time there was no answer.

What kind of mother would allow her daughter to walk home in the cold at such a vulnerable time? Why hadn't I foreseen what was going to happen? There had been a number of other times when I had sensed that my children were in danger. I had found them perched precariously on top of the stairs or in the kitchen with a knife, but I had always been there to prevent the accident. This time, when the danger had been the most hostile, I had been preoccupied with cleaning the downstairs.

Why hadn't we been able to convince the police to get out the dogs that night when the scent was fresh? We had done nothing! While she froze to death in a shed, we had been sitting in a warm house just waiting for her to die. It was all my fault. I could have prevented all of it from happening. She had died, and I had the audacity to survive and go on living.

The fingerprints seemed to grow larger.

The whole year my friends had skirted the guilt subject. "Are you blaming yourself?" my sisters had asked cautiously, and I had always answered with such certainty, "No, I didn't do anything wrong. A girl should be able to walk safely from school to her home in the middle of the day. I'm not to blame." They had seemed so relieved, and now I knew why. How do you deal with this kind of guilt? What answer was there for the ugly voices that were making themselves heard for the first time?

I couldn't ignore the voices. I tried to turn them off, but I had ignored them for a whole year, and it had only allowed them to grow stronger and uglier.

It wasn't only guilt from that one decision; it was guilt from everything we had done for Candace, or hadn't done. Every moment, every mistake, every omission loomed up in the shadowy fingerprints.

I had no defense. The hideous voices were totally irrational, but guilt is irrational. It is a feeling and rarely responds to normal rational thinking. No matter how hard I tried to reason with it, I still felt guilty. I needed to deal with this feeling on a feeling level.

I tried to minimize the guilt by arguing that Candace was a teenager. How much influence does a mother have over a teenager?

Then I remembered an incident during Candace's last summer. We had been walking down the back alley to pick up some bread at the corner store. I think we were talking about rock music, and I was laying out my philosophy on it when Candace suddenly burst out laughing. "Mom, you're different."

"What do you mean?" I asked, horrified at being called different.

She shrugged her shoulders. "It's not a bad 'different.' You're just different. You let me do things that my friends can't and don't let me do things they can."

I waited. Our thongs clapped our heels in the quietness.

"You don't really care about some things," she said, groping for words. "But you teach me about life. You pick out the important things."

I was so moved I couldn't say anything.

She continued, "Sometimes when my friends don't know what to do, I tell them things you've told me, and they think I'm wise." She giggled.

Wise? She had called it wise—my advice. But was it wise if it cost her life?

When she was young, she had often complained about the little bully seated next to her in school. There always was a bully in every class, and she seemed to have the misfortune of always being placed next to him. I would tell her, "Candace, he is only trying to get your attention. If you are nice to him, he'll eventually learn to be nice back."

Much later she had told me, "It worked, Mom. I still can't stand him, but he doesn't bother me anymore."

One time she came home and said that the teacher had placed her beside the meanest bully in the class because she was the only one who could handle him.

In every situation, I had always emphasized being loving. I would tell her that love was the most powerful weapon there was.

Had Candace met an oversized bully and tried to use the weapon of love? Had she been so involved with being kind that she hadn't seen an opportunity to escape? If so, then my teaching had been at the scene of the crime, and it hadn't been adequate. My life-skills lessons had not included self-defense or the importance of creative self-preservation.

The police had described the scene to us. They kept mentioning how amazed they were at the seeming lack of a physical struggle. They had concluded that this was evidence that Candace had probably known the person. Each time they said it, I felt the self-accusations. I had taught her not to struggle. I had pushed the voices back then, but they wouldn't stay back anymore.

I tried to whisper that I taught her what I had been taught. But the voices ignored my whispers and took a different twist. Why hadn't our faith in God worked? Why hadn't we been able to prevent the whole situation? Why had we moved into this community to begin with?

I tried to answer.

Why hadn't we been more responsible with our money and provided for our children better? When all our friends had been working and saving for their first house, we had been gallivanting around the country.

I couldn't believe where my thoughts were going. We hadn't been gallivanting around the country; we had been serving God. Was I suddenly feeling guilty because I had put God first? Things that I really believed in were turning against me, and I was totally aghast. The rock I had clung to that first night was slipping.

"And about that first night . . . ," the voices screeched. Why had I been so quick to give in? What kind of mother would accept her child's death so quickly? Maybe Cliff would have continued along those tracks the first night and found her if I had prayed differently. Maybe she would have survived the night!

I could feel that I was losing it. Cliff had been part of all of this. It was his responsibility too!

"Sure," the voices agreed. They loved the idea. "He's guilty too!"

But I couldn't. I had always prided myself on taking responsibility for my own actions. I had vowed I'd never blame Cliff for anything.

Once, when the kids were little, I had blamed him for everything.

Cliff was going camping for a weekend with the young people in our church. I was tired, frustrated, and depressed. I felt housebound. I couldn't do anything, go anywhere. It seemed my whole job description, my whole worth was tied up in following a toddler around the house all day. I was imprisoned in my own home.

I had been furious with Cliff because he could leave. But his last remarks to me were, "Wifey, do you really think I prefer going out among the mosquitoes, sleeping on the hard ground, and trying to control ten high-energy teens for a weekend to being home here with my family and sleeping in my soft bed?"

I hadn't heard him. I just sulked around for the rest of the day.

That night I had dreamed that Cliff was going to kill me. I could hear his footsteps coming to the door, and I went to the door and waited. The doorknob turned, and slowly it opened. But instead of Cliff, it was Satan—ugly, fuming, and swinging an axe.

I woke up screaming. I knew immediately what my subconscious or God was telling me. It was clear that I was blaming Cliff for my suffocation when really it wasn't he at all. He loved me; I knew that. He had always been the best husband—considerate, thoughtful, generous. But there was a force that wanted to inhibit me, intimidate me, kill me. That force was evil itself.

From then on I vowed that I would never blame Cliff for what happened in my own life. I was responsible for my own actions just as Cliff was responsible for his. We were together. We could help and encourage each other, but neither of us had the power to make or destroy the other. That power lies within our hearts.

But I had no power now.

The voices drew very close; they had me and they knew it. "You're a failure," they whispered, and the ominous words swirled and vibrated in the empty stairwell. I finally understood why people bang their heads against the wall. It's to drown out the inside pain.

The voices were right. When we had brought Candace home from the hospital and laid her down in her pink bassinet, our pastor and his wife, who lived across the yard from us, came over, and we dedicated the little baby to God. We vowed we would do our best to protect her and to raise her. Our goal was that she would grow up to be a mature adult. Whatever way I looked at it now, we had failed that goal.

I finally said it. "I failed."

I really think I stunned them. The voices were silenced. And it felt good to say those words.

"I am guilty." I almost felt as if half of the battle was won just by defining it. If I judged myself, then I was free from anyone else's judgment. I didn't need to be protected.

But, oh, the heaviness of those words!

Instinctively I whispered, "God forgive me." I could feel his nod. The load was lighter.

"Oh, Candace," I sobbed. "Forgive me."

I could feel her tears. I could feel her words, "Yes,

Mom." I knew that, from heaven's perspective, she could forgive.

But it wasn't over. The question came back. Could I forgive myself? I was stumped. I didn't think I could. I would have to live with my guilt. I felt the weight of it, the deadness. Even the sharp pain of Candace's memory was better than this dullness, this lifeless emotion of overwhelming despair and rage.

I could see the pattern. At first, my anger had been directed at the murderer, and I had wanted to kill him with my own hands. But I didn't want to hurt others the way I had been hurt, so I had kept the front yard of my life groomed, free of any hint of angry weeds.

Then I had discovered that the anger had grown in the backyard, and it was directed at the police. I was overwhelmed at the enormity of the rage. But the blame hadn't lasted after I discovered that my expectations of them had been unrealistic.

Now I was discovering that I had hauled all that rage, anger, and guilt into the house itself. It was dark and dingy with huge misshapen vines twisted in a grotesque mess of jungle foliage.

Again, I was left with the guilt and rage. What was I to do? Perhaps I was bunching all the anger irrationally. Perhaps, if I divided the responsibility. . . . The police had made some mistakes; I would let them have the responsibility for their errors. Surely the person who had abducted Candace that night was responsible for his mistakes. Cliff was responsible for his own, as the society and the community were responsible for their mistakes. It loosened a branch or two, and I could remove them. It made the load a little lighter. I still carried a whole houseful of my own vengeance, of a lifetime of choices, but at least it was contained now. *I can, with a stiff upper lip, carry this,* I thought to myself. I could carry the burden. I had already carried it for a whole year, and I hadn't even known it. Nowhere had I read that God would hold it against me if I couldn't forgive myself.

I looked up at the fingerprints. They were magnified through my tears. I would leave them. I wouldn't wipe them off. It would be part of the price.

I was getting up to leave when a soft voice said, "Surely, if you have tried to forgive the murderer, the police, and everyone else, you should benefit from some of that forgiveness."

I stopped to listen for more, but it was gone. I noticed that some of the vines had begun to loosen. I could tell that this voice was more powerful than all the rest.

I explored the thought. Surely I could benefit from my own attitude. By giving other people space to make mistakes, surely I was making room for myself. If I had started to forgive the person who had actually done the crime, could I continue to blame the accomplice?

In some weird way, the whole concept of forgiveness wasn't for everyone else, it was for me. I had always thought forgiveness was a means to bridge broken relationships with others. It was a way to acknowledge others' fallibility and give them room to fail. I had never really thought that this same forgiveness would, in some way, be there to heal the broken relationship within me as well. It was the glue that would keep me together and save me from falling into a million different pieces.

The vines had all come undone. I picked up one of the branches to throw it out, but where was it to go? Where does one put a cancerous growth? Two years from now, would I find it all bunched up in my attic?

There was no way around it. I couldn't complete this. I couldn't really forgive my daughter's murderer. It would be a vicious circle. I could try to forgive and forgive, but who could ultimately wipe this guilt away, throw it into the deepest sea? Who could bear this guilt and rage? Who could really deal with it?

In order to vanquish the vine, someone needed to die—someone who was part God, because God was part of the tragedy, and someone who was totally innocent, because Candace had been innocent in her death.

And there in the shadows I saw the cross. Better than ever before, I understood why Christ had to die. I'll never really understand the mystery of what happened on Calvary, but, at that moment, I finally knew where I needed to go with all of the guilt.

The deadness was gone. I was again free to enjoy all the beautiful memories we had of Candace. I could again remember the love, the goodness, the beauty of her life. The memories were no longer framed by guilt.

I remembered the night that Candace had disappeared when I had decided to hold on to my faith regardless of what might come. I had wondered if my faith would hold, if I would have to reorganize it, adapt it, or throw it away.

Now I knew. My faith had been tested, and it had changed slightly. I had gained new insights; I had modified, adapted, and perhaps reorganized it slightly, but it had brought me through.

Blinking away tears, I stood up. The fingerprints that had been tattooed onto the wall needed to be removed. I wondered if it would be possible to remove them. I dampened my cloth and washed them away. There was a clean white wall underneath. The whole house suddenly seemed sparkling clean.

Life is always a test. The minute we think we have grasped some truth, life will test it for us. Often it comes in the form of the smallest choices.

Shortly after Candace disappeared, most of the schools introduced a "street proofing" program, and a trend began for having all the children fingerprinted. The Child Find organization was part of it.

I should have been prepared for it, but I wasn't.

It was a warm winter—almost spring—day. The dogs next door were out, and our neighbor was working on a car in his backyard. Syras and I were just coming home from a shopping trip when he noticed Syras and called out, "Hi there!"

I expected Syras to respond. He always did. He liked people and was usually overly friendly. But he was quiet. He looked at the man in an odd way, reached for the bag I gave him to carry, and walked into the house.

Once inside the house, he got on the kitchen table and looked out the kitchen window at the man and his dogs.

"Mommy," he asked, "is that man a neighbor or a stranger?"

A simple question. It deserved a simple answer. Obviously it came out of the "street proofing" that he had been taught at school: beware of strangers. And he couldn't have chosen a better person, a better relationship, or a better example of just how complicated the whole issue can be.

This neighbor was the kind of person whom you would like to instinctively trust. His place was orderly. His dogs were under control and looked loved, and they had always been friendly. But in all honesty, we knew nothing about him. We didn't know where or even if he worked, or whether he was married or just living with the girl who seemed to come and go. Sometimes he was gone for long periods of time, and we didn't know if it was vacation or business. For all we knew, he could easily be living a double life. He was what one would consider the perfect neighbor-stranger.

But what did I want? Did I want my little son to trust everyone? Was I going to stress loving like I had with Candace? What should my answer be? What should it have been to Candace? I ached to take the safer route. I wanted to end all risks and pronounce this man a stranger.

Syras was waiting impatiently. "Come on, Mom. Is he a stranger?"

I weighed the balances. I reviewed it again. By instilling my children with ideals, I made them and our family vulnerable again. But which was better? Should we live a loving life and risk being hurt or insulate ourselves and never love—or live? I'm not sure that life and love can be separated.

Syras didn't understand my tears when I hugged him as I lifted him off the table and put him down.

"No, sweetheart, he's not a stranger. He's actually a very nice neighbor. And the next time he says hi, the polite thing to do is to say hi back."

"Oh, I will," he said with a big sigh of relief. "I just thought he might be a stranger. I'm glad he's a neighbor. I like to pet his dogs."

He grabbed an apple and went to play.

He had gained a new freedom; I felt as if I had lost some of mine. I was now responsible.

It would have been so much easier to have said, "He's a stranger," and to have taught my children to protect themselves. But because I hadn't painted the world in black and white for him, it was now my responsibility to teach him how complicated life is: how a neighbor can turn into a stranger, how a stranger can turn into a neighbor, and how—stranger or neighbor—we can still love them. I had to teach him how to take reasonable precautions, knowing there would always be risks. A stranger and a neighbor both have the ability to take life or give it. But whether they take our life or give it, we can always respond in love. Because it isn't life that is important—it's love.

CHAPTER 16

Epilogue: Love Endures

Casually, almost too casually, Odia interrupted our Sunday breakfast chatter to urge us to make up our minds about what we were planning to do that Sunday, because she wanted to be on time to attend baptismal classes at our church. Baptismal classes? It was the first time we had heard about it. With one quick look at each other, Cliff and I dropped any alternate plans we were entertaining.

"When did you start this?" I asked, deliberately as casual as she had been, if not more so. Teens are so delicate. If you in any way let on how you feel about anything, you can influence the decision, positively or negatively, without even wanting to. This one I didn't want to. I hardly dared breathe.

"Two weeks ago," she answered.

Cliff cleared his throat. "Well then, let's get going."

In some ways, for five years following Candace's disappearance we had been free-falling through space, wondering where we would land and whether we all would land in the same place.

At first, all we tried to do was keep each other in sight. It was only on rare occasions that we were skilled enough to build a formation and hold each others' hands. Usually it was an undignified fall with just enough control to be careful that we wouldn't bump into each other, knowing that at that speed even the slightest bump would become a major collision. Instead, we called out instructions to each other—where to find the rip cord; where we wanted to land.

I knew my parachute had opened four years ago on the first anniversary day of Candace's disappearance. I had sensed that Cliff's had opened around that time too. But even though we lived so close, talked a lot, and were open with each other, I wasn't sure exactly when he had pulled his rip cord or what that had actually meant to him. All I knew was that he had somehow come to terms with his anger. He had never directed it at any of us. Never once had he blamed me for not picking up Candace from school that day. I knew that at some point he must have had to deal with that question. It would have been so normal, so easy for him to have targeted all his anger against me.

I finally gathered enough nerve to ask him about his journey. I told him how I had written my own experience of guilt into this book. "But before I'm finished with the question, I need to know how you've dealt with it."

He looked away, and immediately I knew he didn't want to talk about it.

I told him that I already knew he must have, at some point, needed to deal with it and that he must have been angry with me. "Why didn't you ever express it? Why didn't you ever blame me?" I pushed.

"I couldn't," he said softly. "I knew that if I did, if I even hinted at it, it could have destroyed you."

He was right. Everyone else could say it—the police could accuse me, the telephone calls could berate me—and I would be hurt but not knocked down. But if Cliff had blamed me, I would have been devastated.

I was still curious. "But surely it must have been hard sometimes to keep those kinds of emotions inside. . . ." Sometimes I hate myself for the questions I need to ask. "What kept you from saying it?"

He looked honestly amazed at my question, as if I should have known. "I love you," he said simply.

The words were the same as the ones he had said so long ago when he asked me to marry him, but the meaning was immeasurably deeper, richer, and more enduring. He had put my needs above his own.

Many have asked what the secret is to our relationship. I think the answer lies right here. We love and trust each other. We never allow ourselves the luxury of playing the blaming game with each other. Our marriage is too important to even once threaten it with accusations. It's not that we have ever been afraid of confronting each other on different issues and on different levels; in fact, I think confrontation is integral to keeping a relationship alive and well. But we have a kind of agreement that we confront each other on things we can change, not on things we can't. Cliff knew without even talking to me that this was one thing I wanted to change, but couldn't. He loved me enough not to say anything.

He couldn't remember specifically when, how, or where he had made those decisions. "Soon after," he said.

Did he deal with it more than once?

Again he looked a little baffled at my question. "No, once I had made up my mind, I didn't have to go through it again."

I envy that kind of confidence. His parachute was in good order.

It was much easier to keep an eye on each other than it was to always know how the children were doing. They don't have the words, the patience, or the desire to keep tabs on their emotional health. But Odia's announcement that she was taking baptismal classes was the first strong indication that her parachute was open. We'd have to wait several more years to see how Syras was faring.

We had always kept our eye on Odia's spiritual life. It was important to us that she sustain a faith in God. Usually if there is any confusion about life, the first target is God. So Odia's interest in joining the church meant much more to us than the actual joining of the local church. To me it meant, at this stage at least, that her view of God, her relationship with her Maker, was not confused. And if she wasn't confused about this fundamental issue, then there wasn't too much in life that was going to catch her off guard.

Then I wondered if she was joining the church out of some need to please Cliff and me, or the pastor, or her friends. If that was the case, then we had all failed.

I waited to see if her interest would continue.

The classes continued. The pastor asked to meet with us. Did we think she was ready?

Yes, as far as we could tell, her action coincided with her words. But this was her choice, we told him. We would encourage but not insist.

He nodded.

The date was chosen. It was a beautiful spring morning. Our lilac bushes had flowered, the tulips were in bloom, and the grass was a lush green. The April showers had worked their magic, and finally the long prairie winter was over.

It was symbolic in many ways.

Our fourteen-year-old daughter, Odia, stood behind the pulpit of our church reading her testimony.

The church was quiet and she appeared relaxed, though I knew better. Even before she began to read her testimony, I knew that this wouldn't be easy for us. This was Odia's moment, and we were going to celebrate it with her. But somewhere deeper, running parallel, I knew that it would also be a time when Candace's presence would come back. And it did.

Odia took a deep breath and read, "When I was about five or six, I dedicated my life to the Lord. I remember I was at Star Lake Lodge and my sister, Candace, was helping me. She was about nine or ten at the time, and we knelt down by the bed and prayed."

That had been a long time ago; I'd almost forgotten about it. Cliff and I had taken an evening stroll along the beach. As we were coming back to our little cabin, Candace came running to meet us, breathless and beaming. She called out to us. "Odia accepted Jesus into her heart," she kept repeating, her eyes shining.

We found Odia sitting on the bed smiling quietly. We asked both of them to describe what had happened. Candace explained that she and Odia had been talking about God and that Odia had wondered how to get to heaven. "I explained to her, Mom, just like you did to me, that all she had to do was pray to Jesus to forgive her and she would go to heaven. She prayed. So now she's going to heaven."

Odia was nodding her head in happy agreement. "I asked Jesus into my heart," she said.

Now, eight years later, Odia was identifying the beginning of her faith with that humble but profound step. My eyes clouded with tears. Candace's spirit continued to live on.

Odia continued. "After that I had a normal childhood until fourth grade."

Yes, it had all been so normal, such a beautiful time in our lives with our two beautiful daughters and our son.

". . . When I was nine, one Friday my sister didn't come home from school. We looked and searched, but Candace had disappeared." She didn't go into detail. She didn't have to; our church had walked through the experience with us.

Five years later we still didn't know what had really happened that day. How did we live with that? Were we afraid? Those were the questions we were often asked, are still asked.

Truthfully, I don't know how we live with the mystery. I think, in faith, we put it out of our minds and into God's hands, knowing that if we dwell on it, it will soon possess us. But mostly, I think we just put one foot ahead of the other and try to make the most of each day, because the tragedy also taught us how important it is to live each day to the fullest.

There are times when I wish that we did know, that all the mystery in our lives would clear up. I didn't realize how strong the need for some kind of emotional closure was until I received a letter from a person in another province whom I had met earlier. Her twin brother had been killed by a drunk driver, and in her letter she described how horrified she was when the man who had killed her brother moved in next door.

Yes, I knew what she was saying. How cruel can life get? She was asking me to commiserate with her, to allow her to be angry, to tell her that she shouldn't have to endure more humiliation—that there should be justice. I felt her anger and her frustration, but because of my own situation I saw it all so differently than she did.

She had what I would never have—the opportunity to get some answers, to face—head-on—her anger and frustrations. She had a physical object to make peace with, which, as difficult as it might be, is still much easier than making peace with a phantom.

After much deliberation, knowing the risk, I wrote her and told her as kindly as I could how envious I was. She had the opportunity to forgive in a tangible way and to find release in that forgiveness. I asked her if she might want to give something to the man who killed her brother as a symbolic act of her forgiveness.

I didn't hear from her for a long time, but eventually a letter came back. She had been angry at my letter but she had taken up the challenge. She had given him the biggest gift of all—her forgiveness. She told me how good it felt to be free.

I was glad for her.

Odia continued, "Now, when I look back, I realized that I blamed God."

My heart stopped. It's one thing to face that question as an adult, but it's another to realize your own children are facing it so young.

After being with Child Find for three years, I had wondered if I was locking myself emotionally into the first six weeks of our search, so I resigned as president and left it in capable hands. At that time a new organization, Family Survivors of Homicide, was just in the beginning stages of operation, and the president asked if I might want to join and help them. It seemed a healthy transition.

It was. It gave me the opportunity to watch other surviving family members go through the ordeal of a trial, a sentence, an appeal, and sometimes an outright acquittal. I saw what the justice system did to the victims. And I was convinced again that though the justice system is valid, offenders need to be brought to justice and made to face the responsibility of their actions. I don't think our system lends itself to giving victims the satisfaction they need that justice has been served.

Right now I have no equity. There is no one paying for what happened to Candace. I could easily ask myself, *Then where does that life, those unlived years, go? Can Candace's life really be unaccounted for? Can we say that those years that were stolen from her don't matter? Who is going to give them back? Who is going to pay for having taken them? There has to be some kind of retribution.*

In life, when a businessman goes bankrupt someone still pays. It's not the person who ran up the debt, but those who loaned to him. In accounting, there is never a penny that isn't accounted for. If I forgive a debt, I have to adjust my own projected budget. Likewise, when a life has been taken, society expects the person who took it to pay with his own life in terms of a given number of years in prison.

When we forgave, what really happened? Did we just obliterate Candace's unlived years? No. Whether we realized it or not, we took responsibility for Candace's life.

It took me a long time to understand why we go when someone asks Cliff and me to speak someplace that is two hours away. We have become caretakers of Candace's life, of her story. Forgiveness has a high price. God forgave us but had to pay with the blood of his own Son.

Isn't this revictimization? Isn't this making the victim pay twice? Is this necessary? Is it a must?

No, it's not necessary. But I don't think I would want it any other way. I couldn't entrust the memory of my daughter to anyone else. Even if the person were caught and sentenced, I think I'd still do it this way. I could never entrust something as precious as Candace to someone who had hurt her.

Taking responsibility for my rage and for her memory has been difficult, but it has also been freeing. It's helped me gain control of my life again and give meaning to hers. And I think that's what God has been trying to tell us all along. The difficult, costly road of giving, dying, and forgiving eventually becomes our salvation.

Odia was still speaking. "But then I realized that a lot of good was coming out of this tragedy."

Just to hear her say that was worth so much. And she was right. There had been a lot of good.

On October 16, 1986, nearly two years after her death, the Candace Derksen Memorial Pool had been completed, and we had participated in a ribbon-cutting ceremony. In some ways it was like the funeral. We again mourned her loss, but we also celebrated the meaning of her life.

The day had been bright and sunny with a cool autumn breeze. The indoor pool was beautiful. The building's walls were completely finished in cedar. The pool and exit doors were painted a lovely blue, and there were plants placed on the spacious deck. In one corner beside a large window was a six-jet Jacuzzi whirlpool. There was a sauna, a shuffleboard, a coat room, and changing rooms for both men and women. One wall was all glass and overlooked the play structure and camp yard.

The memorial fund had grown miraculously in those two years.

At first it had seemed impossible. An enclosed pool, as it would need to be, would cost at least $250,000. Within a year, $22,000 came in from the community, the Manitoba government gave a $30,000 donation, and many suppliers provided material. The day the pool was completed, it was estimated that the final $265,000 cost represented a little more than half of the full value of the building. Virtually every trade or company involved donated part of their cost.

It was a warm, fulfilling feeling to snip the ribbon. I remembered the covenant that Candace and I had talked about. Death was not the worst option; to live a life with no value and no meaning was far more tragic. I had told her that if she committed her life to him, God could use her death to have an impact. Now I knew that, whether I had the right to promise that or not, God had been listening.

We didn't want people to come to the pool and remember all the tragic details of our story. For Cliff and me it would be enough if they just had a good time. It would be an added bonus if they remembered that life is short and very precious. And it would be wonderful if they remembered that there is a God who listens.

The pool became a memorial that we could see and touch, but there were other little things that people told us that were probably much more profound in terms of making a difference in people's lives.

Once when I dropped by to talk to a professor at the college, he told me about a girl who had learned forgiveness through our experience. She had forgiven her family and had decided to quit her life of prostitution.

A young father told us that because of our experience, he had realized that life is too short to miss watching his sons grow up. He dropped his second job.

Two young people decided to rededicate their lives to God and were baptized in their church.

One woman who had been going through a difficult time and felt like giving up decided that, in light of our tragedy, her problems weren't so bad.

A young mother named her daughter after Candace.

And a police officer told us that they have never been able to take a "runaway" call lightly again.

I have a box full of stories like that.

Nature abhors a vacuum, we're told. So do our lives. Candace left a vacuum in our lives that demanded to be filled.

The Old Testament justice that demands a life for a life is inadequate in the long run. The New Testament shows that if we were always to act on the bare bones of justice, everyone would be missing their eyes and teeth.

Christ shows us how to flesh out the skeleton of justice with love and forgiveness; he shows that complete healing can be brought about by using our pain to build hope.

". . . And I've been growing ever since."

Odia had been growing. Her life had been turned upside down, but she was back on her feet. She had found her way through.

Her testimony was short. "I want to be baptized," she concluded.

It was too short; there was so much more I wanted to know. But it was enough. Cliff and I were thrilled.

This was Odia's first independent adult choice, and we wanted it to be all hers. We were just elated that this first choice of her life was a step that would move her closer to God and a believers' community.

As Odia emerged from the water, wet but beaming, I remembered that long ago, during the dark moments of our tragedy, we had given Candace to God. We had resolved to work good out of evil, thinking that the good would impact others, that we were giving it away. But now, five years later, the good that we had tried to do, tried to give away, was coming back to impact our lives. It was the "good" that had kept Odia.

There are no words, just tears of gratitude, to give to the God who gave us the formula by which to live. As Jesus said in John 12:24, "I tell you the truth, unless a kernel of wheat falls to the ground and dies, it remains only a single seed. But if it dies, it produces many seeds."

We've all more or less landed in the same place. That's not to say that in the future, if perhaps the perpetrator is found, we won't be unceremoniously shoved off the plane and find ourselves spinning in a free fall once again. We know that our lives can change completely in one split second.

But right now, for a little while at least, our feet have touched ground. We can laugh, we can cry, and we can now sit under the shade of the blessings that have grown out of the little seeds. In many ways, Candace is still with us.

Love has endured.

Other Living Books Best-Sellers

74 MORE FUN AND CHALLENGING BIBLE CROSSWORDS. This brand-new batch of crosswords features both theme puzzles and general crosswords on a variety of levels, all relating to Bible facts, characters, and terms. 07-0488-6

400 CREATIVE WAYS TO SAY I LOVE YOU by Alice Chapin. Perhaps the flame of love has almost died in your marriage, or you have a good marriage that just needs a little spark. Here is a book of creative, practical ideas for the woman who wants to show the man in her life that she cares. 07-0919-5

ANSWERS by Josh McDowell and Don Stewart. In a question-and-answer format, the authors tackle sixty-five of the most-asked questions about the Bible, God, Jesus Christ, miracles, other religions, and creation. 07-0021-X

ANSWERS TO YOUR FAMILY'S FINANCIAL QUESTIONS by Larry Burkett. Questions about credit, saving, taxes, insurance, and more are answered in this handbook that shows how the Bible can guide our financial lives. 07 0025-2

THE BEST OF BIBLE TRIVIA I: KINGS, CRIMINALS, SAINTS, AND SINNERS by J. Stephen Lang. A fascinating book containing over 1,500 questions and answers about the Bible arranged topically in over 50 categories. Taken from the best-selling **Complete Book of Bible Trivia.** 07-0464 0

THE CHILD WITHIN by Mari Hanes. The author shares insights she gained from God's Word during her own pregnancy. She identifies areas of stress, offers concrete data about the birth process, and points to God's sure promises that he will gently lead those that are with young. 07-0210 0

CHRISTIANITY: THE FAITH THAT MAKES SENSE by Dennis McCallum. New and inquiring Christians will find spiritual support in this readable apologetic, which presents a clear, rational defense for Christianity to those unfamiliar with the Bible. 07-0525-4

COME BEFORE WINTER AND SHARE MY HOPE by Charles R. Swindoll. A collection of brief vignettes offering hope and the assurance that adversity and despair are temporary setbacks we can overcome! 07-0477-0

Other Living Books Best-Sellers

THE COMPLETE GUIDE TO BIBLE VERSIONS by Philip W. Comfort. A guidebook with descriptions of all the English translations and suggestions for their use. Includes the history of biblical writings. 07-1251-X

DARE TO DISCIPLINE by James Dobson. A straightforward, plainly written discussion about building and maintaining parent/child relationships based upon love, respect, authority, and ultimate loyalty to God. 07-0522-X

DR. DOBSON ANSWERS YOUR QUESTIONS by James Dobson. In this convenient reference book, renowned author Dr. James Dobson addresses heartfelt concerns on many topics, including questions on marital relationships, infant care, child discipline, home management, and others. 07-0580-7

GIVERS, TAKERS, AND OTHER KINDS OF LOVERS by Josh McDowell and Paul Lewis. Bypassing generalities about love and sex, this book answers the basics: Whatever happened to sexual freedom? Do men respond differently than women? Here are straight answers about God's plan for love and sexuality. 07-1031-2

HINDS' FEET ON HIGH PLACES by Hannah Hurnard. A classic allegory of a journey toward faith that has sold more than a million copies! 07-1429-6

HAVE YOU SEEN CANDACE? by Wilma Derksen. In this inspiring true story, Wilma Derksen recounts the hope and agony of the search for her missing daughter. Through Wilma's faith, readers will discover forgivness and love that overcome evil. 07-0377-4

THE INTIMATE MARRIAGE by R. C. Sproul. The author focuses on biblical patterns of marriage and practical ways to develop intimacy. Discussion questions included at the end of each chapter. 07-1610-8

JOHN, SON OF THUNDER by Ellen Gunderson Traylor. In this saga of adventure, romance, and discovery, travel with John—the disciple whom Jesus loved—down desert paths, through the courts of the Holy City, and to the foot of the cross as he leaves his luxury as a privileged son of Israel for the bitter hardship of his exile on Patmos. 07-1903-4

Other Living Books Best-Sellers

LIFE IS TREMENDOUS! by Charlie "Tremendous" Jones. Believing that enthusiasm makes the difference, Jones shows how anyone can be happy, involved, relevant, productive, healthy, and secure in the midst of a high-pressure, commercialized society. 07-2184-5

LORD, COULD YOU HURRY A LITTLE? by Ruth Harms Calkin. These prayer-poems from the heart of a godly woman trace the inner workings of the heart, following the rhythms of the day and seasons of the year with expectation and love. 07-3816-0

LORD, I KEEP RUNNING BACK TO YOU by Ruth Harms Calkin. In prayer-poems tinged with wonder, joy, humanness, and questioning, the author speaks for all of us who are groping and learning together what it means to be God's child. 07-3819-5

MORE THAN A CARPENTER by Josh McDowell. A hard-hitting book for people who are skeptical about Jesus' deity, his resurrection, and his claim on their lives. 07-4552-3

MOUNTAINS OF SPICES by Hannah Hurnard. Here is an allegory comparing the nine spices mentioned in the Song of Solomon to the nine fruits of the Spirit. A story of the glory of surrender by the author of **Hinds' Feet on High Places.** 07-4611-2

OUT OF THE STORM by Grace Livingston Hill. Gail finds herself afloat on an angry sea, desperately trying to keep an unconscious man from slipping away from her. 07-4778-X

QUICK TO LISTEN, SLOW TO SPEAK by Robert E. Fisher. Families are shown how to express love to one another by developing better listening skills, finding ways to disagree without arguing, and using constructive criticism. 07-5111-6

THE SECRET OF LOVING by Josh McDowell. McDowell explores the values and qualities that will help both single and married readers to be the right person for someone else. He offers a fresh perspective for evaluating and improving the reader's love life. 07-5845-5

Other Living Books Best-Sellers

STRIKE THE ORIGINAL MATCH by Charles Swindoll. Many couples ask: What do you do when the warm, passionate fire that once lit your marriage begins to wane? Here, Chuck Swindoll provides biblical steps for rekindling the fires of romance and building marital intimacy. 07-6445-5

SUCCESS! THE GLENN BLAND METHOD by Glenn Bland. The author shows how to set goals and make plans that really work. His ingredients of success include spiritual, financial, educational, and recreational balances. 07-6689-X

WHAT WIVES WISH THEIR HUSBANDS KNEW ABOUT WOMEN by James Dobson. The best-selling author of **Dare to Discipline** and **The Strong-Willed Child** brings us this vital book that speaks to the unique emotional needs and aspirations of today's woman. An immensely practical, interesting guide. 07-7896-0

WINDOW TO MY HEART by Joy Hawkins. A collection of heartfelt poems aptly expressing common emotions and thoughts that single women of any age experience. The author's vital trust in a loving God is evident throughout. 07-7977-0

If you are unable to find any of these titles at your local bookstore, you may call Tyndale's toll-free number **1-800-323-9400, X-214** for ordering information. Or you may write for pricing to **Tyndale Family Products, P.O. Box 448, Wheaton, IL 60189-0448.**